Palgrave Studies in Maritime Economics

Series Editors
Hercules Haralambides
Erasmus School of Economics
Erasmus University Rotterdam
Rotterdam, The Netherlands

Elias Karakitsos
EN Aviation & Shipping Research Ltd
London, UK

Stig Tenold
Department of Economics
NHH – Norwegian School of Economics
Bergen, Norway

Palgrave Studies in Maritime Economics is a new, original and timely interdisciplinary series that seeks to be pivotal in nature and improve our understanding of the role of the maritime sector within port economics and global supply chain management, shipping finance, and maritime business and economic history. The maritime industry plays an increasingly important role in the changing world economy, and this new series offers an outlet for reviewing trends and developments over time as well as analysing how such changes are affecting trade, transport, the environment and financial markets. Each title in the series will communicate key research findings, shaping new approaches to maritime economics. The core audience will be academic, as well as policymakers, regulators and international maritime authorities and organisations. Individual titles will often be theoretically informed but will always be firmly evidence-based, seeking to link theory to policy outcomes and changing practices.

More information about this series at
http://www.palgrave.com/gp/series/15187

Niels P. Petersson · Stig Tenold ·
Nicholas J. White
Editors

Shipping and Globalization in the Post-War Era

Contexts, Companies, Connections

Editors
Niels P. Petersson
Sheffield Hallam University
Sheffield, UK

Nicholas J. White
School of Humanities and Social Science
Liverpool John Moores University
Liverpool, Merseyside, UK

Stig Tenold
Department of Economics
NHH – Norwegian School of Economics
Bergen, Norway

ISSN 2662-6551   ISSN 2662-656X (electronic)
Palgrave Studies in Maritime Economics
ISBN 978-3-030-26001-9   ISBN 978-3-030-26002-6 (eBook)
https://doi.org/10.1007/978-3-030-26002-6

© The Editor(s) (if applicable) and The Author(s) 2019. This book is an open access publication.
Open Access This book is licensed under the terms of the Creative Commons Attribution-NonCommercial-NoDerivatives 4.0 International License (http://creativecommons.org/licenses/by-nc-nd/4.0/), which permits any noncommercial use, sharing, distribution and reproduction in any medium or format, as long as you give appropriate credit to the original author(s) and the source, provide a link to the Creative Commons license and indicate if you modified the licensed material. You do not have permission under this license to share adapted material derived from this book or parts of it.
The images or other third party material in this book are included in the book's Creative Commons license, unless indicated otherwise in a credit line to the material. If material is not included in the book's Creative Commons license and your intended use is not permitted by statutory regulation or exceeds the permitted use, you will need to obtain permission directly from the copyright holder.
This work is subject to copyright. All commercial rights are reserved by the author(s), whether the whole or part of the material is concerned, specifically the rights of translation, reprinting, reuse of illustrations, recitation, broadcasting, reproduction on microfilms or in any other physical way, and transmission or information storage and retrieval, electronic adaptation, computer software, or by similar or dissimilar methodology now known or hereafter developed. Regarding these commercial rights a non-exclusive license has been granted to the publisher.
The use of general descriptive names, registered names, trademarks, service marks, etc. in this publication does not imply, even in the absence of a specific statement, that such names are exempt from the relevant protective laws and regulations and therefore free for general use.
The publisher, the authors and the editors are safe to assume that the advice and information in this book are believed to be true and accurate at the date of publication. Neither the publisher nor the authors or the editors give a warranty, expressed or implied, with respect to the material contained herein or for any errors or omissions that may have been made. The publisher remains neutral with regard to jurisdictional claims in published maps and institutional affiliations.

Cover illustration: Hans Berggren/GettyImages
Cover design by Fatima Jadamar

This Palgrave Macmillan imprint is published by the registered company Springer Nature Switzerland AG
The registered company address is: Gewerbestrasse 11, 6330 Cham, Switzerland

Acknowledgements

The editors wish to thank the following individuals and institutions for their support and contributions to the work on this volume: Liverpool John Moores University and Sheffield Hallam University hosted and supported workshops and editors' meetings. The Open Access publication of this book was supported by Sheffield Hallam University, *CBS Maritime* at the Copenhagen Business School, *Norges Handelshøyskoles Publiseringsfond* at the Norwegian School of Economics and the Institute for Mediterranean Studies of the Foundation of Research and Technology. The editors and contributors are grateful for the help in making their research accessible, and they would also like to thank Publisher Rachel Sangster and Editorial Assistant Joseph Johnson at Palgrave Macmillan for their patience and support during the writing process.

Contents

1 Shipping and Globalization in the Post-War Era:
  Contexts, Companies, Connections 1
  Niels P. Petersson, Stig Tenold and Nicholas J. White

Part I Contexts

2 The Declining Role of Western Europe in Shipping
  and Shipbuilding, 1900–2000 9
  Stig Tenold

3 The Emergence of Maritime Governance
  in the Post-War World 37
  Katharina Reiling

4 Thinking Outside 'The Box': Decolonization
  and Containerization 67
  Nicholas J. White

Part II Companies

5 'Containerization in Globalization': A Case Study of How Maersk Line Became a Transnational Company 103
   Henrik Sornn-Friese

6 East Asiatic Company's Difficult Experiences with Containerization 133
   Martin Jes Iversen

7 Shipping as a Knowledge Industry: Research and Strategic Planning at Ocean Group 157
   Niels P. Petersson

Part III Connections

8 The Role of Greek Shipowners in the Revival of Northern European Shipyards in the 1950s 185
   Gelina Harlaftis and Christos Tsakas

9 Regional, yet Global: The Life Cycle of Overnight Ferry Shipping 213
   René Taudal Poulsen

10 Conclusion 249
    Niels P. Petersson, Stig Tenold and Nicholas J. White

Index 275

List of Figures

Fig. 2.1	World shipbuilding around the turn of the century	13
Fig. 2.2	Shares of world shipbuilding, per cent	19
Fig. 2.3	Shares of the world fleet, per cent 1880–2010	21
Fig. 5.1	The establishment of Maersk Line country offices	114
Fig. 9.1	Average number of cabin berths per vessel, by route, 1960–2018	226
Fig. 9.2	Average number of lane metres per vessel, by route, 1960–2018	237
Fig. 9.3	Average age of vessels (in years), by route, 1960–2018	239

List of Tables

Table 2.1	The world fleet of leading countries, 1900	15
Table 2.2	A comparison of the world's busiest ports, Top 15 1910 and 2010	22
Table 2.3	Putting the shipping trajectory into the Sturmey scheme	25
Table 2.4	Putting the shipbuilding trajectory into the Sturmey scheme	28
Table 5.1	Maersk Line's Agency Network in 1958	111
Table 5.2	The Master Plan for the containerization of the Panama line	123
Table 8.1	Tankers built by Greek shipowners in European, American and Asian shipyards, 1948–1960	193
Table 8.2	Tankers built in European and non-European shipyards by Greek shipowners	195
Table 8.3	Loans from American banks for ships purchased, 1949–1959	201
Table 8.4	The Onassis whaling fleet	203
Table 9.1	Decadal changes in the annual number of passengers carried, in percent, by route	225
Table 9.2	Employment of selected ferries, 1957–2018	228

1

Shipping and Globalization in the Post-War Era: Contexts, Companies, Connections

Niels P. Petersson, Stig Tenold and Nicholas J. White

Introduction

In the early autumn of 2016, the major South Korean shipping company Hanjin filed for bankruptcy. The collapse of the company, which had specialized in container shipping, left much of its fleet marooned at sea. More than 60 ships, with cargoes and sailors, were involved. If the ships went to port, it was likely that the creditors would attempt to seize the

---

N. P. Petersson (✉)
Sheffield Hallam University, Sheffield, UK
e-mail: n.p.petersson@shu.ac.uk

S. Tenold
Department of Economics, NHH – Norwegian
School of Economics, Bergen, Norway
e-mail: stig.tenold@nhh.no

N. J. White
School of Humanities and Social Science, Liverpool John Moores
University, Liverpool, Merseyside, UK
e-mail: n.j.white@ljmu.ac.uk

vessels. Some ports were unwilling to admit Hanjin ships out of fear that the company would not be able to pay the costs of docking and unloading, or that the vessels, with disputed ownership, would occupy valuable berths for long periods of time.[1]

The case received substantial publicity. One reason for this was the fact that Hanjin was a leading shipping company, controlling the seventh largest container fleet in the world. Another reason—and the one that brought the case into non-business media outlets—was the timing of the incident. The Hanjin ships were carrying goods intended to fill shop shelves before the Christmas period. A number of large retailers in Europe and North America feared that thousands of containers with valuable cargo on their way from Asia would not reach their destinations on time. Was Hanjin really the Grinch that would steal Christmas, as a Bloomberg journalist suggested?[2]

The incident found a temporary solution, and Christmas was saved. However, there are several aspects of the Hanjin debacle that illuminate the topics that we deal with in this book—shipping and globalization in the period after World War II. First, the example illustrates the crucial role that foreign trade plays in the economies of most nations. Shipping is crucial in ensuring the smooth operation of this trade system. Second, the case shows how East Asian economies have managed to obtain a central position in the global production system, supplying finished goods to consumer markets in Europe and North America. Third, the fact that the company involved was South Korean illustrates that not only manufacturing production, but also a service industry such as shipping has increasingly moved towards Asia. Finally, the sheer amount of cargo involved is a testament to the manner in which the shipping industry has grown in the post-war period, where ships and companies have become ever larger.

Shipping was both an example and an engine of globalization in the post-war era. In turns, the shipping industry experienced and pioneered, mirrored and enabled key developments that led to the present-day globalized economy. Shipping was among the first industries exposed to fierce globalized competition. The shipping industry pioneered many of the

---

[1] See Ilmer (2016) and *The Economist* (2016) for news reports about the case.
[2] Cooper (2016).

organizational models and mechanisms that characterize the current corporate landscape. The slicing up of the value chain and the strategic location of business functions is one example, the use of low-cost and low-tax jurisdictions, often in small countries 'offshore', is another. Meanwhile, many business strategies and dynamics in shipping reflected those in the wider economy: strategic management, outsourcing, the focus on core businesses. As the main means of production—the ship—is mobile, questions of nationality and legal domicile are far more complex in shipping than in other industries. This increasingly transnational nature of the industry in turn stimulated the emergence of new forms of global governance.

Cheap mass transport, first for bulk commodities and oil and then for general cargo, underpinned the growth of world trade, the migration of production to Asia's Newly Industrialized Countries, and the emergence of complex global supply chains. The container is often seen as the 'typical' symbol of globalization, and the rise of container shipping coincided with the strong growth of international trade after World War II. Container shipping 'changed the world' and 'made the world smaller and the world economy bigger', if we are to believe the titles of the books published to commemorate the '50th anniversary' of container shipping in 2006.[3] Yet container shipping, which primarily involves the transport of finished goods, is far from the largest segment of the shipping market. The most important cargoes are raw materials such as oil, ores, grain, etc. The efficient and ever cheaper seaborne transport of such raw materials has been a necessary condition for the increasing division of labour in the world economy. However, such cargoes are primarily transported to and from terminals near mines and factories, and most people never encounter these gigantic ships. On the transport side, shipping has thus contributed to world trade both in a visible and an invisible way.

Without shipping and its ability to forge connections and networks of a global reach, the modern world would look very different. Famously, ships

---

[3]Cudahy (2006) and Levinson (2006); see also Donovan and Bonney (2006). The converted oil tanker *Ideal X* is usually referred to as the 'first' container ship.

nowadays transport 'ninety per cent of everything' we produce and consume.[4] However, shipping's effect on today's society reaches far beyond the provision of low-cost transport links, into what economists call the supply side, creating global markets for labour and finance. Today, Filipino sailors are creating value on German-owned ships built and financed in China and flying the flag of the Marshall Islands on a voyage between Australia and the United States. The wider connections forged by offshore companies developed gradually from roots sometimes stretching back into the interwar years and even earlier, with an acceleration from the 1970s. At the same time, shipping still remains embedded in national frames of reference in important respects, including business and worker cultures, regulations enforced under port state controls and national industrial policies.

How can we understand the interaction between globalization and shipping? This book highlights the importance of dialogue connecting historians of various specialist backgrounds as well as social scientists. It demonstrates the value of interdisciplinary approaches to analysing complex connections across various parts of Europe, Asia, Africa, the Americas and Australasia. It throws new light on the transformations of the period since World War II—political, ideological and technological as well as economic—and stimulates further enquiry. It combines the key benefits of a historical perspective, such as awareness of longer-term structural change, context and the dynamic interplay of continuity and change, with social scientists' interest in the forces shaping the present-day world.

The book is divided into three sections entitled Contexts, Companies and Connections. The first section illustrates the usefulness of a multi-disciplinary approach, investigating three large-scale historical processes, decolonization, the rise of Asia and the emergence of new structures of international governance, through the lens of shipping. The second section analyses one of the important driving forces of these macro-processes—the companies that created new markets and forged new connections. Our case studies of three liner shipping companies, Maersk, EAC and Ocean, and their very different trajectories provide insight into the strategies and performance of both successful and unsuccessful firms. The third section focuses on shipping's role in the emergence of new global connections at a

---

[4] George (2013).

more specific level, studying individual ships' global 'biographies' and how business leaders were breaking down established institutional forms and transcending boundaries between countries and industries. Through the analysis of such examples, the book highlights how shipping was embedded in and contributed to the transformations of business and society in the post-war era.

References

Cooper, C. (2016, September 9). The Ghost Ships of Hanjin and Why They're Spoiling Christmas. *Bloomberg*. https://www.bloomberg.com/news/articles/2016-09-09/quicktake-q-a-the-shipping-line-that-could-spoil-christmas. Accessed 17 January 2019.

Cudahy, B. J. (2006). *Box Boats: How Container Ships Changed the World*. New York: Fordham University Press.

Donovan, A., & Bonney, J. (2006). *The Box That Changed the World: Fifty Years of Container Shipping—An Illustrated History*. East Windsor: Commonwealth Business Media.

George, R. (2013). *Ninety Percent of Everything: Inside Shipping, the Invisible Industry That Puts Clothes on Your Back, Gas in Your Car and Food on Your Plate*. New York: Metropolitan Books; published in the UK as *Deep Sea and Foreign Going: Inside Shipping, the Invisible Industry That Brings You 90% of Everything*.

Illmer, A. (2016). Hanjin Ships, Cargoes and Sailors Stranded at Sea. *BBC News Online*. https://www.bbc.com/news/business-37241727. Accessed 17 January 2019.

Levinson, M. (2006). *The Box: How the Shipping Container Made the World Smaller and the World Economy Bigger*. Princeton: Princeton University Press.

The Economist. (2016). Why Billions of Dollars of Goods Are Stuck at Sea. https://www.economist.com/the-economist-explains/2016/09/21/why-billions-of-dollars-of-goods-are-stuck-at-sea. Accessed 17 January 2019.

Open Access This chapter is licensed under the terms of the Creative Commons Attribution-NonCommercial-NoDerivatives 4.0 International License (http://creativecommons.org/licenses/by-nc-nd/4.0/), which permits any noncommercial use, sharing, distribution and reproduction in any medium or format, as long as you give appropriate credit to the original author(s) and the source, provide a link to the Creative Commons license and indicate if you modified the licensed material. You do not have permission under this license to share adapted material derived from this chapter or parts of it.

The images or other third party material in this chapter are included in the chapter's Creative Commons license, unless indicated otherwise in a credit line to the material. If material is not included in the chapter's Creative Commons license and your intended use is not permitted by statutory regulation or exceeds the permitted use, you will need to obtain permission directly from the copyright holder.

Part I

Contexts

2

The Declining Role of Western Europe in Shipping and Shipbuilding, 1900–2000

Stig Tenold

Introduction

During the twentieth century, and in particular in the period after 1970, Western Europe lost its hegemony in international shipping and shipbuilding. The aim of this chapter is to present this decline, and to discuss its basis. The reduction of the European position was a necessary condition for the international spread—the globalization—of shipping and shipbuilding after World War II.

The chapter consists of three sections. In the first section, Western Europe's dominant position in world shipping and shipbuilding at the start of the twentieth century is presented. Among the factors that are emphasized to explain the hegemony are Europe's (and, in particular, the UK's) leading position within global production, trade and politics; the

S. Tenold (✉)
Department of Economics, NHH – Norwegian School of Economics, Bergen, Norway
e-mail: stig.tenold@nhh.no

superior access to technology and capital; and the cost structure within shipping.

Starting with a quantification of the reduction in the role of Western European countries in world shipping and shipbuilding, the second section of the chapter suggests some factors that can explain the diminishing position. This analysis follows the scheme used in Stanley Sturmey's examination of the decline of the British-registered fleet from 1900 to 1960 in his classic book *British Shipping and World Competition*. Four factors are considered; competitiveness, subsidies, random factors and internal (business) constraints in European shipping and shipbuilding companies.[1]

In his analysis of British shipping, Sturmey largely exonerated the first three factors. He primarily blamed British shipowners and their commercial lethargy for the fleet's decline. The analysis in this paper shows that when we consider the relative reduction of European shipping and shipbuilding as a whole, and extend the time frame to include all of the twentieth century, the other factors take on a much more prominent role. Moreover, the manner in which the shipping industry adapted to, and partly stemmed, the decline, was different from what occurred within shipbuilding.

The final section of the chapter discusses the timing of the transformation of the maritime industry. At the start of the twentieth century, and even in the first years after World War II, the European position should be considered 'abnormally strong'. In the first post-war decades, the hegemony was increasingly challenged. However, a combination of defensive national policies and technological limitations initially muted the decline both within shipping and within shipbuilding. Towards the end of the century, we see that the developments of these two maritime sectors diverged.

In shipping, the manner in which the industry was organized became totally transformed, and the question of nationality became very elusive. Still, behind this veil of stateless business, European capital and competence continued to play a crucial, albeit reduced, role. Within shipbuilding, however, Asian shipyards had managed to acquire a dominance that was similar in scale to the European leadership 100 years earlier.

---

[1] Sturmey (1962/2010, 1–2).

The Starting Point—The European Hegemony

Today, particularly with regard to manufacturing production, the world appears to be borderless and 'global'. Distances used to pose a problem for businesses—in terms of communication and transport costs, and in particular in terms of 'time costs'. This is no longer the case. From the perspective of an enterprise at the start of the twentieth century, transport and communication today would seem unbelievably fast and inexpensive. Information, commodities and products move rapidly, all over the globe. With this current context as the starting point, it may be difficult to fathom how 'European' most of the maritime industry was around the year 1900.

The establishment and growth of the international economy during the nineteenth century had primarily been a European endeavour.[2] Of course, the economic integration with other parts of the world (North America, in particular, but also the other continents) was the defining factor of this 'first era of globalization'. However, it happened largely on European terms, on European keels and with European capital and technology. The only area that had provided a short-lived challenge to the European maritime dominance—the North-American continent—preferred landward expansion and during the last decades of the nineteenth century gradually built down its presence within shipping and shipbuilding.[3]

Europe determined the scale, the scope and the speed of the world maritime industries, and nowhere was this more evident than in the case of the United Kingdom.

In 1900 the global shipbuilding industry had two centres: The Clyde and The Tyne and Wear-region—the west of Scotland and the northeast

---

[2]This paragraph can—rightly—be criticized for being Eurocentric. However, such an orientation is not 'wrong', as developments in intercontinental shipping to such a large degree had their basis in Europe. There were of course important and interesting maritime connections and expansion in other parts of the world. Yet, when we look at the construction of ocean-going ships and the ownership of the world fleet, the data show European market shares of more than 90%—confer Figure 1 and Table 1. It would thus be misguided to put the main emphasis elsewhere.

[3]With regard to the US 'withdrawal', the initial economic explanation—profits were higher on land than at sea—was shortly after World War I given a political justification as well. 'The Jones Act'—formally the Merchant Marine Act of 1920—imposed restrictions that ensured that US shipping could not possibly be competitive, and thus profitable, in the international market, at least for new ships flying the American flag.

of England.⁴ More than 70% of the world's steamship fleet at that time had been produced in the United Kingdom, and most alternatives to British-built ships were relatively expensive, technologically inferior vessels that found willing buyers mainly as a result of nationalistic attitudes or government initiatives.⁵

The basis for the strong position of UK shipyards was primarily technological; The Industrial Revolution had given them a first-mover advantage that lasted well into the twentieth century. The UK had the right combination of capital and competence—both skilled and unskilled labour—and could take advantage of their technological lead. Moreover, the country's shipbuilding industry had the size that was necessary to fully utilize the economies of scale in both steel and ship production.⁶

In the period 1901–1905, British yards produced almost 60% of the world's new shipping tonnage. As Pollard points out, this market share underestimates the British position, due to the fact that 'the tonnage launched in the United Kingdom was of a higher quality, ton for ton, than that of the rest of the world'.⁷ Although the United States was the second-largest producer, the European market share was close to 85% of the market for merchant ships. However, much of the non-British production was subsidized; 'Britain kept her share of the world market because few of the shipyards abroad were truly competitive'.⁸ This was particularly evident with regard to labour productivity; annual output per shipyard worker in the UK was 12.5 tons at the start of the century, the United States came second with 6.8 tons and Germany third with 3.3 tons. For France and Holland, the figure was less than

---

⁴In 1911–1912, yards on the Tyne and the Wear produced around 35% of the UK output, while yards on the Clyde produced 31.5%; data from *Fairplay* in Slaven (2013, 51).
⁵Calculated on the basis of Table 4 in *Lloyd's Register* (1901, supplement, 758–759). The followers were Germany with 6.8%, the United States with 6.5% and Sweden with 4.3%. See also Schwarz and von Halle (1902), quoted in Pollard (1957, 428).
⁶At times, British yards also benefitted from US steel producers dumping steel abroad; Pollard (1957, 439).
⁷Pollard (1957, 426). Calculations based on data from Lloyd's. Though the 60% market share was impressive, it was down almost 20 percentage points relative to the period 1892–1896. For a statistical presentation of the development of British shipbuilding, see Buxton et al. (2015).
⁸Pollard (1957, 431).

2 The Declining Role of Western Europe in Shipping ...

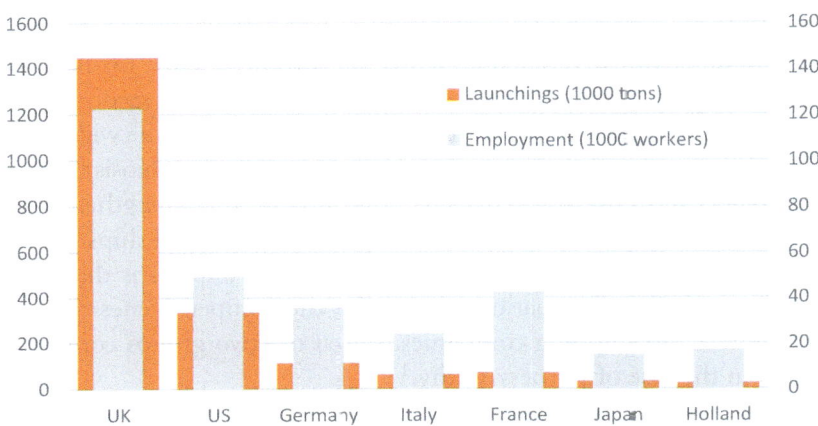

Fig. 2.1 World shipbuilding around the turn of the century—production (1000 tons, left axis) and employment (1000 men, right axis) (Chart based on Board of Trade data in Pollard [1957, 438], referring to five-year averages around the following specific years: 1895 [Germany]; 1896 [France]; 1899 [Holland]; 1900 [US]; 1901 [UK and Italy] and 1902 [Japan])

two.[9] Figure 2.1 shows shipbuilding production and employment around the turn of the century.

Shipbuilders in the UK derived an undisputed advantage from their proximity to the principal market for ships: British shipowners. By 1900, the British owners controlled around half of the world fleet, and almost 55% of the new steamships delivered that year went to British owners.[10] British shipping companies had been pioneers in the long-lasting transformation from sail to steam and from wood to iron and then steel hulls, and they were loyal to British yards. In 1900 four ships from Dutch yards were added to the British fleet; they were the only foreign-built newbuildings that year. The previous year there had been none.[11] Having the world's major shipowners as 'captive customers' clearly helped British shipbuilding, at least in the short term.

---

[9] Board of Trade data in Pollard (1957, 438). The classic article on the gradual decline of the British superiority is Lorenz (1991). For more extensive discussions, confer Slaven (2013) or Johnman and Murphy (2002).
[10] Calculated on the basis of Table 7 in *Lloyd's Register* 1901, supplement, 764–765.
[11] *Lloyd's Register* 1901, supplement, Table 3, 756–757 and Table 7, 764–765.

As Robertson points out in his article on the Scottish shipbuilding and shipping company William Denny and Brothers, 'close financial ties between shipbuilders and shipowners were common in the second half of the nineteenth century'.[12] Such relationships continued to be widespread and important also after the turn of the century. This symbiosis between shipbuilders and shipowners reflected, but initially also strengthened, the British advantage. Standardization—long series of identical ships—information and knowledge exchange, as well as intergroup loans that could even out cash flow fluctuations, improved the competitiveness of both shipbuilders and shipping companies. Often the two groups converged, such as in the case of Furness Withy.[13]

Within shipping, the concentration was lower than within shipbuilding and the UK presence not as dominant. Other countries—primarily within Europe—had managed to build up market shares in areas where they had political or colonial control. Alternatively—in the case of shipowners from less 'territorial' nations such as Greece and the Scandinavian countries—they had managed to acquire important positions in certain niche markets. Still, the UK in general, and London in particular, continued to play crucial roles as the centre of a global system of shipping.

As world historians like to remind us, there were of course similar trading, financial and political hubs in other parts of the world. However, with regard to global trade—the intercontinental voyages, whose strong growth distinguishes the second half of the nineteenth century from previous periods—London was the undisputed engine. At this time, more than fifty per cent of the world merchant marine was registered in the UK, and

---

[12] Robertson (1974, 36).

[13] For a good schematic overview of the closeness of the links between shipowners and yards, see Boyce (1995, 181–182), and specifically on Furness Withy, Boyce (2012b). A similar, but slightly different, type of relation is seen in the case of the shipbuilders John Scott & Co., who 'built and helped finance ships' for Alfred Holt & Co. (Ocean Steam Ship Co.). Milne (2009, 19) argues that 'the shipowner-shipbuilder link was crucial to expanding shipping firms'. It could, however, be argued that the symbiosis subsequently turned from positive to negative. Conservative British shipowners did not encourage the country's yards to transform production from ships running on coal, of which they had plenty, to ships with diesel engines. Similarly, British yards with outdated thoughts about technology did not facilitate a shift from steam to motor ships in the country's fleet. The neighbourhood or cluster effect—positive in good times, detrimental in bad times—is one of the main arguments used to explain the problems of British shipbuilders in Todd (2011). See also Ingram and Lifschitz (2006) on the relations among various shipbuilders and between the shipyards and their subcontractors.

the British fleet had more of the modern steamship tonnage than the rest of the nations combined.

Table 2.1 shows the distribution of the world fleet at the start of the twentieth century. The first columns show the sailing and steamship fleets, respectively, while the third column shows the 'Estimated' or 'Compensated' tonnage—a measure that takes into account differences in productivity between the two dominant technologies. As such, it is the best measure of the carrying capacity of the various countries' merchant marines. The fourth column shows the share of steam tonnage in the various fleets, and clearly illustrates that the transformation from sail to steam progressed at very different speeds in different countries.

The final column in Table 2.1 shows the countries' tonnage divided by the number of inhabitants. This figure can be seen as a measure of the extent to which the countries had channelled their resources into the

Table 2.1 The world fleet of leading countries, 1900[a]

	Sail tons (t)	Steam tons (t)	Estimated tons (t)	Steam share (%)	Tons per inhabitant
GB & Ireland	1923	7150	27,663	78.8	0.667
Germany	558	1347	5407	70.7	0.096
The United States	1405	938	4782	40.0	0.063
Norway	930	499	2725	34.9	1.227
France	394	597	2543	60.2	0.066
Italy	483	374	1830	43.6	0.056
Spain	91	435	1657	82.7	0.091
Japan	148	330	1336	69.0	0.031
Sweden	256	257	1181	50.1	0.230
Br. Australia	164	234	1006	58.8	0.182
Denmark	111	245	993	68.8	0.405
The Netherlands	68	252	949	78.8	0.186
Br. America	446	103	817	18.8	0.109
Russia	152	173	774	53.2	0.007
Greece	176	165	770	48.4	0.298
Other European	336	424	1864	55.8	
Other non-European	226	235	1072	50.1	

[a]Based on data from Statistics Norway (1902) *Statistisk aarbog for kongeriget Norge* (pp. 168–169). Kristiania: Det Statistiske Centralbureau and H. Aschehoug & Co, Tables I and K. See Tenold (2019, 22–23), for a detailed presentation of the data

shipping sector. When it comes to the relative importance of shipping, Norway is in a special position, where each inhabitant owned more than a ton of shipping tonnage. The United Kingdom, Denmark and Greece also had invested disproportionately in shipping.[14]

London's role as a global centre for trade and finance—which together with shipping were the dominant service industries—is an important explanation of the British hegemony. Around these service industries, a number of auxiliary businesses surfaced, gradually becoming more professionalized. The typical example of such a spin-off business would be Lloyd's, where the small beginnings in a coffee shop gradually evolved into one of the most important institutions in shipping's commercial infrastructure.[15] Similarly, ship brokers, ship agents, banks, insurance companies and world-leading institutions such as The Baltic Mercantile and Shipping Exchange ensured the city's pre-eminence in global trade and shipping. 'The Baltic', for instance, 'acted as the unofficial regulator of the shipping business and significant segments of commodity trading'.[16]

The pride of the British merchant marine was the elegant vessels that served British shipping lines around the globe. These shipping lines can be considered—in tandem with the telegraph network—as the tentacles of the empire; permanent connections that facilitated both the economic and the political role that the United Kingdom played in the global arena. By 1914 the submarine cables that Britain controlled were almost twice as large as those of the two next powers (The United States and France) combined, and the extensive telegraphic system contributed decisively to the City of London's position as the world capital of trade, shipping and finance.[17] The shipping lines were to cargo transport what the telegraph was to information—a manifestation of British power, which contributed to preserving the very same dominance that it reflected.

Any explanation of the dominant European role within the maritime industries at a global level echoes the explanation of the British dominance

---

[14] Interestingly, three of these four countries—Denmark, Norway and Greece—are among the leading shipping nations even today, when we look at the size of their fleets relative to the countries' own needs.

[15] Boyce (2012a, 108–114).

[16] Boyce (2012a, 115).

[17] Scholl (1998, 201–202).

at the European level. Key factors are the leading position within production and trade; the superior access to technology, capital and sufficiently skilled labour; and imperial ambitions and structures that ensured political support for maritime activities. Indeed, when we look more closely at the cost structure and the demands for competence within shipping, it is evident that there were few challengers outside Europe, even at the hypothetical level.

In shipping, success is defined by being internationally competitive. To succeed at the beginning of the twentieth century, a country needed funds to invest in tonnage, technological skills and competent labour to operate the vessels, as well as efficient commercial and political networks that could support shipping at home and abroad. It is evident that European countries had this—and that other parts of the world did not. Moreover, the UK satisfied these criteria better than the other European countries.

In international shipping, like in the case of industrialization and modernization more generally, Japan was the only contender outside Europe and its Western offshoots (The United States, Canada, Australia and New Zealand). This statement does not only pertain to the pre-twentieth-century period, but rings true all the way until well after the Second World War. The combination of an outward-looking strategy and a fear of being colonized created a 'shipping-political complex' in Japan that spurred the growth of the country's fleet.[18] Helped by the involuntary withdrawal of much European shipping during the First World War, Japanese shipping companies laid the foundation for a strong expansion in the interwar period.[19]

Within shipbuilding, the explanation of the European dominance was almost purely related to capital—not only 'capital' in its technological and its financial sense, but also in its human guise. Outside Europe—with the exception of North America and Japan—the technology needed to produce large steam vessels was missing. Moreover, the funds necessary

---

[18] See Chida and Davies (2012) and Davies (2008).

[19] An early example of contra-factual thinking, from the British Board of Trade, reprinted in Berglund (1926, 647), suggests that the disruptions caused by the First World War reduced the fleets of the UK, Germany, Norway and France by 5 million, 3.5 million, 1 million and 500,000 tons, respectively. At the same time, 'the United States showed a gain of nearly 7,000,000 gross tons over her normal growth; and Japan 20,000 tons'.

to establish shipyards capable of building such vessels were absent, as were the requisite knowledge and the needed skill base. Even the shipyards in the most advanced European countries had a productivity that was less than a third of the productivity in British yards around the turn of the century.

With regard to auxiliary services, closeness to the most important market—and to the informal institutions of shipping—plays an important part. Gradually, the British way of doing business—the types of contracts, the accepted forms of insurance and the standardized clauses—became the established rules and regulations throughout the shipping market. Even today, the main framework covering maritime contracts is British, and agreements between businesses that have no relationship to the United Kingdom refer to British laws and institutions in the case of disagreement. The crucial role that was played by Western Europe/the United Kingdom/London in the development of the merchant economy and the transport and trade infrastructure undoubtedly casts long shadows, even after the dominance had disappeared.

Lost Continent

Europe's dominant position within shipping and shipbuilding was eroded throughout the twentieth century, though there appears to have been some acceleration towards the end of the millennium. Early challenges were related to the two wars. During these difficult years, the United States took over tasks within shipping and shipbuilding that the fighting European countries could no longer perform. Subsequently, and in particularly in the last decades of the twentieth century, the challenge came from the East. This time the competition was both stronger and more permanent.

The first warning shot came as early as the 1950s. Japan rose from the ashes of the Second World War to displace the UK as the world's leading shipbuilder in 1956. After the middle of the 1970s, South Korea and then China managed to grab massive market shares. At the beginning of the twenty-first century, the Asian presence in the high-volume shipbuilding

2 The Declining Role of Western Europe in Shipping ...   19

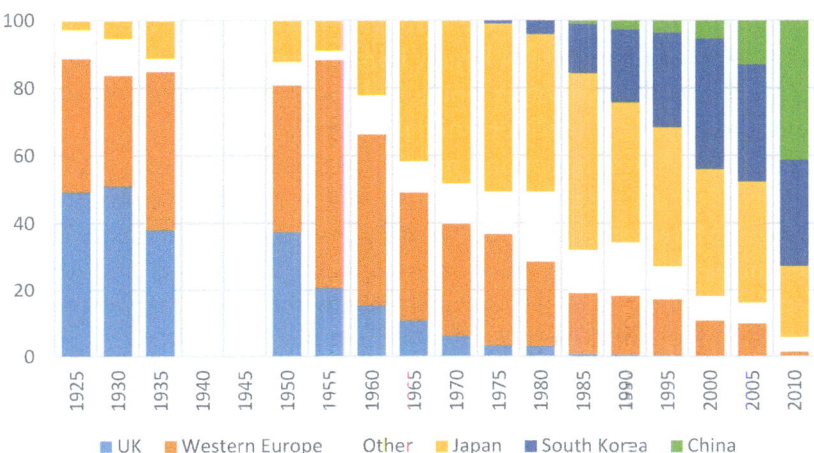

Fig. 2.2 Shares of world shipbuilding, per cent (Compiled on the basis of various issues of *Lloyd's Statistical Tables*. Based on Gross Register Tonnage, except for the 2010 figures which are based on Dead Weight Tonnage, and thus likely to slightly underestimate the European market shares. Although some countries are missing, the chart gives a representative overview of the shift)

market was even more dominant than Europe's had been one hundred years earlier.[20]

Figure 2.2 shows the spectacular decline in the European share of the world market for newbuildings after 1955. Moreover, it is clear that the hegemony was transferred to Asian yards, led by Japan, then followed by South Korea and China. By December 2008, only eight of the world's leading 100 yards, based on the size of the order book, were European. Some of these have subsequently closed down or have been taken over by other European or Asian yards. Given the dominant British position a century earlier, it is worth noting that not a single British yard warranted inclusion among the Top 100 shipbuilders in the world by 2008. The

---

[20]This is partly a matter of interpretation; in pure tonnage terms—measured as dead weight tons of shipping capacity produced or ordered—the three leading Asian shipbuilders (South Korea, Japan and China) were more dominant at the beginning of the twenty-first century than Europe had been at the beginning of the twentieth century. However, if we look at the value of the production, the continued construction of smaller high-technology vessels and luxury cruise ships at European yards skews the picture and increases the European share of the shipbuilding market.

leading European yard—the German Meyer Werft—was number 38 on the list. At that time, the ten largest European yards had about three per cent of the total world order book—in sum less than half of what the world leading South Korean Hyundai group had.[21]

The shipbuilding hegemony moved from Europe to Asia during the twentieth century. In shipping the geographic shift has not been as pronounced. Moreover, changes in the manner in which the industry is organized make the transformation more difficult to quantify and identify. In some ways, many of the national traits within shipping were washed away during the twentieth century. This implies that while it is possible to identify a European decline, it is far more difficult to say something precise about where the business in fact moved.

At the start of the twentieth century, a ship's flag would reflect the nationality of the owners, the managers, the crew and officers and often the cargo owners as well. At the end of the twentieth century, it is usually the case that investors, managers, crews and officers come from different countries, and neither of these necessarily have any relationship to the flag that the ship is flying and the nationality of the owner of the cargo that it is carrying. For two-thirds of all merchant tonnage, the flag of the vessel reveals absolutely nothing about the real nationality of the main economic agents involved. Consequently, it is increasingly difficult to find a meaningful measure of 'the European share'.

The decline in Europe's share of the world fleet, as seen in Fig. 2.3, is clearly dramatic. At the same time, this occurred against a backdrop of reduced European importance in the international economy. Around 1900, the international economy—in terms of cross-border flows of trade and factors of production—was dominated by Western Europe. This region was responsible for more than three quarters of all manufacturing exports and more than two-thirds of the imports of primary products.[22] Consequently, while the share of almost 97% of the world fleet was an overrepresentation, it to some extent reflected a real European dominance

---

[21] Based on data from ECORYS (2009, 55).

[22] Estimated on the basis of data for the United Kingdom and northwest Europe in Yates (1959), reprinted in Kenwood and Lougheed (1999, 84).

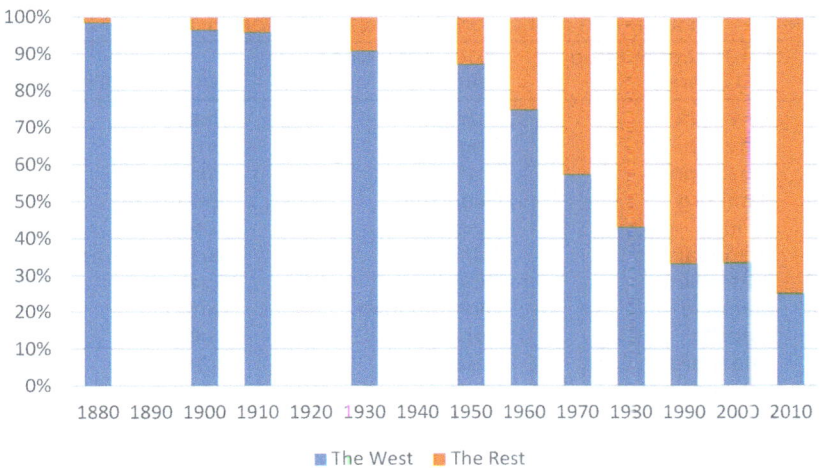

Fig. 2.3 Shares of the world fleet, per cent 1880–2010 (Based on a combination of definitions and sources from SSB, Lloyd's, UNCTAD and OECD. As the results are sensitive to the choice of tonnage measure, size restrictions and so on, this figure should be seen as an indication of the development, rather than as a precise measure)

in the international economy. While it is difficult to find comparable figures for the end of the twentieth century, it is evident that Western Europe's contribution to seaborne trade is far smaller. Data from the United Nations Conference on Trade and Development suggest that the Western European share of the volume of seaborne imports and exports in 2000 was less than a third and around a fifth, respectively.[23]

Table 2.2 is a good illustration of the manner in which the balance of international trade in general, and seaborne trade in particular, has shifted from Western Europe and the North-Atlantic economy to East and Southeast Asia. In 1910 more than half of the world's 15 busiest ports, measured by cargo volume, were European. By 2010 there was only one left. The United Kingdom had four ports in the Top 15 in 1910, and none 100 years later. It was little consolation that the country had four ports in the Top 100—Grimsby and Immingham at 68th, London at 82nd, Milford Haven at 93rd and Southampton at 98th. In fact, the

---

[23] Calculated on the basis of data from 2000 in UNCTAD, *Maritime Transport 2006*, 133–136.

Table 2.2 A comparison of the world's busiest ports, Top 15 1910 and 2010[a]

	1910—tons entered and cleared	2010—total cargo volume	2010—container traffic
1	New York	Shanghai	Shanghai
2	Antwerp	Singapore	Singapore
3	Hong Kong	Rotterdam	Hong kong
4	Hamburg	Guangzho	Shenzhen
5	London	Ningbo	Busan
6	Shanghai	Tianjin	Ningbo-Zhouzhan
7	Rotterdam	Qingdao	Guangzho
8	Marseille	Qinhuangdao	Qingdao
9	Cardiff	Hong Kong	Dubai
10	Singapore	Busan	Rotterdam
11	Constantinople	South Louisiana	Tianjin
12	Liverpool	Houston	Kaohsiung
13	Colombo	Shenzhen	Port Klang
14	Tyne	Dalian	Antwerp
15	Kobe	Port Hedland	Hamburg

[a]The 1910-list has been calculated on the basis of Bureau of Statistics, 1911, 753; see the source for details. The 2010-lists are taken from American Association of Port Authorities, 2011

biggest British port in the year 2000, would have been number 12 on the list of Chinese ports or number 34 on a list of Asia's busiest ports.

The data in the charts and tables above clearly illustrate the reduced European role within shipping and shipbuilding. In order to discuss the basis for this decline, we will use the analytical framework in Stanley Sturmey's seminal book *British Shipping and World Competition*—which deals with the period from the start of the twentieth century to 1960. Here, Sturmey presents four factors that might explain why the British share of the world fleet 'declined from over forty-five per cent of the world total in 1900 to about sixteen per cent of that total in 1960'. His possible culprits are (1) a transformation of the basis for the competitive situation, caused for instance by changes in the cost structure within shipping; (2) subsidies or other mechanisms that interfered with the competitive market mechanism; (3) random factors such as wars, changes in the trade pattern, taxation or non-shipping policies; and (4) internal constraints.[24]

---

[24]Sturmey (1962/2010, 1–2). There have of course been plenty of research and numerous public and privately commissioned reports dealing with the same problems. For an 'approved' explanation,

Sturmey claims that in the case of British shipping, the first three factors were not unimportant, but 'neither separately nor together can these answers be regarded as more than partial'.[25] He finds that the main basis for the British decline was internal constraints—the attitudes of the industry—which fostered inadequate and inhibiting reactions to a changing shipping market. Contemporary sources concur—the problem was business decisions, rather than comparative advantage, macroeconomic developments, policy issues or random factors. This idea is supported by *The Economist*, which in the early 1960s suggested that British shipping companies committed 'suicide by commercial timidity and sheer bad judgment'.[26]

It is not possible to magnify Stanley Sturmey's explanation of the British decline, give it a European setting, and claim that it is valid for all of the twentieth century. Even the British experience was diverse, and this variation increases even more when we look at the whole continent and extend the time period. At the same time, Sturmey's analysis can be very useful, as it provides us with a set of potential explanatory factors, and these can be applied to the longer and broader perspective.

Perhaps surprisingly, if we extend the basis for the analysis like this, Sturmey's explanations are turned on their heads. In the case of the decline of European shipping and shipbuilding during the twentieth century, the culprits are the factors that Sturmey largely dismissed.[27] Internal constraints or business lethargy is not the main factor behind the European decline. In fact, for shipping, the result is quite the opposite; European shipping companies managed to adapt wisely to the new circumstances, but the other forces were too strong.

This finding is not necessarily in opposition to one of Sturmey's main arguments. He actually points out that it is exactly because of the improved

---

see UK Parliament (1987–1988) Transport Committee, First report: 'Decline in the UK-registered merchant fleet'. However, few—if any—studies have been as influential and systematic as that of Sturmey, which makes it a good starting point for the discussion.

[25] Sturmey (1962/2010, 328).

[26] *The Economist*, 9 February 1963, 519.

[27] Subsequent analyses, including Jamieson (2003), have a more nuanced view of British shipowners than Sturmey, pointing out that they succeeded in certain segments.

competitive abilities and the successful strategic decisions in other countries—and his examples are primarily found in Europe—that the United Kingdom lost out in the years from 1900 to 1960. A similar contrast between under-geared British owners and their more expansive European cousins is made by Richard Goss, in his analysis of British shipping companies' business strategies in the post-war period.[28] Elsewhere, Goss has pointed out the linkage between the decline and non-shipping policies, for instance, the manner in which governments supported and subsidized industries that competed with shipping. All things equal, such preference is likely to reduce the role of shipping.[29]

European Shipping in Sturmey's Scheme

With regard to shipping, the factors that Sturmey dismisses, or at least downplays, have played a much more important role when we look at all of Western Europe and when we extend the time period to include all of the twentieth century. Table 2.3 provides a schematic overview of how the various elements developed, and how they influenced the competitiveness of European shipping. Changes in the cost structure, subsidies (and their counterpart, taxes), the transformation of the trade pattern and cargo restrictions were all important in an explanation of the European decline.

The main reason for the declining European presence in world shipping has been the combination of the general reduction in Europe's importance and the manner in which the competitive picture has shifted. During the 1950s and 1960s, the skill premium paid for European seafarers was not exorbitant, and national(istic) regulations limited the use of foreigners in most fleets. Moreover, the combination of labour-saving economies of scale, strong demand growth and frequent reinvestment in inexpensive tonnage (including efficient and value-for-money ships built in Japan) ensured that European shipping companies continued to make profits.

Europe's superior position at the start of the twentieth century, as discussed in the first section of the chapter, was largely maintained well

---

[28] Goss (2011, 246).
[29] Richard Goss interviewed in UK Parliament (1998–1999), The Environment, Transport and Regional Affairs Committee, 12th report: 'The future of the UK shipping industry'.

Table 2.3 Putting the shipping trajectory into the Sturmey scheme

Factor	Effects on twentieth-century European shipping
The competitive situation/costs	Increasing wage costs in Europe originally offset by economies of scale, subsequently by the use of foreign labour
Market interference	Nationalist pressures, particularly in the liner sector Cargo preference, bilateral agreements and cabotage restrictions
Random factors	
Wars	Temporary loss of ships and markets during wars, not fully recouped in peacetime
Changes in the trade pattern	Shifts in world production and trade—in particular the integration of Asia in the world economy—reduced Europe's importance
Taxation	Part of the reason for the rise of the Flags of convenience, but became less important with the erosion of the national dimension Today most European countries have a system with low rates
Non-shipping policies	Protection of competing industries reduced domestic competitiveness R&D in technology and marketing improved competitiveness
Internal constraints	Skilful adaptation to the new situation, although solutions partly undermined the European flags in the long term Large intra-European differences (the UK particularly lacklustre)[a]

[a]See Ojala and Tenold (2017) for an illustration of how a handful of European countries (specifically, Greece, Norway and Denmark) have involved into 'super-exporters' of shipping services, while the majority of European countries import such services from others. On Greece, see Harlaftis (1995) and Theotokas and Harlaftis (2009). For Denmark and Norway, see Sornn-Friese et al. (2012), Tenold (2012) and Tenold (2019)

into the post-war period. After the wars, the United States retreated from shipping and shipbuilding again, gradually selling off surplus tonnage, or including it in the reserve fleet, while rapidly winding down shipbuilding capacity as part of the return to a peacetime economy. Within Europe, there were changes, however. The British decline was as inevitable within shipping and shipbuilding as it had been within manufacturing—the market share was simply too large to be sustainable in the long run. Still, until the last part of the 1960s, the retired empire-builder controlled the world's largest fleet.

The challenge to the British market share initially came from other industrialized countries, both as a result of expanding national fleets and as a result of the increasing use of Flags of convenience by American and Greek owners, in particular. In the first post-war decades, the main competitors were found among the Traditional Maritime Nations of Europe. The cost structure of international shipping continued to favour relatively capital-abundant and technologically advanced countries that had the necessary networks and knowledge. However, in the last part of the century, this description no longer applied only to European countries—by then several Asian counties had managed to acquire the capital and skills needed to succeed in shipping. Moreover, as the centre of gravity of the world economy moved to East and Southeast Asia, networks in this region became far more important.

The political and macroeconomic forces were powerful, but European shipping companies showed a great deal of ingenuity and adaptability in order to alleviate the decline. In particular they used foreign inputs—primarily seafarers—strategically, while at the same time maintaining some functions at home. Such manoeuvres were helped by authorities that liberalized the policy regime and also introduced measures—both futile and successful—to strengthen the countries' shipping policies.[30]

Shipbuilding in Sturmey's Scheme

Institutional innovations—a combination of maritime enterprise and accommodating policies—ensured that Europe maintained some of the activity within shipping. A stronger and more fundamental challenge came within shipbuilding. The UK had gradually lost market shares to other European countries from the start of the twentieth century—yards in Germany, France, the Netherlands and Scandinavia challenged Great Britain

---

[30] A good example of a futile policy is the British investment grants, which temporarily stemmed the decline of the British fleet in the late 1960s and early 1970s. These grants were costly and had no long-term effect. More successful policies have been the introduction of second registries in Norway and Denmark.

through low costs, second-mover advantages, government financing and close links to 'their own' compatriot shipowners, who were often more expansive and less conservative than their British counterparts.

In the 1950s another—and in the end far more threatening—competitor turned the shipbuilding industry on its head. Before World War II the Japanese shipbuilding industry—with a minor exception during World War I—had produced ships almost solely for the Japanese market. After the war, international demand was actively sought. Based originally on US investments and technology, Japan's shipbuilding industry expanded rapidly.[31]

Indirect government support, low wages and limited unionization helped the Japanese effort—a strategy that was echoed decades later in South Korea and China. In Europe in general—and in the UK shipbuilding industry in particular—high wages and frequent confrontations between workers and management had become the norm, and the combination of European sclerosis and Japanese stamina can explain the rapid transfer of orders to Japanese yards. However, it is also important to point out that the transfer of orders to Japan enabled the European shipping companies to survive—if they had been forced to buy more expensive and inferior European tonnage, they would have found it much more difficult to remain competitive.

Table 2.4 puts the development of the shipbuilding industry into the Sturmey scheme. It suggests that the shipbuilding industry was particularly suited for a transfer of production to Japan and the Newly Industrialized Countries in Asia. The technology was relatively simple. The main input—in addition to inexpensive labour—was steel, and the shipyards grew in tandem with the domestic supply of steel, ensuring an outlet for the countries' nascent steel production. At the same time, the liberal economic trading regime ensured that there were relatively few restrictions on the import of ships, effectively meaning that the whole world was a potential market for the Asian tonnage. Moreover, shipbuilding found its place within the relatively controlled economic development model seen in many Asian countries, where government directives and guided credit and currency 'nudged' the economic structure in the right direction.

---

[31] See Blumenthal (1976), Davies (1992) or Chida and Davies (2012) for a more detailed account.

Table 2.4 Putting the shipbuilding trajectory into the Sturmey scheme

Factor	Effects on twentieth-century European shipbuilding
The competitive situation/costs	Uncompetitive labour costs in Europe and standardized, easily transferable technology
Market interference	Government attempts to stem the decline (beggar-thy-neighbour in Europe) and nurture infant industries (in Asia)
Random factors	
Wars	Cold War support helped South Korean and Japanese industrialization and capacity-building
Changes in the trade pattern	Improved communication reduced the 'home bias', that is, the advantage of proximity between shipowners and yards
Taxation	Subsidies (negative taxation) have been important; defensive support in Europe, offensive support in Asia
Non-shipbuilding policies	Credit, currency, employment and unemployment policies have facilitated the growth, as well as industrial policies
Internal constraints	Reliance on government support, even in the growth phase

The main reason for the decline of European shipbuilding was the change in the competitive situation. With labour costs such a large part of the picture, and a technology that was easy to transfer, European shipyards were unable to compete. Even generous public support—countercyclical subsidies to deal with a structural crisis—was unable to do more than stem the decline in the orders for large ships. Although Europe still has an important position in certain shipbuilding niches, the high-volume production has disappeared.

The analyses above have illustrated that while the European conditions for both shipping and shipbuilding deteriorated, shipping companies were able to adapt to the new competitive situation in a way that shipyards could not.

When Did Europe Lose Its Maritime Hegemony?

The analysis of the declining role of European shipping and shipbuilding in the twentieth century suggests the following broad pictures. Within shipping, Europe gradually lost its position, with particularly large temporary drops during the two world wars. Moreover, in the period from around the middle of the 1970s, the decline accelerated. In the last quarter of the century there was a pronounced relative reduction; the European-registered share of the world fleet fell rapidly. However, part of the declining market share was offset by European-owned ships flying foreign flags, which are hard to identify in the data.

In shipbuilding, there was a more or less continuous British loss of market share, initially taken over by other European countries, then by Japan as well. The continental European competitiveness evaporated in tandem with the new orders after 1975, and shipyards were forced to rapidly reduce their productive capacity. For a while, governments supported the industry, recognizing neither the structural shift nor how the potential for competitive high-volume shipbuilding in Europe had disappeared.

Why was the 1970s such a watershed? It could be argued that this decade was a turning point for Europe in general. The end of the Golden Age and the deepening *Eurosclerosis* was the local part of the story. This was exacerbated by concerted—and successful—efforts at economic modernization in a number of Asian countries, including China, where Deng Xiaoping started crossing the river 'one stone at the time'. The sheer number of people—and the potential increases in income—meant that the Asian advances, if successful, would overwhelm the international economy.

The turning point—where the downward-sloping trend began to accelerate—was the OPEC-orchestrated oil price increases of the 1970s. These triggered an unprecedented crisis in shipping and shipbuilding. As a result, the European decline picked up speed—tonnage was transferred to foreign flags and shipyards were closed. From 1973 to 1987 the British-flagged fleet declined by more than 75%, as did the fleets of Norway and Sweden.

Over the same period, the fleets of the main Flags of convenience doubled, while the five leading Asian nations (except Japan) saw their fleets multiply by a factor of more than seven.[32]

The collapse was just as severe in shipbuilding. Due to the lag between ordering and delivery, the European deliveries peaked a couple of years after the shipping market had collapsed. In 1975, shipyards in Europe delivered more than 14 million gross tons. Ten years later, the figure was 3.6 million tons and the trend continued downwards—'European shipbuilding production never recovered to the pre-crisis level'.[33]

Governments in Europe initially attempted to support European yards in the anticipation that the downturn was temporary. The shipyards were more pragmatic: as European shipbuilding was gradually being built down, the scraps were sold abroad. For instance, the world's largest shipbuilder—Hyundai Heavy Industries—entered shipbuilding on the basis of South Korean determination and labour, but with crucial contributions from European capital (credit) and competence (technology and consultancy).[34]

In shipping, the shift from growth to stagnation in demand led to a new focus on costs, and ushered in a number of technological and institutional innovations. The crisis forced shipowners to cut costs wherever possible, and although manning costs had become a very small proportion of total costs, paying four to five times as much for labour as the competitors still made a difference.[35] Moreover, the types of businesses engaged in the industry changed, with myopic speculators and financial investors taking the place of the old traditional 'shipowners', who had a long-term view both on their business and on its role in the local maritime community.

Both within shipping and shipbuilding, the European decline was taken to the extreme in the case of the UK. As Sarah Palmer points out, the downfall was not a gradual process; there was a loss of market shares in the

---

[32] See the analysis in Tenold (2006, 92–101). The term 'Flags of convenience' refers to Bahamas, Bermuda, Cyprus, Liberia and Panama, while the five rapidly growing Asian fleets are those of China, Hong Kong, The Philippines, Singapore and South Korea.

[33] OECD (2017, 52).

[34] See Kang et al. (2015, 2016).

[35] Awkwardly, despite the current universal use of labour from low-cost countries, a lot of research funding is spent on 'crew-less ship design'. For a 165,000 ton container ship, valued at some 175 million USD, even a crew of thirteen Filipinos appears to be too expensive.

first part of the century, but after 1975 'the UK flagged fleet [...] went into free fall'.³⁶ British shipbuilding, which had been even more dominant, was at the end of the century 'reduced to rump status in international terms and struggling for its very existence'.³⁷ By the end of the century, merchant shipbuilding had 'all but ended' in the United Kingdom.³⁸

Conclusion: Was Western Europe Doomed to Lose Its Maritime Hegemony?

Inequalities in economic development—an industrialized and politically dominant Europe and a relatively underdeveloped periphery—can explain the European/Western leadership in shipping and shipbuilding at the start of the twentieth century. Europe had the capital and competence necessary to gain and maintain the maritime hegemony. The hegemony was—rightly or wrongly—a reflection of Europe's leading position within international trade, manufacturing production and global politics.

The maritime industries were particularly vulnerable to competition. The reason is simple: despite improvements in communications, there are still transport and transaction costs in most industries, although they are low compared with previous times. In international shipping and shipbuilding, however, such costs are largely irrelevant, as 'mobility' is the fundamental aspect of the product. It is extremely difficult to tax and to regulate objects that can easily be moved from one jurisdiction to another.

The term 'globalization', at least in its economic guise, is often depicted as a process where relations between nations are tightened and international trade and investment increase. However, in addition to the growth in general terms, this process may entail a significant element of dislocation. Like customs unions have both a *trade creating* and a *trade diverting* effect, 'globalization' has had both a *production creating* and a *production diverting* effect. In the case of shipping and shipbuilding, activities and

---

³⁶Palmer (2012, 124); see also Palmer (2008).
³⁷Johnman and Murphy (2002, 244).
³⁸Buxton et al. (2015, 305).

production have been transferred from Europe to other parts of the world, in particular to East and Southeast Asia.

The net effect for Europe has varied among the different types of activities. In shipbuilding, there has been a substantial decrease in activity in European yards since the peak in the middle of the 1970s, particularly with regard to the construction of the largest tankers and dry bulk ships. In most European countries, the number of merchant ships under construction has declined, and in terms of tonnage, the reduction has been even more spectacular.

Within shipping, there has also been a substantial loss in the European market share during the twentieth century, with an acceleration in the last quarter. However, the European position was 'abnormally high' at the start of the century—Western Europe had around 15% of world population, but controlled more than 85% of the world fleet in 1900. Moreover, even though the market share has declined, the European tonnage has increased substantially—the *production creation* has been higher than the *production diversion*.

Despite this growth, Europe's development in shipping and shipbuilding is one of relative decline. The undisputable leader at the start of the century—Great Britain—has been hit harder than most. In 1988, the Transport Committee of the UK Parliament recognized that the British shipping industry had 'declined to such an extent that action was needed to remedy the situation'. Despite political efforts, ten years later the very same committee acknowledged that 'the industry's decline has continued'.[39]

The nineteenth century was characterized by the dominance of Europe in general, and the UK in particular, in international politics and trade. During the twentieth century, the world became more balanced—the European leadership disappeared as new regions were integrated into the world economy. Nevertheless, for most of the century, Europe determined the direction and the speed of international shipping and shipbuilding. The Japanese challenge started in earnest in the 1950s, but it was not until the last decades that the Europeans were replaced by Asians within

---

[39] UK Parliament (1998–1999), The Environment, Transport and Regional Affairs Committee, 12th report: 'The future of the UK shipping industry'. The reference in the 1998 report is to UK Parliament (1987–1988) Transport Committee, First report: 'Decline in the UK-registered merchant fleet'.

shipbuilding. The conditions for modern, low-cost production are much better in Japan, South Korea and China, and the technology was easy to transfer.

By the end of the twentieth century, Europe's commercial and political networks were no longer the quasi-monopolies they had been at the start of the century. Faced with increased foreign competition, European shipping companies managed to remain profitable by reducing the European contents of their services, moving to low-tax flags and utilizing low-cost labour from Asia. At the same time, some activities remained in Europe, though the market share was lower than before. Consequently, due to the slicing up of the value chain within shipping, it is difficult to determine the true nationality of a ship or a shipping company. A global, often unidentifiable, fleet has become the norm.

The growing share of Asia in world production and trade has been one of the most important developments in the international economy after the Second World War. Developments in shipping and shipbuilding made this integration possible. The European hegemony had been based on a combination of technological leadership, superior investment capacity and skill and knowledge advantages. It was unlikely to last.

References

Berglund, A. (1926). Our Merchant Marine Problem and International Trade Policies. *Journal of Political Economy, 34*(5), 642–656.

Blumenthal, T. (1976). The Japanese Shipbuilding Industry. In H. Patrick & L. Meissner (Eds.), *Japanese Industrialization and Its Social Consequences* (pp. 129–160). Berkeley: University of California Press.

Boyce, G. (1995). *Information, Mediation and Institutional Development: The Rise of Large-Scale Enterprise in British Shipping, 1870–1919*. Manchester: Manchester University Press.

Boyce, G. (2012a). The Development of Commercial Infrastructure for World Shipping. In G. Harlaftis, S. Tenold, & J. M. Valdaliso (Eds.), *The World's Key Industry—History and Economics of International Shipping* (pp. 106–123). Basingstoke: Palgrave Macmillan.

Boyce, G. (2012b). *The Growth and Dissolution of a Large-Scale Business Enterprise: The Furness Interest, 1892–1912*. St. John's: IMEHA.

Buxton, I., Fenton, R., & Murphy, H. (2015). Measuring Britain's Merchant Shipbuilding Output in the Twentieth Century. *The Mariner's Mirror, 101*(3), 304–322.

Chida, T., & Davies, P. (1990/2012). *The Japanese Shipping and Shipbuilding Industries—A History of Their Modern Growth*. London and New York: Bloomsbury.

Davies, P. (1992). The Role of National Bulk Carriers in the Advance of Shipbuilding Technology in Post-war Japan. *The International Journal of Maritime History, 4*(1), 131–142.

Davies, P. (2008). A Guide to the Emergence of Japan's Modern Shipping Industries. In L. R. Fischer & E. Lange (Eds.), *International Merchant Shipping in the Nineteenth and Twentieth Centuries* (pp. 105–124). St. John's: IMEHA.

ECORYS. (2009). *Study on Competitiveness of the European Shipbuilding Industry*. Rotterdam: ECORYS.

Goss, R. O. (2011). Strategies in British Shipping, 1945–1970. *The Mariner's Mirror, 97*(1), 243–258.

Harlaftis, G. (1995). *A History of Greek-Owned Shipping: The Making of an International Tramp Fleet, 1830 to the Present Day*. London: Taylor & Francis.

Ingram, P., & Lifschitz, A. (2006). Kinship in the Shadow of the Corporation: The Interbuilder Network in Clyde River Shipbuilding, 1711–1990. *American Sociological Review, 71*(2), 334–352.

Jamieson, A. (2003). *Ebb Tide in the British Maritime Industries: Change and Adaptation, 1918–1990*. Liverpool: Liverpool University Press.

Johnman, L., & Murphy, H. (2002). *British Shipbuilding and the State Since 1918—A Political Economy of Decline*. Exeter: University of Exeter Press.

Kang, J. Y., Kim, S., Murphy, H., & Tenold, S. (2015). Old Methods Versus New: A Comparison of Very Large Crude Carrier Construction at Scott Lithgow and Hyundai Heavy Industries, 1970–1977. *Mariner's Mirror, 101*(4), 426–457.

Kang, J. Y., Kim, S., Murphy, H., & Tenold, S. (2016). British Financial, Managerial and Technical Assistance in Establishing the Global Shipbuilding Giant, Hyundai Heavy Industries. *The International Journal of Maritime History, 28*(1), 81–101.

Kenwood, A. G., & Lougheed, A. L. (1999). *The Growth of the International Economy 1820–2000*. London: Routledge.

Lorenz, E. H. (1991). An Evolutionary Explanation for Competitive Decline: The British Shipbuilding Industry, 1890–1970. *The Journal of Economic History, 51*(4), 911–935.

Milne, G. J. (2009). North East England Shipping in the 1890s: Investment and Entrepreneurship. *The International Journal of Maritime History, 21*(1), 1–26.

OECD. (2017). *Imbalances in the Shipbuilding Industry and Assessment of Policy Responses* (C/WP6(2016)6/FINAL). Paris: OECD Working Party on Shipbuilding.

Ojala, J., & Tenold. S. (2017). Maritime Trade and Merchant Shipping: The Shipping/Trade Ratio Since the 1870s. *The International Journal of Maritime History, 29*, 838–854.

Palmer, S. (2008). British Shipping from the Late Nineteenth Century to the Present. In L. R. Fischer & E. Lange (Eds.), *International Merchant Shipping in the Nineteenth and Twentieth Centuries* (pp. 125–142). St. John's: IMEHA.

Palmer, S. (2012). Government and the British Shipping Industry in the Later Twentieth Century. In G. Harlaftis, S. Tenold, & J. M. Valdaliso (Eds.), *The World's Key Industry—History and Economics of International Shipping* (pp. 124–141). Basingstoke: Palgrave Macmillan.

Pollard, S. (1957). British and World Shipbuilding, 1890–1914: A Study in Comparative Costs. *The Journal of Economic History, 17*(3), 426–444.

Robertson, P. L. (1974). Shipping and Shipbuilding: The Case of William Denny and Brothers. *Business History, 16*(1), 36–47.

Scholl, L. U. (1998). The Global Communication Industry and Its Impact on International Shipping Before 1914. In D. J. Starkey & G. Harlaftis (Eds.), *Global Markets: The Internationalization of the Sea Transport Industries Since 1850* (pp. 195–215). St. John's: IMEHA.

Schwarz, T., & von Halle, E. L. (1902). *Schiffbauindustrie in Deutschland und im Auslande*. Berlin: Mittler.

Slaven, A. (2013). *British Shipbuilding: A History 1500–2010*. Lancaster: Crucible Books.

Sornn-Friese, H., Poulsen, R. T., & Iversen, M. J. (2012). "Knowing the Ropes": Capability Reconfiguration and Restructuring of the Danish Shipping Industry. In S. Tenold, M. J. Iversen, & E. Lange (Eds.), *Global Shipping in Small Nations—Nordic Experiences After 1960* (pp. 61–99). Basingstoke: Palgrave Macmillan.

Statistics Norway. (1902). *Statistisk aarbog for kongeriget Norge* (pp. 168–169). Kristiania: Det Statistiske Centralbureau and H. Aschehoug & Co, Tables I and K.

Sturmey, S. G. (1962/2010). *British Shipping and World Competition*. St. John's: IMEHA.

Tenold, S. (2006). *Tankers in Trouble—Norwegian Shipping and the Crisis of the 1970s and 1980s*. St. Johns: IMEHA.

Tenold, S. (2012). Boom, Crisis and Internationalised Revitalisation: Norwegian Shipping 1960–2008. In S. Tenold, M. J. Iversen, & E. Lange (Eds.), *Global Shipping in Small Nations—Nordic Experiences After 1960* (pp. 26–60). Basingstoke: Palgrave Macmillan.

Tenold, S. (2019). *Norwegian Shipping in the 20th Century—Norway's Successful Navigation of the World's Most Global Industry*. Cham: Palgrave Macmillan.

Theotokas, I., & Harlaftis, G. (2009). *Leadership in World Shipping: Greek Family Firms in International Business*. Basingstoke: Palgrave Macmillan.

Todd, D. (2011). Going East: Was the Shift in Volume Shipbuilding Capacity from Britain and Continental Europe to the Far East and Elsewhere During the Latter Half of the Twentieth Century Inevitable? *The Mariner's Mirror, 97*(1), 259–271.

Yates, P. L. (1959). *Forty Years of Foreign Trade: A Statistical Handbook with Special Reference to Primary Products and Under-developed Countries*. London: Allen & Unwin.

Open Access This chapter is licensed under the terms of the Creative Commons Attribution-NonCommercial-NoDerivatives 4.0 International License (http://creativecommons.org/licenses/by-nc-nd/4.0/), which permits any noncommercial use, sharing, distribution and reproduction in any medium or format, as long as you give appropriate credit to the original author(s) and the source, provide a link to the Creative Commons license and indicate if you modified the licensed material. You do not have permission under this license to share adapted material derived from this chapter or parts of it.

The images or other third party material in this chapter are included in the chapter's Creative Commons license, unless indicated otherwise in a credit line to the material. If material is not included in the chapter's Creative Commons license and your intended use is not permitted by statutory regulation or exceeds the permitted use, you will need to obtain permission directly from the copyright holder.

3

The Emergence of Maritime Governance in the Post-War World

Katharina Reiling

Introduction

Shipping highlights some of the adverse effects of globalization as can be seen in examples such as oil spills resulting from maritime accidents, seafarers reduced to 'modern slaves' and the risk of pandemics spread through seaborne trade and cruise trips. These observations raise the question of what, if anything, the public regulation of maritime shipping can achieve today. Regulation is usually understood as emanating from states, but the nation-state faces difficulties in coping with cross-border phenomena such as modern shipping. The obvious solution seems to be a close cooperation of states in regulatory matters; however, the issue of Flags of convenience illustrates the practical limitations of this approach in maritime matters.

K. Reiling (✉)
Universität Konstanz, Konstanz, Germany
e-mail: katharina.reiling@uni-konstanz.de

Against this background, this chapter aims to show that experiences from shipping can reveal some of the legal challenges presented by globalization. The development of the regulation of shipping reveals that globalized industries do not operate in a legal vacuum,[1] but that they require a more subtle form of regulation than the traditional state-centred perspective implies. The chapter describes the regulation of shipping as 'conglomeratic' because it is characterized by the involvement of a wide and growing range of different actors in creating and enforcing shipping standards, and attributes its conglomeratic structure to the fact that maritime shipping fully developed its global nature in the post-war era. On the basis of these observations, the chapter argues that an analysis of the shipping industry can serve as a means of better understanding the role of law in processes of globalization.

Regulating Global Shipping: From the Primacy of the Flag State to the 'Conglomeratic Approach'

Maritime shipping is a prime example of an increasingly globalized industry.[2] A ship is a highly mobile industrial plant and can readily be transferred to other jurisdictions. The different types of ships, such as bulk carriers, container ships, tankers or reefers transport cargo throughout the world, thus enabling the intercontinental trade of goods. Since the post-war era, the transboundary character of shipping has gradually become more and more pronounced. On the one hand technological advances such as containerization have increased the effectiveness, volume and thus importance of shipping, on the other hand the mobility of maritime shipping has been systematically used by shipowners to inhibit effective regulation, in particular through what has become known as 'flagging out'.[3] This began after the First World War as US shipping interests, seeking to evade US

---

[1] Simmel (2001, 684) regarding seafarers. Very sceptical: Roe (2013).
[2] See Alderton et al. (2004).
[3] Stopford (2009, 164, 191, 438–440).

3 The Emergence of Maritime Governance in the Post-War World

regulations, registered their ships first in Panama and then, after the Second World War, also in Liberia.[4] Such 'open registries', as UNCTAD has called this phenomenon since the early 1970s[5] and which is by now the international standard term,[6] are especially popular with shipowners[7] from industrial nations[8] because they offer lower tax levels and allow the recruitment of low-cost crews from countries around the world. This shift to open registries was accelerated by the 1973 oil price increases, the related economic crisis, drastic temporary reductions in world trade and the continued production of ships built under subsidies which added to already existing worldwide surplus capacity. As a consequence, shipowners sought to reduce costs. Today, not only Liberia and Panama but even land-locked states such as Bolivia have set up open registries. In addition to flagging out, many shipowners have begun to use subcontracting and single-ship companies with addresses in offshore jurisdictions, in order to conceal ownership and limit their legal responsibilities.[9]

Thus, maritime shipping is a typical globalized industry, with multiple countries and cultures involved in every single voyage.[10] A typical ship

> may be owned by a Greek national through a Liberian Company. The ship may well have been built in Japan, but powered by Danish engines. It will no doubt be manned by a crew of mixed nationality, including for example, some Italian officers and Philippino ratings. It may have been financed through a New York bank and insured in London, time chartered to an oil multinational corporation for three years to carry Saudi Arabian crude oil from the Gulf to Rotterdam.[11]

As a globalized industry, shipping is also highly competitive with shipowners under continuous pressure to reduce costs. Moreover, the international

---

[4] Carlisle (1981, 2).
[5] First UNCTAD (1972–1973, 13).
[6] Sturmey (1983, 9).
[7] For analyses of their decisions Bergantino and Marlow (1997).
[8] Ownership of the world shipping fleet is highly concentrated. Shipowners from Greece, China, Japan and Germany together account for 41% of world tonnage: UNCTAD (2016).
[9] Gereffi et al. (2005, 461), see also Harlaftis and Tsakas, in this volume.
[10] DeSombre (2009).
[11] Odeke (1984, 10).

setting offers shipowners many opportunities for disreputable practices. Traditionally, flag states were regarded as responsible for enforcing regulation. However, widespread regulatory avoidance by shipowners and the lack of interest shown by 'open registry' states in enforcing regulation demonstrate that the flag state principle fails in a highly globalized industry such as shipping.

To facilitate maritime shipping, the principle of freedom of the seas—prominently formulated by Hugo Grotius—was established.[12] Under this principle, ships are free to use the open seas to sail anywhere they want.[13] Nevertheless, this does not imply freedom from regulation. Under the flag state principle, maritime shipping regulation lies in the hands of the flag state, that is, the state where a ship is registered. The flag state has full jurisdiction over the ship, its crew and its operations and this jurisdiction is exclusive while the ship is on the high seas.[14] In this sense, the flag state principle can be seen as an expression of national sovereignty and thus of the traditional so-called Westphalian system of international law.[15]

The 1982 United Nations Convention on the Law of the Sea (LOSC), the overarching framework regarding ocean issues, sticks with the flag state principle (Articles 91, 92 LOSC). The LOSC recognizes the problem of open registries and seeks to address it by imposing obligations on the flag state regarding its shipping regulation (Articles 94, 217 LOSC)[16] and by extending the authority of coastal and port states over foreign flagged ships[17] (see, for example, Articles 218, 220 LOSC). However, because the LOSC continues to assert that the flag state is the principal authority, the international law of the sea only insufficiently addresses the conditions of the regulation of maritime shipping, especially since

---

[12] For historical accounts, see Gidel (1932), Fulton (1911), and Stier-Somlo (1917).

[13] It remains legally disputed if the ship or its flag states use the freedom of the sea. In one of its first cases, ITLOS stated that both are the users, MV Saiga (Saint Vincent and the Grenadines v. Guinea), 1 July 1999, ILR 120 (1999, 143).

[14] An exception is when the ship engages in piracy.

[15] The famous 'Lotus principle' referred to a shipping case. In this context the Permanent Court of International Justice considered a foundation of international law, says that sovereign states may act in any way they wish so long as they do not contravene an explicit prohibition, P.C.I.J. (ser. A) No. 10 (1927, 18) *The Case of the S.S. Lotus (France v. Turkey)*.

[16] Witt (2007).

[17] Molenaar (1998), Yang (2006), and Marten (2014).

3 The Emergence of Maritime Governance in the Post-War World

open registries have neither the capacity nor the inclination to regulate shipping properly[18] (capacity is often a problem regarding popular open registries with large fleets like Panama[19]). It is argued here that (a) the worldwide impact and the regulatory avoidance which are widespread in the maritime shipping industry demand an involvement of all the multiple actors that are concerned by maritime shipping rather than the monolithic approach implied by the flag state principle, and (b) that a regulatory regime involving these multiple actors is indeed emerging.

Since the 1970s, the time during which the open registries became more and more popular, the monolithic approach inherent in the flag state principle was progressively replaced by a conglomeratic approach to the regulation of maritime shipping. This conglomeratic approach can be characterized as follows: First, standard setting and law enforcement are no longer concentrated in the hands of the flag state, but are distributed across different actors. Secondly, there is a multiplication of actors involved in the regulation of shipping, and there is no hierarchical link between these actors. In the following, the key features and the emergence of the conglomeratic approach will be put in concrete terms by describing the actors of maritime governance and their regulatory roles.

International Organizations and Their Procedures

There is a long history of transnational decision-making in the maritime shipping sector, which greatly contributed to the development of a cross-border transportation system. However, the twentieth century is specific because it is characterized by a proliferation of international organizations, which created an extensive treaty-making system and numerous treaties

---

[18] Rothwell and Stephens (2016, 168).
[19] For social matters ITF (2016a, 25).

establishing international standards.[20] The technique whereby international law ensures such an international harmonized legislation is the delegation of standard-setting to international organizations.[21] Alongside this quantitative aspect of a more 'international' standard-setting, a further feature is the fact that the states' influence on the standard-setting process has been reduced more and more.

The most important international shipping standards are the International Convention for the Safety of Life at Sea (SOLAS), 1974, as amended; the International Convention for the Prevention of Marine Pollution from Ships, 1973, as modified by the Protocol of 1978 relating thereto and by the Protocol of 1997 (MARPOL); the International Convention on Standards of Training, Certification and Watchkeeping for Seafarers (STCW), as amended, including the 1995 and 2010 Manila Amendments and the Maritime Labour Convention (MLC). These conventions are often called the four pillars of the international maritime regulatory regime. They were concluded under the auspices of two international organizations.

The SOLAS, adopted in 1914 in the wake of the *Titanic* disaster, was created in a mixed multilateral diplomatic and technical arena and turned out to be a milestone for international maritime standard-setting. This form of standard-setting was institutionalized with the establishment of the Intergovernmental Maritime Consultative Organization (IMCO) in 1948, which eventually became the International Maritime Organization (IMO) in 1982.[22]

The IMO has a broad mandate; its purpose is summarized in Article 1 of the Convention on the International Maritime Organization as

> To provide machinery for co-operation among Governments in the field of governmental regulation and practices relating to technical matters of all kinds affecting maritime shipping engaged in international trade, and

---

[20] See Chirop et al. (2012, 1).

[21] In LOSC, when it comes to shipping regulation, a standard wording is 'generally accepted international rules and standards established through the competent international organization or general diplomatic conference' (for instance, Article 213, similar Article 94 Paragraph 5). This reference empowers the international level to set standards.

[22] Librando et al. (2014, 577).

3 The Emergence of Maritime Governance in the Post-War World

to encourage the general adoption of the highest practicable standards in matters concerning maritime safety, efficiency of navigation and prevention and control of marine pollution from ships; and to deal with administrative and legal matters related to the purposes set out in this Article.[23]

Within the IMO, national delegations composed primarily of technical experts work closely with observers from all areas of industry, trade unions and environmental organizations. This system created a global community of experts working through the IMO's system of committees, sub-committees and other expert groups, on a sessional and inter-sessional basis.[24] By 2018, the IMO had 174 member states and had produced over fifty international maritime conventions covering, among other issues, safety of life at sea, including construction, equipping, operation and maintenance; vessel-source pollution including liability and compensation for damage; preparedness for and response to maritime accidents; wreck removal; ship recycling; limitation of liability for maritime claims; training standards for seafarers; facilitation of maritime traffic; and salvage.[25]

Another international organization that plays an important role in maritime activities is the International Labour Organization (ILO).[26] The ILO was founded in 1919 to pursue a vision based on the premise that 'universal and lasting peace can be established only if it is based on social justice', and became the first specialized agency of the UN in 1946.[27] Its so-called tripartite structure gives an equal voice to workers, employers and governments of 187 member states[28] to ensure that the views of the social partners are closely reflected in labour standards. More than sixty conventions that have been adopted cover nearly all aspects of seafarers' working and living conditions. The MLC, adopted in 2006 and entered into force in 2013, updates and consolidates these earlier ILO conventions.

---

[23] IMO.
[24] Simmonds (1994).
[25] See IMO.
[26] Roach (2016).
[27] Constitution of the ILO, Preamble.
[28] ILO.

Under domestic legal systems, if the majority votes in favour of a provision, the minority is bound by this decision. In contrast, public international law is not governed by the majority principle but by the consent principle. This reflects the fact that the foundation of public international law is national sovereignty. Therefore, as a general rule, an international convention only becomes legally binding when a state gives consent, namely signs and, normally, also ratifies the convention and implements it into its national legislation. In the modern maritime shipping world with its rapid technological development and the advent of open registries, this state-based solution has become unsatisfactory because the conclusion and implementation of international standards is often refused or stalled by the states. Since the established mode for the introduction of international standards is a highly time-consuming process, two instruments have been used to solve this problem by limiting the states' influence on the standard-setting process.

The first one is the 'tacit acceptance procedure' which was first stipulated in IMO conventions and can now also be found in those of the ILO.[29] IMO committees regularly draft and adopt the technical parts of international conventions mostly contained in amendments. These amendments become binding if within a certain period of time, a certain number of contracting parties (usually at least one-third representing at least 35% of global tonnage) have not explicitly rejected them—silence means consent. The tacit acceptance procedure enables amendments of international treaties to enter into force within as little as a year after being adopted. Although the requirement for consent is thereby not waived, consent becomes the default position and unless states issue a declaration of the contrary, they are bound by the amended treaty.[30] Furthermore, the tacit acceptance procedure is no longer solely used for strictly technical issues; shipping standards with far-reaching consequences have been introduced via this instrument.[31]

---

[29]See IMO; in detail König (2013, 8). The MLC has adopted this IMO procedure for MLC amendments (Article XV), see Servais (2011, 75, 105).
[30]Kachel (2006, 34).
[31]For example, the mandatory introduction of the International Safety Management Code, with further instances Pamborides (1999, 110).

The second instrument is the clause of 'no-more-favourable treatment' which also can be found in both IMO and ILO conventions.[32] Essentially, a no-more-favourable-treatment clause requires that each contracting party shall apply such conventions to a foreign ship in its ports even if the flag state of the ship has not ratified the respective convention. The clause is designed to prevent ships flying the flags of states that have not signed the convention—in particular, open registries—from having an unfair advantage. The no-more-favourable-treatment clause is not regarded as prejudicial to the sovereignty of states that are not party to the respective convention, because while it obliges signatory states to apply the convention to ships registered in non-signatory states, it does not place any direct obligations on non-signatories.[33] Furthermore, the no-more-favourable-treatment clause does not extend the jurisdiction of the signatory states since the right of port states to prescribe conditions for the entry into port already exists under public international law.[34] However, this is a point of form rather than of substance because from the perspective of the non-party states, it does not make any difference if an international treaty directly obliges it to comply with its provisions or if an international treaty obliges other states to apply its provisions to ships registered in non-party states.[35]

To summarize, the combination of international standard-setting with the tacit acceptance procedure and the no-more-favourable-treatment principle has diminished the role of flag states and increased that of international organizations and port states. International organizations have become the key players in shipping legislation. Nevertheless, there remain many weak points because international standard-setting still relies on a state-centred approach. For instance, regarding the tacit acceptance procedure, every state has the possibility to opt out of a convention and implementation likewise still relies on states. As a consequence of the remaining influence of states in international standard-setting, maritime

---

[32] For example, Article II SOLAS; Article 5 Paragraph 4 MARPOL, see Boisson (2016, 212) and Oral (2012, 219).
[33] Regarding the so-called *pacta tertiis* rule of Article 34 of the 1969 Vienna Convention on the Law of Treaties, see with further references Proelss (2018, 16).
[34] Molenaar (1998, 119).
[35] Proelss (2018, 17).

conventions are reactive rather than proactive as they are often adopted in response to particular accidents or incidents, as the SOLAS convention shows.[36] Furthermore, they are of a compromise nature, thus only setting minimum standards.[37] Hence, standard-setting activities by regional actors such as the EU who can push through their own agendas, as well as incentive-based instruments of intermediate actors that foster higher standards in maritime shipping are very important.

The Role of Public Authorities in Port State Control and IMO Compliance Procedures

In standard-setting, the flag states' primary responsibility has been substantially reduced by the activities of international organizations. Regarding the enforcement of standards, the situation is a similar one. Although the IMO and the ILO are not empowered to enforce their standards, the monopoly of flag states has been pushed back by complementing it with inspections carried out by port states and with IMO procedures which foster compliance of the flag states with their international obligations.

Port state control refers to the control of foreign-flagged ships by the public authorities of a port state.[38] Where a port state control officer finds deficiencies, the officer may require their rectification. In serious cases, the ship may be detained or even banned from returning to a country's ports. It is by no means a recent phenomenon that vessels entering a foreign port are subject to standards mandated by local laws. A well-known example is the Merchant Shipping Act of 1876, which appears to be the United Kingdom's first regulation relying on port state jurisdiction to address the safety of foreign vessels engaged in international trade.[39] This initiative of port state control can be explained by the fact that the UK, the world's leading maritime power in those days, was witnessing great technological changes in the expanding maritime shipping industry. In recent decades,

---

[36] Chirop et al. (2012, 5).
[37] For the MLC Pineiro (2015, 48). For IMO Conventions Carlin (2002, 347).
[38] Kasoulides (1993), Marten (2014), and Molenaar (2015, 291).
[39] Marten (2014, 37–41).

3 The Emergence of Maritime Governance in the Post-War World

the role of port states in enforcing international shipping standards has expanded vastly.[40] International law reflects this development, as several IMO and ILO conventions now give port states powers to inspect foreign vessels.[41]

However, port state control does not displace the flag state's control. Rather it follows a subsidiarity-based approach, compensating for deficits of the flag state.[42] Thus, the public authorities of flag states are still involved in the enforcement of shipping standards. To hold them to their obligations, the IMO has begun to establish several procedures aiming to guarantee that flag states properly implement and enforce international standards. The point of reference for these IMO compliance procedures is Article 94 LOSC, establishing flag states' fundamental duties and requiring them to take the steps necessary to secure compliance with international requirements (mainly ensuring periodic surveys and issuing and renewing ships' certificates).[43]

IMO compliance procedures against flag states have been widely introduced in the 1990s.[44] The most recent step has been the introduction of the so-called IMO Member State Audit Scheme (IMSAS), which entered into force in 2016. IMSAS which is mandatory[45] is intended to provide an audited member state with a comprehensive and objective assessment of how effectively it administers and implements mandatory IMO instruments.[46] Such IMO compliance procedures demonstrate that the flag states have lost their primacy in shipping regulation.

These compliance procedures differ from the traditional compliance procedures of international law. The traditional compliance mechanisms are actions taken unilaterally by individual states against other states. Thus,

---

[40] Marten (2014, 37).
[41] For instance SOLAS, Part B, Regulation 6 (c); MLC, Title 5, Regulation 5.2.1. But there is no international obligation to do so.
[42] For this interconnection, see Marten (2014, 225).
[43] LOSC Article 94 Paragraph 1 and 5; Article 94 Paragraph 4; Article 217 Paragraph 1 and 3.
[44] Lemke (2011, 268).
[45] Amendments to COLREG 1972, MARPOL Annexes I through to VI. SOLAS, 1974, as amended (adding a new chapter XIII) International Convention on Standards of Training, Certification and Watchkeeping for Seafarers, 1978.
[46] IMO.

it is upon each state to determine whether other states are fulfilling obligations owed to it, and whether there is non-compliance that cannot be rectified by means of negotiations or diplomatic measures, such as retortions, to induce the other state or states to comply with its or their obligations. In contrast, the new IMO compliance procedures have been characterized as 'collective' measures. This stems from the fact that not an individual state, but an international body has the competence to ascertain whether there is compliance and to take action in the case of non-compliance.[47] The background of such 'collective' compliance procedures is the fact that individual states regularly lack the interest and the information to consider taking measures against fellow states.[48]

Regional Actors

Since the 1970s, the regulation of maritime shipping is subject to processes of regionalization.[49] Regional actors are involved by implementing and enforcing international standards, setting stricter standards and contributing local knowledge in the international standard-setting process. The LOSC considers the IMO the predominant intergovernmental organization,[50] but regarding the protection of the marine environment it recognizes the importance of regional cooperation, as Article 237, 197, 127 LOSC show. The key regional actors are port states' agency networks, the EU and Regional Seas Organizations (RSOs).

Port states regularly act through agency networks. A historic example of such networks can be found in the incident of the *Amoco Cadiz*, a major oil spill in 1978 that followed a tanker running aground off the coast of France. Subsequent to this incident, networks of public authorities of the port states have emerged in order to enforce international shipping standards more effectively. The underlying idea is that the elimination of

---

[47] Churchill (2012, 777).
[48] Beyerlin and Marauhn (2011, 318).
[49] For an in-depth analysis of the development of regionalism in the law of the sea Franckx (1998, 307) and, specifically on Europe, van Leeuwen (2015, 23).
[50] Critical: Ringbom (2015, 124).

3 The Emergence of Maritime Governance in the Post-War World

substandard shipping, meaning ships that are not compliant with international standards, would be best achieved by regional alliances of public authorities. These agency networks do not act on the basis of an international treaty, but on that of agreements among the public authorities within a region, known as Memoranda of Understanding (MoUs). They embody a common database with shipping and inspection information, common inspector training and a code of conduct. The earliest and best-known regional cooperation of this kind is the 1982 Paris Memorandum of Understanding on Port State Control (Paris MoU). It includes twenty-seven public authorities from Europe including the Russian Federation and from Canada.[51] Paris MoU is the model upon which eight other regions of the world have based their agreements on port state control.[52]

Establishing their own institutions such as a Secretariat and a Member Committee,[53] these agency networks, also known as PSC MoUs, can be regarded as regional actors in maritime shipping issues because their status is between a formal international organization and a mere agreement.

The growing number of sub-standard ships trading with the EU and several maritime shipping accidents off European coasts, such as the *Erika* and *Prestige* accidents, have spurred the EU to develop its own regulation of maritime shipping, notably starting with the Communication on a Common Policy on Safe Seas in 1993.[54] At first, the EU aimed to improve implementation and enforcement of international standards. A prominent example is the Directive on Port State Control adopted in 1995[55] and extended after the tanker accidents of the *Erika* and the *Prestige*.[56] In 2002,

---

[51] Paris MoU.

[52] Asia and the Pacific (Tokyo MoU); Latin America (Acuerdo de Viña del Mar); Caribbean (Caribbean MoU); West and Central Africa (Abuja MoU); the Black Sea region (Black Sea MoU); the Mediterranean (Mediterranean MoU); the Indian Ocean (Indian Ocean MoU); and the Riyadh MoU. The United States Coast Guard maintains its own port state control regime, see IMO.

[53] Paris MoU.

[54] EU Commission (1993), see Urrutia (2006, 202).

[55] Directive 95/21/EC of 19 June 1995 concerning the enforcement, in respect of shipping using Community ports and sailing in the waters under the jurisdiction of the Member States, of international standards for ship safety, pollution prevention and shipboard living and working conditions (port state control), OJ L 157/1 of 7 July 1995. See in detail Salvarani (1996, 225).

[56] See Keselj (1999, 127). In detail van Leeuwen (2010, 75).

the EU established the European Maritime Safety Agency (EMSA),[57] providing technical assistance and support to the European Commission and Member States in the development and implementation of EU maritime shipping legislation.[58] For this purpose, EMSA assesses the functioning of the port state inspection systems and collects and analyses maritime shipping information.

The tendency in the EU's current regulation is to create its own regulatory concepts in order to push forward difficult negotiations on the international level. Thus, this form of European shipping legislation also includes standards which are stricter than the international ones in terms of time scales and content.[59] A well-known example is the issue of phasing out single hull tankers and replacing by them with double hull tankers; here, the EU's proposals forced the IMO to adopt a faster schedule.

RSOs are regional bodies that have been established for a specific and limited purpose, the protection and preservation of the marine environment of particular regional seas.[60] In general international environmental law, RSOs are called regional Multilateral Environmental Agreements (MEAs).[61] With their local knowledge and their specific interest in solving local problems, regional MEAs can offer solutions for environmental issues, implement international standards and negotiate their own standards. Even though they are based on intergovernmental agreements, MEAs have acquired a measure of autonomy, with their own institutions such as a Secretariat, a Conference of the Parties and scientific bodies to enable them to fulfil their functions.[62] Due to their organizational structure, they are called 'autonomous institutional arrangements'.[63]

Initially, RSOs were established in Europe in the 1970s: The Convention for the Protection of the Marine Environment of the North-East Atlantic (OSPAR Convention) and the Helsinki Convention for the Baltic

---

[57] Regulation 1406/2002 of the European Parliament and of the Council of 27 June 2002 establishing a European Maritime Safety Agency, OJ L 208/1.
[58] EMSA.
[59] See Höltmann (2012, 73).
[60] Tetzlaff (2015, 112).
[61] Birnie et al. (2009, 84).
[62] Birnie et al. (2009, 86).
[63] Scott (2011, 12).

3 The Emergence of Maritime Governance in the Post-War World   51

Sea are the central conventions for the protection of the sea. OSPAR started in 1972 with the Oslo Convention against dumping and was broadened to cover land-based sources and the offshore industry by the Paris Convention of 1974. These two conventions were unified by the 1992 OSPAR Convention, with the OSPAR Commission as the forum through which the contracting parties cooperate, as well as a Secretariat, five main committees and several working groups.[64] Regarding the Helsinki Convention, the Helsinki Commission (HELCOM) adopts recommendations for the protection of the marine environment, which is supported by a Secretariat, the Heads of Delegation and eight main groups.[65] Following the examples of the OSPAR and the Helsinki Convention, the UNEP's Regional Seas Programme (UNEP RSP) was established in 1974 in order to promote the preservation and protection of the marine environment worldwide. The UNEP RSP provides a framework for regional cooperation through a network of currently eighteen Regional Seas Programmes, which implement action plans and are often supported by regional seas conventions.[66] In contrast to the EU's taking the initiative in developing its own sets of standards, these RSOs have mostly focused on implementing international shipping standards.[67] However, in recent years, they have started to pursue their own environmental policies and provide impulses at the international level. To give an example, the organs of the OSPAR, the Helsinki and the Barcelona Convention have worked together to put in place voluntary guidelines[68] for the maritime shipping industry that request vessels entering the waters concerned to exchange all their ballast water at least 200 nautical miles from the nearest land in water at least 200 metres deep. The background for these guidelines is the fact that maritime shipping is a key vector of invasive species due to the discharge of ballast water and the sediments that it carries. The IMO Ballast Water Management Convention preventing the transfer of invasive species entered into

---

[64] OSPAR Commission.
[65] HELCOM.
[66] UNEP.
[67] Ringbom (2015, 124).
[68] The General Guidance on the Voluntary Interim application of the D1 Ballast Water Exchange Standard, see OSPAR.

force in 2017. Thus, the RSOs have anticipated international standards in their regions.

In recent years, the institutions of the Antarctic Treaty System (ATS) as well as the Arctic Council have fostered their regulatory roles, because both polar areas have very fragile environments susceptible to externally-inflicted damage, while global climate change has stimulated interest in making use of these regions' resources and transport routes. The ATS, consisting of three treaties[69] and one comprehensive Protocol on Environmental Protection, builds the framework for a regional MEA,[70] with the Antarctic Treaty Consultative Meetings, the Committee for Environmental Protection and a Secretariat as main organs. In the Arctic space, the Arctic Council, its Working Groups and its Secretariat can be regarded as a RSO.[71] The work on a so-called Polar Code, regarding navigation in polar waters, is a result of the regulatory cooperation of these two arctic actors and the IMO.[72]

Intermediate Actors

Intermediate actors are non-state actors fulfilling public functions. Similar to the regional actors mentioned above, they support the regulation of maritime shipping by implementing and enforcing international standards, setting stricter standards and contributing expertise in the process of international standard-setting. They differ from the regional actors in that regional actors are essentially state actors. The involvement of intermediate actors is said to constitute a form of 'hybrid governance' because, despite their private nature, they are involved in public regulation.[73] The

---

[69] The treaties are the Antarctic Treaty (AT, Washington, 1959), the Convention for the Conservation of Antarctic Seals (CCAS, London, 1972), and the Convention on the Conservation of Antarctic Marine Living Resources (CCAMLR, Canberra, 1980).

[70] Steiner et al. (2003, 236).

[71] However, the Artic Council is a result of soft law, because the 1996 Ottawa Declaration established the Arctic Council as forum for promoting cooperation, coordination, and interaction among the Arctic States and not a legally binding international treaty. For the role of the Arctic Council Fife (2013, 355).

[72] Mucci and Borgia (2014, 505).

[73] A well-known example is ICANN, see Möllers (2015, 124).

major intermediate actors are port authorities, classification societies, P&I clubs and the International Transport Workers' Federation (ITF).

Modern seaports are not mere interfaces between sea and land, but operational hubs for the logistics supply chain and, as such, play a significant role for seaborne trade. At the same time, the adverse impacts of expanding maritime transport are particularly tangible in the local area of a port.[74] Combining interest in the regulation of maritime shipping with the ability to do so, seaports, or strictly speaking the port authorities, have created their own instruments to foster environmentally friendly 'green shipping' since the 1990s. Their key instruments are financial incentives such as differentiated port fees to encourage ships to comply with or even go beyond existing environmental standards, e.g. for ships using cleaner fuels.[75] Often, differentiated port fees are used in combination with voluntary certification schemes or with environmental indexes. Such certifications and indexes provide information about the environmental impact of individual ships. Relying on a certificate or index that documents how environmentally friendly a ship is is obviously easier for ports than developing and enforcing a new metric.[76] One of the first certification schemes was the Green Award, initiated in 1994 by Rotterdam Municipal Port Management and the Dutch Ministry of Transport.[77] The Environmental Shipping Index (ESI) established in 2010 is a project within the World Ports Climate Initiative (WPCI).[78] It identifies seagoing ships that perform better in reducing air emissions than required by the current emission standards of the IMO.

The legal nature of port authorities differs from region to region. In Europe, most seaports remain in public ownership, but they are moving towards a more independent private sector-like management.[79]

---

[74] Becker et al. (2011, 5).
[75] Lister et al. (2015, 191).
[76] European Commission (2017, 44).
[77] Green Award (2019).
[78] ESI.
[79] ESPO.

The main function of classification societies is the technical surveillance of seagoing ships.[80] Classification societies set standards for the design, construction and inspections of ships, carry out periodic surveys and ultimately issue so-called class certificates confirming whether or not a certain ship meets specific standards. Traditionally, the purpose of these classification societies, which arose in England in the second half of the eighteenth century, is to protect the property interests of shipowners and operators, insurers and other private parties directly affected by a ship's seaworthiness. Today, however, classification societies also carry out public functions, because flag states frequently delegate the fulfilment of their international obligations imposed by IMO conventions and IMO resolutions to specifically recognized classification societies.[81] On behalf of flag states, classification societies perform surveys and issue so-called statutory certificates which confirm that a ship complies with IMO standards.

This brief overview reveals the characteristic features of classification societies[82]: While remaining essentially private actors, classification societies perform a dual role. They have both a private aspect—classification or voluntary services on behalf of the maritime industry—and a public aspect—certification or statutory services on behalf of flag states. Thus, they can be described as intermediate actors.

Protection and Indemnity (P&I) insurance provides cover for named risk marine liabilities common to the maritime shipping industry. This type of insurance has its origin in London in the middle of the nineteenth century[83] and can be seen as a consequence of third party claimants succeeding in their attempts to file claims for damages against shipowners. The resulting P&I Clubs were an adjunct to the commercial Hull & Machinery underwriters already established in the market.[84] The P&I Clubs work on a mutual, not-for-profit basis (mutuality) and are owned and controlled by the shipowners.[85] Currently, there are thirteen P&I Clubs covering

---

[80] For a synopsis of the historical role and development of classification societies, see Boisson (1999, 353).
[81] See Thorpe et al. (1997, 521).
[82] Boisson (1999, 371).
[83] For the history of the Clubs, see Young (1995).
[84] See Young (1995).
[85] Bennett (2001, 15).

90% of the world's ocean-going fleet (by tonnage), which are coordinated by the International Group of P&I Clubs (IG P&I).[86]

In theory, mutuality provides an incentive for shipowners to minimize risk by adhering to maritime safety and environmental standards. In practice, mutuality is not, in itself, effective in raising safety and environmental standards, especially due to the problems of moral hazard and adverse selection.[87] Thus, the Clubs employ managers who control entry and attempt to set premiums that are commensurate with the riskiness of each member so as to give an incentive to minimize risk.[88] Insurance payouts are conditional upon the ship's compliance with international standards, and the Clubs can also set their own stricter standards.[89] Moreover, the Club Rules state that a ship may be required to be submitted to survey by a surveyor appointed by the Club. Hence, they can foster safe and environmentally friendly shipping.

Especially since the 1990s, international organizations and regional actors have made attempts to involve P&I Clubs more closely in the regulation of maritime shipping.[90] One option is a strict liability regime and compulsory insurance, but these measures can be hard to find support for on an international level[91] and are only reluctantly accepted by P&I Clubs.[92] A further approach for getting the Clubs into the regulatory process is the so-called Quality Shipping Campaign of the EU, launched in 1998. This Campaign makes use of a range of incentives and sanctions to ensure that private actors such as the P&I Clubs are more sensitive to adopting and enforcing high shipping standards.[93]

The ITF, an international trade union federation of transport workers' unions representing over 600,000 seafarers, plays a vital role in improving

---

[86] IG P&I (2019).
[87] Bennett (2001, 15).
[88] For the Clubs' instruments to foster safe and clean shipping, see Riley (1998, 107).
[89] Eivendstad and Petire (2012, 327).
[90] On this issue, see Bennett (2000, 875).
[91] Originally, only regarding oil pollutions from tankers, known as Civil Liability Convention 1969. The Bunker Convention entered into force in 2008, but has only 58 contracting parties; the Hazardous and Noxious Substances by Sea Convention from 1996 has not entered into force due to signatory states not meeting the ratification requirements.
[92] For this point, Eivendstad and Petire (2012, 340).
[93] For this concept, see Haralambides (1998).

living and working conditions for seafarers since its beginnings.[94] The ITF coordinated trade union action against open registries in one of the earliest reactions against capital mobility. Its focus has shifted from the elimination of open registries in the 1950s to enhancing the living and working conditions for seafarers on ships flying the flag of an open registry since the 1970s.[95] Shipowners sailing under what the ITF considers a 'flag of convenience' have been pushed to sign one of the standard collective agreements drawn up by the ITF. Shipowners agreeing to do this are given a 'blue certificate'. A blue certificate means that the ITF inspectors will refrain from impeding the respective vessel from sailing. In the case that shipowners refuse to cooperate with the ITF, hurdles might crop up in the form of boycotts or other industrial actions if the minimum living and working conditions on board as guaranteed by the collective agreement are not respected.[96]

The ITF works closely with public actors in setting international standards and enforcing them. The ITF organizes seafarers' representation at the tripartite negotiations at ILO Maritime Sessions and meetings in the ILO Joint Maritime Commission. Under the MLC 2006, trade unions have their own right of complaint against the port state control authorities which are obliged to enforce the MLC.[97] In practice, the global network of ITF inspectors supports public authorities with its information and expertise in enforcing international shipping standards like the MLC.[98]

---

[94] It was founded in 1896 as the International Federation of Ship, Dock and River Workers. In 1898 it expanded to include non-maritime transport workers. After the First World War, the federation was re-established in 1919 as the ITF, see ILO (2019), see also Fink (2011, 145).
[95] Koch-Baumgarten (1997), see further Koch-Baumgarten (1998, 36; 1999) and Simon (1993).
[96] Koch-Baumgarten (1997).
[97] Standard A.5.2.1 no. 3 and no. 1 lit. d.
[98] ITF (2016b, 8).

From State-Centred Regulation to Conglomeratic Global Governance

The above description of the current international regulation of maritime shipping has shown that flag states no longer are the key actors in maritime issues. Instead, a 'conglomeratic' regulatory structure has emerged as a number of international organizations, public authorities of port states, regional and intermediate actors have become increasingly involved in maritime standard setting and enforcement. This conglomeratic regulation is not just a variation upon the governance once provided by the liner conference system[99]: The liner conference system represents a form of self-governance by selected groups of producers pursuing their own commercial interests, whereas the conglomeratic regulation represents public regulation, still influenced by states and international organizations despite the growing role of intermediate actors such as classifications societies and P&I clubs. Therefore, the conglomeratic regulation represents a new and different way of making and enforcing rules at sea, characterized by the interaction of a multitude of actors.

The LOSC hints at these regulatory changes: The preamble of the LOSC emphasizes the importance of a 'cooperation of the states', and Art. 94 LOSC gives rule-making competences to international organizations and mentions the right of port states to control ships. Primarily, however, the conglomeratic structure has been created not through legislation but through the practice of state and non-state actors responding to the failure of flag states to meet their responsibilities.

Thus, in response to globalization and to the shortcomings of a state-centric approach, namely the failures of flag states in maritime regulation, a conglomeratic approach to regulation has emerged in the maritime world. Perhaps the most important period in this process was the period from the early 1970s and extending to the early 1980s when the most important IMO conventions and their core elements, the tacit acceptance procedure and the no-more-favourable-treatment clause, were adopted.[100] Furthermore, in that period the first steps were taken to harmonize port

---

[99] See Premti (2016) and OECD (2015).
[100] Pamborides (1999, 100).

state control inspections. However, the growth of conglomeratic regulation was neither abrupt nor even and linear; rather, shipping disasters can be identified as the key drivers of the increased regulatory activities.[101] The sinking of the *Titanic* (1912), the *Torrey Canyon* (1967) and the *Amoco Cadiz* (1978) resulted in the adoption and revision of the conventions SOLAS and MARPOL. The *Amoco Cadiz* oil spill also stimulated the introduction of the tacit acceptance procedure and the establishment of agency networks on port state control. The expansion of the EU's regulatory activity can be traced back to the incidents of the *Erika* (1999) and the *Prestige* (2002). Regulatory reform proceeded in a slow and still unsteady manner. Therefore, it cannot be excluded that in the future new actors and new instruments will complement the international shipping regime.

Despite these shortcomings and limitations, the changing conception of international regulation that can be observed in maritime shipping issues can be acknowledged as an example of global governance. Global governance is commonly defined as 'the complex of formal and informal institutions, mechanisms, relationships, and processes between and among states, markets, citizens and organizations through which collective interests on the global plane are articulated and duties, obligations and privileges are established'.[102] Thus, the concept of global governance implies that while states do remain key actors in addressing global problems, a multitude of other actors beyond and below the state have evolved in parallel and engage in international regulation. These actors range from international non-governmental organizations, multinational corporations and international economic institutions to transnational social movements. The conglomeratic structure of regulation that has emerged in the shipping world over the past decades is one example of such global governance[103]

---

[101] Pamborides (1999, 12).

[102] Rosenau (1999).

[103] In this sense van Leeuwen (2015, 23): 'maritime governance is defined as the sharing of policy making competencies in a system of negotiation between nested governmental institutions at several levels (international, supranational, national, regional and local) on the one hand, and state actors, market parties and civil society organizations on the other hand'. Also Bloor et al. (2006, 535).

and may throw light on the mechanisms, achievements and challenges to be faced in areas other than shipping.

References

Academic Literature

Alderton, T., Bloor, M., Kahveci, E., Lane, T., Sampson, H., Thomas, M., et al. (2004). *The Global Seafarer: Living and Working Conditions in a Globalized Industry*. Geneva: ILO.

Becker, A., Inoue, S., Fischer, M., & Schwegler, B. (2011). Climate Change Impacts and Adaption: A Challenge for Global Ports. *Journal of Climate Change, 110,* 5–29.

Bennett, P. (2000). Environmental Governance and Private Actors: Enrolling Insurers in International Maritime Regulation. *Political Geography, 19,* 875–899.

Bennett, P. (2001). Mutual Risk: P&I Clubs and Maritime Safety and Environmental Performance. *Marine Policy, 25,* 13–21.

Bergantino, A. S., & Marlow, P. B. (1997). *Econometric Analyses of the Decision to Flag Out*. Cardiff: SIRC.

Beyerlin, U., & Marauhn, T. (2011). *International Environmental Law*. Oxford: Hart Publishing.

Birnie, P., Boyle, A., & Redgwell, C. (2009). *International Law and the Environment* (3rd ed.). Oxford: Oxford University Press.

Bloor, M., Datta, R., Gilinskiy, Y., & Horlick-Jones, T. (2006). Unicorn Among the Cedars: On the Possibilities of Effective 'Smart Regulation' of the Globalized Shipping Industry. *Social & Legal Studies, 15,* 534–551.

Boisson, P. (1999). Classification Societies and Safety at Sea: Back to Basics to Prepare the Future. *Marine Policy, 18,* 363–377.

Boisson, P. (2016). Law of Maritime Safety. In D. J. Attard (Ed.), *The IMLI Manual on International Maritime Law* (Vol. 2, p. 347). Oxford: Oxford University Press.

Carballo Pineiro, L. (2015). *International Maritime Labour Law*. Berlin and Heidelberg: Springer.

Carlin, E. M. (2002). Oil Pollution from Ships at Sea. In E. L. Miles, A. Underdal, S. Andresen, J. Wettestad, J. B. Skjaeseth, & E. M. Carlin (Eds.), *Environmental Regime Effectiveness*. Cambridge and London: The MIT Press.

Carlisle, R. P. (1981). *Sovereignty for Sale—The Origins and Evolution of the Panamanian and Liberian Flags of Convention*. Annapolis: Naval Institute Press.

Chirop, A., Letalik, N., McDorman, T. L., & Rolston, S. J. (2012). Introduction to the Regulation of International Shipping. In A. Chirop, N. Letalik, T. L. McDorman, & S. J. Rolston (Eds.), *The Regulation of International Shipping* (pp. 1–13). Leiden and Boston: Martinus Nijhoff.

Churchill, R. (2012). Compliance Mechanisms in the International Law of the Sea: From the Individual to the Collective. In H. P. Hestermeyer, D. König, N. Matz-Lück, V. Röben, A. Seibert-Fohr, P.-T. Stoll, & S. Vöneky (Eds.), *Coexistence, Cooperation and Solidarity* (Vol. 1, pp. 777–806). Leiden and Boston: Martinus Nijhoff.

DeSombre, E. R. (2009). *Flagging Standards: Globalization and Environmental, Safety and Labour Regulations at Sea*. Cambridge and London: MIT Press.

Eivendstad, K., & Petire, C. (2012). Safer Ships and Cleaner Seas: The Insurers Role. In A. Chirop, N. Letalik, T. L. McDorman, & S. J. Rolston (Eds.), *The Regulation of International Shipping* (pp. 325–341). Leiden and Boston: Martinus Nijhoff.

Fife, R. E. (2013). Cooperation Across Boundaries. In P. A. Berkman & A. N. Vygzhanin (Eds.), *Environmental Security in the Arctic Ocean* (pp. 345–358). Heidelberg, NY: Springer.

Fink, L. (2011). *Sweatshops at Sea: Merchant Seamen in the World's First Globalized Industry from 1812 to the Present*. Chapel Hill: University of North Carolina Press.

Franckx, E. (1998). Regional Marine Environment Protection Regimes in the Context of UNCLOS. *International Journal of Marine and Coastal Law, 3*, 307–324.

Fulton, T. W. (1911). *The Sovereignty of the Sea*. Edinburgh: Blackwood.

Gereffi, G., Humphrey, J., & Sturgeon, T. (2005). The Governance of Global Value Chains. *Review of International Political Economy, 12*, 461–487.

Gidel, G. (1932). *Le droit international public de la mer* (Vol. 1). Chateroux: Mellotée.

Haralambides, H. E. (1998). *Quality Shipping*. Rotterdam: Erasmus Publishing.

Höltmann, M. (2012). *Schiffssicherheit und Meeresumweltschutz in der EU nach Erika und Prestige*. Baden-Baden: Nomos.

Kachel, M. J. (2006). Competencies of International Maritime Organisations. In P. Ehlers & R. Lagoni (Eds.), *International Maritime Organizations and Their Contribution to a Sustainable Marine Development*. Hamburg: LIT Verlag.

Kasoulides, G. (1993). *Port State Control and Jurisdiction*. Dordrecht: Martinus Nijhoff.

Keselj, T. (1999). Port State Jurisdiction in Respect of Pollution from Ships. *Ocean Development & International Law, 30,* 127–160.

Koch-Baumgarten, S. (1997). Vom Mythos Internationaler Solidarität. *Zeitschrift Für Kritische Sozialwissenschaft, 27,* 263–290.

Koch-Baumgarten, S. (1998). Trade Union Regime Formation Under the Conditions of Globalization in the Transport Sector: Attempts at Transnational Trade Union Regulation of Flag-of-Convenience Shipping. *International Review of Social History, 43,* 369–402.

Koch-Baumgarten, S. (1999). *Gewerkschaftsinternationalismus und die Herausforderung der Globalisierung: Das Beispiel der Internationalen Transportarbeiter-Föderation (ITF)*. Frankfurt am Main. and New York: Campus.

König, D. (2013). Tacit Consent. In R. Wolfrum (Ed.), *Max Planck Encyclopedia of Public International Law (MPEPIL)* (para. 8). Oxford: Oxford University Press.

Lemke, M. (2011). *Erfüllungsdefizite von Flaggenstaaten*. Baden-Baden: Nomos.

Librando, G. (2014). The International Maritime Organization and the Law of the Sea. In D. J. Attard (Ed.), *Manual on International Maritime Law* (Vol. 1, pp. 557–606). Oxford: Oxford University Press.

Lister, J., Poulson, R., & Ponte, S. (2015). Orchestrating Transnational Environmental Governance in Maritime Shipping. *Global Environmental Change, 34,* 185–195.

Marten, B. (2014). *Port State Jurisdiction and the Regulation of International Merchant Shipping*. Heidelberg, NY, Dordrecht, and London: Springer.

Molenaar, E. (1998). *Coastal State Jurisdiction Over Vessel-Source Pollution*. The Hague, Boston, and London: Kluwer Law International.

Molenaar, E. (2015). Port and Coastal States. In D. Rothwell, A. O. Elferink, K. Scott, & T. Stephens (Eds.), *Oxford Handbook of the Law of the Sea* (p. 291). Oxford: Oxford University Press.

Möllers, C. (2015). Constitutional Foundations of Global Administration. In C. Sabino (Ed.), *Research Handbook on Global Administrative Law* (p. 124). Cheltenham: Edward Elgar.

Mucci, F., & Borgia, F. (2014). The Legal Regime of the Antarctic. In D. J. Attard (Ed.), *The IMLI Manual on International Maritime Law* (Vol. 1, p. 505). Oxford: Oxford University Press.

Oral, N. (2012). Climate Change and Shipping. In M. Nordquist, J. Moore, A. Soons, & H. S. Kim (Eds.), *The Law of the Sea Convention* (p. 219). Leiden and Boston: Martinus Nijhoff.

Odeke, A. (1984). *Protectionism and the Future of International Shipping*. Dordrecht, Boston, and Lancaster: Springer, Netherlands.

Pamborides, G. P. (1999). *International Shipping Law*. The Hague, London, and Boston: Kluwer Law International.

Premti, A. (2016). *Liner Shipping: Is There a Way for More Competition?* Geneva: UNCTAD.

Proelss, A. (2018). Article 34. In O. Dörr & K. Schmalenbach (Eds.), *Vienna Convention on the Law of Treaties: A Commentary*. Berlin: Springer.

Riley, J. C. W. (1998). Ship Operating Standards and the Role of the P & I Clubs. In H. E. Haralambides (Ed.), *Quality Shipping* (p. 107). Rotterdam: Erasmus Publishing.

Ringbom, H. (2015). Vessel-Source Pollution. In R. Rayfuse (Ed.), *Research Handbook on International Environmental Law* (p. 124). Cheltenham: Edward Elgar Publishing.

Roach, J. A. (2016). The Role of Global Organizations. In R. Warner & S. Kaye (Eds.), *Routledge Research Handbook of Maritime Regulation and Enforcement* (pp. 86–106). London: Routledge.

Roe, M. (2013). *Maritime Governance and Policy-Making*. London: Springer.

Rosenau, J. N. (1999). Toward an Ontology for Global Governance. In M. Hewson, T. J. Sinclair (Eds.), *Approaches to Global Governance Theory*. New York: State University of New York Press.

Rothwell, D. R., & Stephens, T. (2016). *The International Law of the Sea*. Oxford and Portland: Hart.

Salvarani, R. (1996). The EC Directive on Port State Control. *International Journal of Marine and Coastal Law, 11*, 225–231.

Scott, K. N. (2011). International Environmental Governance. *Melbourne Journal of International Law, 12*, 177.

Servais, J.-M. (2011). *International Labour Law*. New York: Wolters Kluwer.

Simon, H. (1993). *Die Internationale Transportarbeiter-Föderation. Möglichkeiten und Grenzen internationaler Gewerkschaftsarbeit vor dem Ersten Weltkrieg*. Essen: Klartext.

Simmel, G. (2001). *Soziologie*. Frankfurt am Main: Suhrkamp.

Simmonds, K. R. (1994). *The International Maritime Organization*. London: Simmons & Hill Publishing.

Steiner, A., Kimball, L. A., & Scanlon J. (2003). Global Governance for the Environmental and the Role of Multilateral Environmental Agreements in Conservation. *Oryx, 37*, 227–237.

Stier-Somlo, F. (1917). *Die Freiheit der Meere und das Völkerrecht*. Leipzig: Veit.

Stopford, M. (2009). *Maritime Economics*. London: Routledge.

Sturmey, S. (1983). *The Open Registry Controversy and the Development Issue*. Bremen: Institute of Shipping Economics.

Tetzlaff, K. (2015). The Role of Regional Organizations. In R. Warner & S. Kaye (Eds.), *Routledge Handbook of Maritime Regulation and Enforcement* (pp. 106–121). London: Routledge.

Thorpe, R., McAlea, R., & Leback, W. (1997). The Changing Role of Ship Classification Societies. *SNAME Transactions, 105*, 521.

Urrutia, B. (2006). The EU Regulatory Action in the Shipping Sector: A Historical Perspective. *Maritime Economic & Logistic, 8*, 202–221.

van Leeuwen, J. (2010). *Who Greens the Waves? Changing Authority in the Environmental Governance of Shipping and Offshore Oil and Gas Production*. Wageningen: Academic Publishers.

van Leeuwen, J. (2015). The Regionalization of Maritime Governance. *Ocean & Coastal Management, 117*, 23–31.

Witt, J.-A. (2007). *Obligations and Control of Flag States*. Berlin: LIT Verlag.

Yang, H. (2006). *Jurisdiction of the Coastal State Over Foreign Merchant Ships in Internal Waters and the Territorial Sea*. Berlin and Heidelberg: Springer.

Young, P. (1995). *Mutuality: The Story of the UK P&I Clubs*. Chesterton: Granta Editions.

Publications of International Institutions

Baltic Marine Environment Protection Commission (HELCOM). (2017). http://www.helcom.fi/. Accessed 8 February 2019.

Commission of the Oslo and of the Paris Convention (OSPAR Commission). https://www.ospar.org. Accessed 20 July 2018.

Environmental Ship Index (ESI). http://www.environmentalshipindex.org. Accessed 8 February 2019.

European Commission (1993). *A Common Policy on Safe Seas: Communication from the Commission* COM (93) 66.

European Commission. (2017). *Study: Differentiated Port Infrastructure Charges to Promote Environmentally Friendly Maritime Transport Activities and Sustainable Transportation*. https://ec.europa.eu/transport/modes/maritime/news/

2017-06-27-study-differentiated-port-infrastructure-charges-promote_en. 8 February 2019

European Maritime Safety Agency (EMSA). http://www.emsa.europa.eu/. Accessed 8 February 2019.

European Sea Ports Organisation (ESPO). http://www.espo.be. Accessed 8 February 2019.

Green Award. http://www.greenaward.org. Accessed 8 February 2019.

Institute for International Law and Justice. (2017). *Global Administrative Law.* www.iilj.org/GAL. Accessed 8 February 2019.

International Group of Protection & Indemnity Clubs. http://www.igpandi.org. Accessed 8 February 2019.

International Labour Organization (ILO). http://www.ilo.org. Accessed 8 February 2019.

International Maritime Organization (IMO). http://www.imo.org. Accessed 8 February 2019.

International Transport Workers' Federation (ITF). (2016a). *MLC: Making a Difference?* (Seafarers' Bulletin No. 30, 25).

International Transport Workers' Federation (ITF). (2016b). *Successful Use of MLC and PSC Co-operation on Detaining Vessels* (Seafarers' Bulletin No. 3, 8).

Organisation for Economic Co-operation and Development (OECD). (2015). *Working Party No. 2 on Competition and Regulation: Executive Summary of the Roundtable on Competition Issues in Liner Shipping.* Paris: OECD.

Paris Memorandum of Understanding (Paris MoU). https://www.parismou.org/. Accessed 8 February 2019.

United Nations Conference on Trade and Development (UNCTAD). (1975). *Review of Maritime Transport.* http://unctad.org/en/PublicationsLibrary/rmt1972-73_en.pdf. Accessed 8 February 2019.

United Nations Conference on Trade and Development (UNCTAD). (2016). *Review of Maritime Transport.* http://unctad.org/en/PublicationsLibrary/rmt2016_en.pdf. Accessed 8 February 2019.

United Nations Environment Program (UNEP). http://www.unep.org/regionalseas/. Accessed 8 February 2019.

3 The Emergence of Maritime Governance in the Post-War World

Open Access This chapter is licensed under the terms of the Creative Commons Attribution-NonCommercial-NoDerivatives 4.0 International License (http://creativecommons.org/licenses/by-nc-nd/4.0/), which permits any noncommercial use, sharing, distribution and reproduction in any medium or format, as long as you give appropriate credit to the original author(s) and the source, provide a link to the Creative Commons license and indicate if you modified the licensed material. You do not have permission under this license to share adapted material derived from this chapter or parts of it.

The images or other third party material in this chapter are included in the chapter's Creative Commons license, unless indicated otherwise in a credit line to the material. If material is not included in the chapter's Creative Commons license and your intended use is not permitted by statutory regulation or exceeds the permitted use, you will need to obtain permission directly from the copyright holder.

4

Thinking Outside 'The Box': Decolonization and Containerization

Nicholas J. White

The Box, Levinson's influential maritime history bestseller, demonstrates that the shift from break-bulk to container shipping offered huge cost savings. Gathering pace from the mid-1960s, the intermodal transport of freight in boxes—highly automated and by ship, rail and truck—eliminated up to a dozen separate handlings of cargo and simultaneously reduced the risks of pilferage and damage. Capital was substituted for labour in an era when dockworkers were prone to strikes which resulted in escalating wage costs and frequent delays in port. Lines that failed to take up the new technology faced extinction. The prospects of the principal innovators, US companies (Malcom Maclean's Sea-Land Service, Inc. especially), capturing the lion's share of Pacific and Atlantic trade pushed European shipping lines into phasing out their conventional

---

N. J. White (✉)
School of Humanities and Social Science, Liverpool John Moores University, Liverpool, UK
e-mail: n.j.white@ljmu.ac.uk

vessels.[1] Broeze's earlier, posthumously published study came to similar conclusions, emphasizing 'indispensable' computerization (for documentation) and the reduction of insurance premiums (through reduced cargo loss).[2] According to the recollections of a leading British naval architect, involved in the design and procurement of the first container ships for the Overseas Containers Ltd (OCL) consortium, the technology shift arrived 'none too soon'. At 'about half the ship's year', the 'time a ship spent in port loading and discharging was becoming ridiculous'. Break-bulk liners were more like 'floating warehouse[s] than efficient transportation vehicles'.[3] For OCL's Australian service after 1968, a BBC journalist discovered that 'nine ships will replace the forty which used to exist and the speed with which ships can be unloaded and loaded (forty-eight hours instead of two or three weeks) means that each ship can make five round trips a year…instead of two-and-a-half'.[4]

These standard interpretations of containerization's origins focus on the Anglo-world. Technological change is blamed on the obstructiveness of British, American and Australian dockworkers (as well as the forcing ground provided by US logistical demands in Vietnam). This, however, neglects the wider-world situation; the process of decolonization of which the Vietnam conflict was symptomatic. As Hopkins argues: 'Instead of fitting decolonisation into the Cold War…the Cold War needs to be fitted into decolonisation…[T]he effective decolonisation of China…fuelled the Cold War in Asia, drew the superpowers into the region and…pulled the rug from under the colonial order'.[5]

Influenced by Hopkins, this chapter regards decolonization as much more than a constitutional act. Decolonization was part of a bigger process that preceded and exceeded the lowering and raising of flags at independence ceremonies. Decolonization, for Hopkins, went hand-in-hand with the 'changing character and accelerating pace of globalization after the Second World War' in which 'horizontal' concepts of racial equality

---

[1] Levinson (2006, 8, 10–11, 92, 103, 161). Levinson's influence can be seen in Bott (2009, 21), D'Eramo (2015, 90–92), and Bernhofen et al. (2016, 38–40).
[2] Broeze (2002, 11–12, 23, 25, 28, 35, 42).
[3] Meek (2003, 104).
[4] Turner (1971, 315).
[5] Hopkins (2017, 736–737).

4 Thinking Outside 'The Box': Decolonization and Containerization 69

and universal democracy, as well as the breakdown of complementarities between industrial metropoles and primary-producing peripheries, undermined vertical, hierarchic imperial systems.[6] In this shift from colonial to post-colonial globalization, the study of decolonization can be extended from formal dependencies in Africa, Asia and the Caribbean to include those territories 'that retained their formal independence but were clearly [previously] subordinated to an external power' (notably China but also the 'White' Dominions of Australia, Canada, New Zealand and South Africa).[7] The Dominions achieved political independence in the interwar years, but disengagement (economic, cultural and geo-strategic) from Britain was delayed until the 1960s. As Lindblad demonstrates for Indonesia, meanwhile, the process of economic decolonization, through the indigenization of business in the 1950s and 1960s, had a longer trajectory than the achievement of political independence from the Netherlands in 1949.[8] Lindblad pays little attention to international shipping, but the expansion of Indonesia's national line, Djakarta Lloyd (DL), during the 1950s and 1960s (often through links to Japan and the Soviet bloc) was part of this wider devolution beyond the transfer of political power.[9]

An overarching argument of this chapter, therefore, is that post-colonial globalization, in tandem with economic decolonization, created a multi-centred maritime system no longer automatically dominated by European conglomerates (a phenomenon identified in the rise of Asian shipping and shipbuilding in Tenold's chapter in this volume). Non-Europeans (wittingly and unwittingly) played significant roles in the remaking of shipping forms by the 1970s. The focus is on British shipping lines and how the challenges of decolonization affected their take-up of containerization after 1965. This is justified on two levels. Firstly, the 'thalassocracy' which was the British Empire meant that UK steamship companies were leading beneficiaries of the European-topped economic, political and social hierarchies of colonial globalization.[10] For example, Britain's largest shipping group, the Peninsular and Oriental Steam Navigation Company

---

[6] Hopkins (2008, 241–242).
[7] Hopkins (2017, 736).
[8] Lindblad (2008).
[9] Jamieson (1995, 138–139, 143–144).
[10] Jackson (2006, 28).

(P&O), has been called the 'bloodstream of the British Raj'.[11] Hence, the levelling and multi-centring tendencies of post-colonialism threatened the pre-eminence of UK ocean shipping. Secondly, although British lines were not the original innovators, they were at the forefront of developing containerization on a global scale, 'devising and promoting a vast array of changes to all its aspects'.[12] The post-colonial context, moreover, was central to this redeployment. Kerry St. Johnston, joint managing director and one of the 'founding pioneers' of OCL, recalled in 1971 that 'the seeds of political and economic change sown as a result of the war were soon to have a profound impact'.[13]

St. Johnston was also a managing director of the Ocean Steam Ship Company (OSSCo; otherwise known as the Blue Funnel Line or Alfred Holt & Co and renamed Ocean Transport & Trading Ltd [OTT] in 1973). The Ocean Group archive at the Merseyside Maritime Museum supplies the primary-source base for this analysis. This is appropriate because OSSCo, the leading British line in East and Southeast Asia, with an offshoot to Australia, was embroiled in the end-of-empire experience 'east of Suez'. Blue Funnel, from 1936, was also the major shareholder in Elder Dempster, the dominant UK shipping interest in West Africa. Additionally, the Ocean Group encompassed a Dutch subsidiary in the Indonesia trade. As late as the 1970s, Malaysia/Singapore constituted the Ocean Group's 'biggest revenue area' with eastern Asia as a whole contributing 63% and western Africa 32% of operating profits.[14] Moreover, as St. Johnston's career trajectory emphasizes, Ocean was a key driver of containerization after 1965 as one of the four founder companies of OCL. Blue Funnel's management persuaded P&O, the other lead partner in the first British ocean-going container consortium, to take the plunge.[15]

The first section of this chapter does find evidence to support the existing literature's focus on developed-world competition and costs pushing British containerization. But, the bulk of the discussion focuses on the

---

[11] Bott (2009, 31).
[12] Bott (2009, 23).
[13] Bott (2009, 15); 'Shipping—The Six Year Revolution', reprinted from *Ocean: The Journal of the OSSCo* (December 1971), 16–21, OA/832.
[14] *Annual Report and Accounts* (hereafter *AR&A/Cs*) *1970*, 5–8, OA/4031/1.
[15] Bott (2009, 13, 27–30).

wider decolonization picture. The second part shows the pressures (both real and perceived) which arose from the emergence of national shipping lines throughout the decolonizing world, critiques of the conference system, and the potential for decolonized states to exploit the shipping services of newcomers from outside the established European rings. Moreover, the third section shows how shipping costs were also rising in the developing world through sovereign risks associated with decolonization; not only in terms of labour, but also through port congestion, pilferage and the declining position of European agency houses. The OCL strategy allowed British companies to exploit the lower risks of Australasian trade. Yet, as the final part argues, the agency of the ex-Dominions and Asian Commonwealth states needs to be incorporated into the containerization story.

The OCL Solution

In line with the established explanation, OCL's birth did partly reflect competitive threats in international shipping unrelated to political change. Lindsay Alexander, a managing director of OSSCo from 1955 recalled the situation when he became chairman in 1971. By 1965, it was clear that Sea-Land, due to start trans-Atlantic operations in 1966, was designing larger and faster container ships which had the carrying capacity to cover the entire trade. '[S]evere over-tonnaging' on the Atlantic was a 'grave likelihood'. Sea-Land's anticipated response was entry into the Pacific with its excess vessels. Pushing west, Sea-Land had an existing network of trucks and depots in the US, as well as Pacific Coast terminals and experience in pivot transhipment. Sea-Land could offer shippers in both Europe and East Asia through-transport door-to-door across both the Atlantic and the Pacific. Sea-Land's low rates would also attract cargo, and OSSCo would be 'under severe attack'.[16] In this counter-containerization, St. Johnston likewise highlighted the 'unmistakable signs' that American coastal container operators were 'going international'. There 'is no greater spur to rapid economic assessments leading to investment decisions than the threat of

---

[16] 'Liner Shipping at the Crossroads. Part V—OCL and All That', c. 1971, OA/750.

having your business flinched from under your nose', OCL's CEO wryly observed.[17]

Competition dovetailed with cost-cutting. Blue Funnel's managers reported in 1951 that '[i]n Australia the ships are held up on idleness for long periods through lack of labour and port facilities, and by strikes'. Blue Funnel ships to Australia covered about 50,000 miles a year against 75,000 miles for vessels in the UK–Japan trade. Moreover, the 'home ports' experienced labour indiscipline: 'Strikes, and bans on overtime, by both dockers and ship repairers…caused much delay and rising costs in sea carriage'.[18] Blue Funnel executives were still besmirching Australian labour two decades later. In the Australia–Malaysia service, the May 1970 pay-award on the waterfront entailed a 20% increase in cargo costs, absorbing over half Blue Funnel's revenue and leaving 'barely sufficient to break even'.[19]

Meanwhile, the huge capital costs of containerization led to combinations and consortia.[20] As Alexander explained, if containers were 'the proper answer', OSSCo was 'not large enough to be able to go it alone'. Single-handed, Blue Funnel would be reduced to 'no more than a sailing a fortnight' to reap 'economies of scale'. That was insufficient to remain competitive: joint-sailing agreements would beef up frequency. It was decided to link with P&O since the Australian and Far Eastern activities of the two groups were 'perfectly complementary'. P&O was dominant in Australasia, where OSSCo was 'relatively weak', and vice versa in eastern Asia.[21] Sir John Nicholson, Blue Funnel's chairman in 1965, recalled similar in 1977: 'our established Australian and Far Eastern trade shares were too small to sustain the frequency of container service…needed to attract shippers'; the 'overhead costs could only be met if spread over several trades'.[22]

But, technological diversification was also a strategy to reduce sovereign risk in the post-colonial world, a phenomenon often overlooked in the existing literature. British shipowners believed that, under pressures from

---

[17]'Six Year Revolution'.
[18]Annual Meeting, 6 June 1951, 'Report for 1950', OA/4003/8.
[19]*AR&ACs 1970*, 5–8, OA/4031/1.
[20]Levinson (2006, 215) and Broeze (2002, 42).
[21]'Liner Shipping', OA/750.
[22]Note in Nicholson to Alexander, 21 October 1977, OA/1582.

national shipping lines and the holding down of freight rates by independent states, the returns on capital from conventional liners were limited.[23]

Decolonization and Competitive Pressures

A consequence of political decolonization, and the accompanying drive for economic liberation, was the encouragement given to indigenous shipping companies (often government-subsidized and -protected through cargo reservation). National carriers were embraced for a variety of reasons: as status symbols and strategic necessities, to save hard currency, to help employment generation, trade expansion and technology transfer and to control freight rates.[24] This was part-and-parcel of rectifying imbalances in global trading regimes deemed to favour Europe. Denial of an indigenous merchant marine was described by an Indian shipowner in 1944 as a 'grave act of tyranny of England over India'. Citing Gandhi's adage that 'Indian shipping had to perish so that British shipping might flourish', political independence would allow India to operate its own merchant marine as a key element in economic development, halting the 'drain' of invisible earnings to the UK and lowering rates to boost 'industries at home' and 'markets for national products abroad'.[25]

By the 1960s, British companies were sharing the Indian and Pakistani trades with the national lines with the former demoted to 'the rank of junior vice-admiral'.[26] Throughout Asia, 'political independence' proved a 'prerequisite for systematic fleet development and expansion'.[27] The claustrophobia of post-colonial shipping markets was epitomized by developments in the wake of the separation of Singapore from Malaysia in 1965 and the emergence after 1968 of the Malaysian International Shipping Corporation (MISC) and Singapore's Neptune Orient Line (NOL). The

---

[23] Note by Sir Donald Anderson, Chairman P&O, 29 September 1971, CA/JLA/22/3.
[24] Turner (1971, 313), Dharmasena (1989, 86–88), and Evans (2012).
[25] Hirachand (1944, 193–199).
[26] Turner (1971, 307).
[27] Broeze (1987, 90).

plan put up in 1962 by British shipowners to form their own Malayan-registered subsidiary was scuppered. The UK lines ended up with their nightmare scenario: 'two Lines extra instead of only one'.[28]

National lines were usually contained within existing conferences which regulated sailings and apportioned freights. Nonetheless, they were difficult partners. In Ghana, an obvious advantage for the Black Star Line (BSL) was the marketing of cocoa, the country's major export, by a state-owned enterprise. In securing cocoa parcels to the Baltic, BSL was said to be 'overcarrying' by 1964 in the northbound trade in an arrangement that did not represent 'true sharing'. A similar situation existed southbound, particularly with cargo for the Volta River development project 'specifying BS[L]'.[29] By the end of 1964, a change in Ghana Cocoa Marketing Company policy, making arrangements with individual lines rather than the conference pool, likewise tended to favour BSL. Simultaneously, the German Woermann Line appeared to be getting extra cargo by appointing BSL as its Ghana agents.[30] In April 1965, Elder Dempster's chairman regarded these arrangements in favour of BSL as 'having a very dampening effect on present earnings'.[31] In Southeast Asia, meanwhile, MISC was considered by Blue Funnel 'likely [to] fiddle conference rules'.[32]

For St. Johnston, an inordinately 'unproductive' time in the postwar era was spent by the 'best brains' defending conferences.[33] In the 'ideological-political revolution' post-1945, conferences were in danger of being bypassed.[34] They were suspect as 'neo-colonial' price-fixing cartels, allegedly inflating freight rates and preventing newcomers (both national lines and cross traders) from entering routes. By 1962, the leading UK shipowners reported to their Minister of Transport about 'considerable

---

[28] Thomson, Ben Line to Nicholson, 18 August 1965, OA/2116.
[29] Cotton to Lucas, 27 September 1962, OA/2078/1.
[30] Muirhead to Tilby, Palm Line, 19 November 1964; Muirhead to Quarshie, BSL, 13 November 1964; Muirhead to Lagos, 5 October 1964; Lane to Gorick, Chamber of Shipping, 20 May 1965, OA/2273.
[31] Lane to Lucas, Joyce and Ogley, 23 April 1965, OA/2273.
[32] Blue Funnel Line (BFL) Minutes, 28 April 1972, OA/1773.
[33] 'Six Year Revolution'.
[34] Broeze (2002, 70–72).

misunderstanding and criticism' of conferences from governments, shippers and international bodies.[35] In Indonesia, OSSCo was incensed by the UN's appointment of an 'anti-Conference' Australian as shipping adviser to the Jakarta government in 1961. He sympathized with the Indonesian commonplace that 'the word "Conference" suggests…a foreign body with a complete hold on shipping'. The adviser's subsequent report was 'a scarcely veiled attack on the [Europe-Indonesia] Conference on the grounds that it keeps the rates up to support chronic over-tonnaging'.[36] In Confrontation with British-backed Malaysia after 1963, the increasingly radical tone of Indonesian economic nationalism was epitomized by the Minister of Sea Communications, Major-General Ali Sadikin, in singling out the Europe-Indonesia Conference as the 'tool of imperialist domination in the field of international shipping'. Indonesia remained in the conference, but through developing a 'strong fleet' of its own would 'have the power … to transform the … imperialist "tool" into a tool for our nationalist stride'.[37]

World-wide there were alarming pressures (as UK shipowners saw it) from developing countries and the Eastern bloc, culminating in an enquiry into conferences and rates by the UN Conference on Trade and Development (UNCTAD).[38] To break the cartels, meanwhile, decolonized states could also turn to the Soviet bloc whose 'substantial national fleets of merchant-cum-military sealift ships … were under no obligation to show a profit and could therefore undercut the freight-rates [offered by the conferences]'. Espousing 'the creed of brotherly love', and with 'no connections with the old imperial powers', the Comecon lines 'found customers in the newly independent states, particularly in Africa'.[39]

---

[35] Shipping Advisory Panel (SAP) Minutes, 12 December 1962, OA/1870.
[36] 'Djakarta, June–Dec', Holt to Day, 21 June 1961; '1962. Private Djakarta, April to July', Graham to Holt, 25 June 1962, OA/1961; 'Ministry of Transport Correspondence', Holt to Hosegood, 24 August 1963, OA/1869/2.
[37] 'Indonesia: Dutch Disputes', confidential translation, 13 November 1964, OA/1696.
[38] SAP Minutes, 3 June 1964, OA/1870.
[39] Woodman (2010, 339). In 1965, Elders highlighted Polish competition in Northern Europe and an oilseeds contract with the Nigerian Produce Marketing Company at an 'uneconomic' rate. Lane to Gorick, 20 May 1965, OA/2273.

Furthermore, the intrusion of newcomers as partners to the new national lines was unwelcome to the established expatriates. To the chagrin of Elder Dempster, as Ghana became independent, the Nkrumah government chose the Israeli Zim Line to establish BSL as a joint venture in 1957.[40] Zim also assisted Burma in establishing a national line which entered the Burma shipping conference at the end of 1959 while Sudan turned to Yugoslavia.[41] Additionally, developing-world producers could exploit non-conference interlopers. By mid-1968, Blue Funnel faced stiff competition in the Malaysian palm oil trade from Stolt-Nielsen, the Norwegian parcel-tanker outfit, offering rates lower than the conference.[42] In a buyer's market, Malaysian palm-oil shippers, as well as Singapore rubber dealers, used their muscle to reduce conference rates in the early 1970s.[43]

To paraphrase Robinson, political independence allowed Third World states to effectively pick and choose which Big Brother (or combination of Big Brothers) exploited them in future as what Kleiman called the 'enforced bilateralism' of colonialism broke down.[44] On top of the massive subsidized growth of the US merchant marine during World War II, what disappointed European shipping lines was the encouragement given to regulation in Washington. Blue Funnel's chairman informed shareholders in 1966 that: 'American policy is still dictated by Congressional determination to impose on international shipping a pattern of control solely derived from the singularities of national beliefs and commercial habits'.[45] Drawing upon anti-trust ideology and encouraged by the Department of Justice, the Federal Maritime Commission during the 1960s was particularly concerned, for the benefit of US consumers, exporters and importers, that America's external trade 'was open to all nations on fair and equitable terms'. In particular, that entailed the scrutiny of common carrier agreements to ward off 'cosy cartel[s]'.[46] St. Johnston recalled in 1971

---

[40] White (2011, 197–198).
[41] Memorandum on Burma Trade, 31 December 1962, OA/2610; Jamieson (1995, 139).
[42] BFL Minutes, 21 June 1968, OA/1772/2.
[43] Levinson (2006, 255–256).
[44] Robinson (1984) and Kleiman (1976, 462, 471).
[45] *AR&A/Cs 1965*, 15, OA/4031/1.
[46] Cafruny (1987, 151) and Turner (1971, 309).

that for much of the decade after 1955, the 'overwhelming preoccupation' of European shipowners was 'attempting to restrain the monstrous worm of American regulatory zeal'. A 'new aura' of rate-making, 'at best of increased consultation and formalism, at worst of blatant political muscle' emerged.[47] Reflecting the growth of US global power, Latin American countries were also part of the process of using 'restrictive practices to establish and develop national merchant shipping fleets'.[48] By the late 1960s, South American regimes added 'thirty per cent to customs duties for goods carried in foreign ships'.[49]

Developing-world shipping proved ineffectual. From 1974, UNCTAD's Liner Code included the sharing of cargoes between shipping companies of importing and exporting countries, and cross traders, in a 40:40:20 ratio. But the code was only operative from 1983, and its universality was undermined by US non-ratification plus European governments, following Britain's lead, only applying the code in shipping with developing countries.[50] By the early 1990s, national shipping lines throughout West and Central Africa were in a dreadful state. None were capable of carrying even 40% of their national export trades.[51] MISC, though commanding a fleet of 44 vessels in excess of 1.3 million dwt in 1982, still carried 'but a small share of Malaysia's overseas trade'.[52] Given the poor performance of national lines. Ocean faced a far greater challenge from the outsiders of the industrialized world. Japan's Mitsui-OSK or Norway's Hoegh, for example, were greater menaces because they undercut conference rates.[53] Despite the presence of BSL and the Nigerian National Shipping Line (NNSL), Elder Dempster was still capable of making spectacular returns in the late 1970s given the Nigerian oil boom.[54]

---

[47]'Six Year Revolution'.
[48]Iheduru (1992, 297).
[49]Turner (1971, 309).
[50]Broeze (2002, 70–71), Sturmey (1986, 185, 197–198), and Cafruny (1987, 224–226).
[51]Iheduru (1992, 308–11).
[52]Broeze (1987, 88).
[53]I am grateful to Nicholas Barber, a key strategist at OSSCo/OTT in the 1970s (and later chairman of the group) for this insight. Email communication, 18 February 2013. See also White and Evans (2015, 232); note on ICI, undated (c. 3 September 1965) and telex, 7 September 1965, OA/2273.
[54]Email communication from Nicholas Barber, 18 February 2013; Davies (2000, 382).

But the weaknesses of the national lines proved a liability for the expatriate companies. By July 1965, the profitability 'actual' of BSL was doubtful and Elder Dempster was already aware that the Ghanaian line had 'difficulty in paying its debts'. In May 1967, a BSL cheque was 'returned unpaid', prompting discussion of Black Star's 'overall indebtedness'.[55] After 1968, Elders was increasingly hostage to the inefficiencies of BSL and NNSL in the joint service it was obliged to run with the national line in the UK West Africa Lines conference (UKWAL), making Elders vulnerable to takeover by the 1980s.[56]

Moreover, fear of the possible rather than the actual after 1945 drove decision-making in international shipping. Highly apprehensive about the prospect of maritime nationalism in their traditional domains, the adoption of containerization by European shipping companies was part of a wider picture of increased cooperation and combination. As Poulsen argues, the trend towards consolidation in Scandinavian shipping during the 1960s and 1970s was not primarily a response to the costs of technological change but was designed instead to counter discriminatory practices (not just in developing countries but in the US and Australia too). Fear 'had a very real impact at the time' and in corporate strategy the 'issue of protectionism' proved 'pivotal'.[57]

This defensive strategy in light of the trend towards post-colonial state intervention in shipping was driven home by F. L. Lane, Elder Dempster's chairman, in his justification of a full merger with OSSCo in August 1965:

> Shipping being an international business, those engaged in it face a wide diversity of competitive arrangements, many of which have the backing of individual Governments in favour of their respective shipping lines …
>
> [T]he financial results of shipping … will inevitably depend more and more on specialisation and the use of modern techniques … The greatest

---

[55] Cotton to Accra, 28 July 1965, OA/2078/2; Management Committee Minutes, 16 May 1967, OA/1587/8.

[56] In 1986, for example, as a consequence of mechanical failures, classification disputes and ship seizures, and the resulting refusal of shippers to use Nigerian vessels, NNSL temporarily withdrew from the conference. In 1989, Elders was taken over by France's Delmas Vieljeux. Davies (2000, 390–392).

[57] Poulsen (2010, 76–83, 84).

4 Thinking Outside 'The Box': Decolonization and Containerization 79

benefits ... will accrue to those organisations which are large enough to be able to justify the expenditure of time and money ... which the far reaching changes ... entail.[58]

Those 'modern techniques' and 'far reaching changes' clearly included containerization which was now being seriously considered by the Ocean Group (including as we'll see below in West Africa). Moreover, the essence of OCL was a combination of four leading British shipping companies searching out new means to defend market shares and reduce political risk. OCL was primarily a partnership between OSSCo and P&O, both agitated by political and economic change in their former domains outside Europe. The first serious moves in British containerization were taken around 1960 by the British India Steam Navigation Company (BI), owned by P&O. BI faced constraints in South Asia, deriving from the partition of India and Pakistan and its expulsion from the coastal trade through pro-indigenous regulations. BI's headquarters transferred from Calcutta to London in 1957, and 1960 was the year that P&O sold its last remaining interests in Bombay and Calcutta, and in which black-majority rule in East Africa became imminent.[59] Through a study of UK-East Africa trade, BI's new technical department in London demonstrated that containerization could pay in regions of low as well as high wages. BI senior manager R. B. Monteath became a 'key figure in the early development of OCL'.[60]

Furness Withy and B&C were the other partners (albeit junior) in OCL. Furness Withy's Royal Mail Lines was increasingly unprofitable through flag discrimination on top of import restrictions, exchange controls and currency manipulations in South America (and in Argentina specifically a desire to reduce dependency on the UK by diverting exports to continental Europe).[61] B&C's Clan and Union-Castle lines were likewise facing the squeeze from national lines in India and east-southern Africa. By 1966, they also had to contend with South African import restrictions,

---

[58] 'Acquisition', memorandum for senior staff, 13 August 1965, OA/1696.
[59] Howarth & Howarth (1986, 164–165, 173, 174, 176–177).
[60] Bott (2009, 23–24).
[61] Forrester (2014, 195, 197–198, 207–208, 214–215).

devaluation of the Indian rupee and the 'unresolved problems' of Rhodesia's Unilateral Declaration of Independence, all of which were 'having a serious effect on [B&C's] carryings'.[62] The sense of uncertainty was exacerbated by additional costs and inconveniences associated with changing conditions in the decolonizing Afro-Asian world: labour relations, port security and congestion, and, the general retreat of European merchant firms. 'Safe' colonial investments were being transformed into 'risk capital', the 'crux of the international revolution labelled decolonization' as Fieldhouse argued.[63]

Decolonization, Political Risk and Containerization

Disputes between maritime labour and capital, and rising labour costs, were certainly not unique to post-war Liverpool, New York or Brisbane. Labour militancy in the tropics was often a product of the reformist zeal of late colonialism. In the 'partnership' era after World War II, French and British colonial administrations attempted to stabilize labour through promoting European-style 'responsible' trade unionism in the hope that productivity increases would accrue. This usually spiralled out of control, pushing up labour costs in a wave of strikes for pay increases as well as pension and other benefits, particularly among port and transport workers.[64] Trade unions became 'organs of anti-colonial protest' as nationalist leaders drew upon organized labour for mass mobilization.[65] In 1956, Sir John Hobhouse, OSSCo's chief executive, reported that Asia was 'in various stages of ... progress towards self-government' and a general accompaniment was the emergence of trade unions which believed they were 'not up to the best Western standards unless [they] organise[d] frequent stoppages'.[66]

---

[62] Chairman Nicholas Cayzer in B&C *AR&A/Cs 1966* cited in Sinclair (2010, 264).
[63] Fieldhouse (1978, 601).
[64] Cooper (1987, 1996).
[65] Low (1991, 238).
[66] 'South East Asia in 1956'.

There was also trouble at sea against the backdrop of decolonization, encapsulated in a strike led by Nigerian stewards on the Elder Dempster mail boat *Apapa* while berthed in Liverpool in the summer of 1959. This followed a series of allegations of racial discrimination on the part of African crews and occurred in the midst of attempts to establish an employers' federation in Lagos to deal with the Nigerian Union of Seamen (NUS), believed to be under communist influence. The only way to get the ship away was to promise a full inquiry in Lagos.[67] With Nigeria on the cusp of full independence, and concern on the part of the end-of-empire government in Lagos to avoid further labour unrest, the inquiry ruled in the stewards' favour. The Board conceded that African crews experienced worse conditions than European ones, identifying inequalities in wages, hours of work and leave arrangements. Elders was advised to end the loosely regulated system of work hours, and institute overtime payments.[68] The shift from 'vertical' notions of racial and social hierarchy to 'horizontal' ideas of racial equality and universal democracy, as in Hopkins's post-colonial globalization schema, were clearly making the management of maritime labour more costly (or, at least, time-consuming and formalized).[69]

Ongoing concerns about communist influence in the Nigerian labour movement persisted into the 1960s (as did strikes).[70] Seafarer militancy intersected with that of Nigerian waterfront labour. The NSU's 'considerable truculence', for example, in insisting that a pay award of September 1964 be backdated to the beginning of the year, was encouraged by 'knowing [its] strong position after the success of the Dockworkers in obtaining all their demands through strike action', reported Elder Dempster director Bruce Glasier.[71]

Port labour forces were also caught up in the competing nationalisms which characterized late- and post-colonial politics. Hobhouse noted in

---

[67] Managers' Meeting Minutes, 15 June 1959, OA/1060/1/1.
[68] Schler (2016, 92–93); Salubi Report summarized in *The Newsletter: The Weekly Journal of the Socialist Labour League*, 'Nigerian Seamen Win Concessions', 5 March 1960, OA/1908/3.
[69] Hopkins (2008, 241–242).
[70] Gale to Glasier, 14 May 1960; Paxton to Holt, 10 August 1962, OA/1908/3.
[71] Managers' Meeting Minutes, 21 September 1964, OA/1060/1/3.

1956 that Ceylon was 'wrestling with internal disputes between the Sinhalese majority and the Tamil minority' which had 'disorganised the labour force at Colombo so that the port is in a constant state of congestion'.[72] Indeed, Ceylon's decolonization dramatically changed port conditions. To independence in 1948, Colombo was largely worked by itinerant 'coast coolies' from South India who were not much bothered about their terms and conditions since they frequently returned home after a year to two. This allowed the development of a casual labour pool which could be drawn upon by the mainly Indian stevedores at times of high demand (and equally discharged in less busy periods). An affirmative action trend in favour of indigenous Sri Lankans began in the 1930s downturn, intensified by the political imperatives of independence. Whereas one-third of labour was Sri Lankan in 1948, it was 80% by 1957.[73] Local dockworkers who replaced the immigrants 'lacked the stamina required for [strenuous] dock work'.[74] Colombo's famed efficiency disappeared as the labour force decasualized and unionized, and industrial disputes became commonplace. As Liverpool's Bibby Line discovered, Colombo became a 'politicians' playground' as the unions wooed the national parties, culminating in the nationalization of the port in 1958.[75] '[S]hipping circles and general trade in all corners of the world can only speak in terms of despair and disgust of the pathetic daily tonnage output' stated a report on Colombo's cargo handling in 1959.[76]

Port congestion intersected with labour unrest. The Liverpool Steam Ship Owners' Association (LSSOA) conducted surveys of its members in the 1950s on the 'wastage of carrying power' arising from slow turnaround. The UK and Australian ports were deemed outmoded but so was maritime infrastructure in South Asia, the Caribbean and East and West Africa, which was unable to keep pace with the upsurge of trade. This also reflected restrictive labour practices, go slows and strikes. A cargo liner company engaged in trade between the UK and India, Pakistan and Ceylon ran

---

[72] 'South East Asia in 1956', *Blue Funnel and Glen Lines Staff Bulletin* (July 1956, 171–172), OA/692/2.
[73] Dharmasena (1985).
[74] Dharmasena (1998, 77–78).
[75] Watson (1990, 47) and Dharmasena (1985, 112).
[76] Dharmasena (1985, 113).

4 Thinking Outside 'The Box': Decolonization and Containerization

before the war, on average, three voyages a year for each ship in its fleet. In 1951, 2.25 voyages only were averaged, despite the fact that a large proportion of the fleet had more engine power and improved cargo-handling gear. This figure declined further to 1.9 voyages per annum by 1955. In the UK-West Africa trade, voyages as a whole were taking 25% more time than pre-war. Per annum, that entailed a loss of nearly thirty round voyages. In the Caribbean, it was said to be taking six weeks or more to effect turn round in a number of ports, which pre-war took no more than four weeks (a 50% deterioration).[77] For Southeast Asia in 1956, Hobhouse was sure of 'continued trouble in keeping the ships to anything like fixed dates' given labour unrest, bottlenecks and political instability. Maintaining regular scheduled services, the meat-and-drink of Blue Funnel's competitive advantage, was increasingly costly. The agents and ships' personnel surmounted difficulties 'with ingenuity and cheerfulness' but, as Hobhouse revealingly quipped, 'you should see our cable bill!'[78]

Political upheaval interlinked with port congestion. Blue Funnel experienced 'difficult and disappointing' trade with China at the end of 1968 due to the 'political tensions' of the anti-western Cultural Revolution and the 'impossibility of maintaining liner schedules through chronically congested ports'.[79] Blue Funnel would withdraw from the China trade altogether by 1970. It was not only the British dock strike in July 1970, but also Nigerian delays caused by the civil war which cost OSSCo group about £1.1 million during that year.[80]

Fraught labour–management relations leading to theft was not unique to ports in the Global North either.[81] In the late 1960s, the problems of the Sierra Leone Port Authority were blamed on 'inefficiency and large scale pilferage due to lack of firm top management'. In Freetown, the general secretary of the dockworkers' union was believed to be in cahoots in this criminality with the port authority's personnel officer.[82] Mass pilferage was

---

[77] *Annual Report for 1950*, 18; *Annual Report for 1951*, 18–24; *Annual Report for 1952*, 12–13; *Annual Report for 1955*, 19–24, LSSOA, D/SS/2/7.
[78] 'South East Asia in 1956'.
[79] *AR&ACs 1968*, 15–18, OA/4031.
[80] *AR&ACs 1970*, 5–8, OA/4031.
[81] Levinson (2006, 26–27).
[82] Notes on visit to West Africa, 15–24 January 1969 by E. Storey, 7 February 1969, OA/1296/2/13.

an Asian phenomenon too. Six months into Indonesian independence in June 1950, the 'main difficulties' for Blue Funnel were 'the complete lack of disciplined control over the men loading and discharging the cargo', involving 'much stealing of cargo and considerable risk of injury to the crew on watch'.[83] In Indonesia's economic meltdown from the end of the 1950s, things only got worse, reflected in an extreme incident of pillage at the port of Balikpapan in Kalimantan in March 1965. Thirty to forty local police and army personnel boarded *Lycaon*, a steamship owned by the Nederlandsche Stoomvaart Maatschappij 'Oceaan' (NSMO), OSSCo's Dutch wing. Along with the dockworkers loading and discharging the vessel, the armed intruders ransacked the cargo (including the personal effects of the passengers valued at £8000; equivalent to about £147,000 at 2017 prices).[84] This was a striking example of the unpredictability, uncertainty and fragility of ex-imperial business in post-colonial states. However far expatriate interests attempted to appease assertive nation-states, there were no guarantees. The pillage at Balikpapan was baffling because Blue Funnel had apparently secured its Indonesian trade by cloaking its UK status. Given Confrontation with British-supported Malaysia, OSSCo withdrew its British-registered tonnage and re-engaged the Dutch-flag NSMO vessels in Indonesian waters as tensions between Jakarta and The Hague eased (following the settlement of the West New Guinea/Irian Jaya dispute).[85]

The Balikpapan incident also underscored how information networks unravelled through economic decolonization. NSMO/OSSCo lost access to vital information flows as Dutch shipping agencies were nationalized in the late 1950s, and British ones were taken over during Confrontation.[86] In military-controlled Balikpapan, Blue Funnel lacked an agent. It was only when *Lycaon* reached Sumatra that the Balikpapan outrage could be reported to Amsterdam and Liverpool.

---

[83] Annual Meeting, 6 June 1950. Report for 1950, OA/4003/8.

[84] Djakarta File. January, February, March 1965, Boerstra to Amsterdam, 10 March 1965 enclosing 'Visit to the Musi, 4–7 March 1965'; Boerstra to Amsterdam, 12 March 1965; notes on discussion in Amsterdam, 5–6 March 1965, OA/1869/1. Purchasing-power comparators are derived from MeasuringWorth.com.

[85] White (2012, 1306).

[86] White (2012, 1293, 1298–1299).

4 Thinking Outside 'The Box': Decolonization and Containerization

Miller views intelligence flows, particularly via close links between shipping lines and trading companies/agency houses in the port cities of the colonial and semi-colonial world, as central to the European-dominated maritime system.[87] Expatriate merchant firms, which scouted out and booked cargoes, were prime targets of indigenization measures throughout the developing world. This is illustrated by two examples from the apparently opposite ends of the post-colonial spectrum in eastern Asia: Communist China and the 'highly Americanised' Philippines.[88]

The former's assault upon British merchant firms supports Hopkins's view that China should be incorporated into end-of-empire narratives given its 'effective decolonization' in 1949.[89] In 1954, Butterfield & Swire (B&S) was replaced in Shanghai by the China Ocean Shipping Agency (COSA) as Blue Funnel's agents.[90] Breaking down, therefore, was a British-dominated shipping-cum-trading chain along the Yangtze in which OSSCo's intimate relationship with John Swire & Sons, B&S's parent, provided access to the feeder services of the China Navigation Company (CNC) as well as indigenous comprador networks.[91] COSA was an offshoot of the Ministry of Foreign Trade and, in contrast to B&S, viewed itself 'as the mouth-piece of the shippers rather than the representative of the shipping companies'. COSA's quasi-monopoly cut Blue Funnel off from shippers and receivers. By the late 1950s, OSSCo had no means of 'knowing how we get what cargo we do'. Cargo flows could be 'turned off at will for political reasons'. Meanwhile, the state corporations had 'a well-developed technique of refusing to accept rates which they have not themselves explicitly accepted'.[92] As Manila's leadership sought a greater Asian identity, there would be indigenization legislation by the late 1950s.[93] Blue Funnel's British agents in Manila, Smith, Bell & Co,

---

[87] Miller (2012, 4, 31–32, 70–71, 171–172).
[88] Sir John Hobhouse, 'British Interests in Eastern Asia', Lecture delivered at the University of Liverpool, 26 May 1952, OA/74.
[89] Hopkins (2017, 737).
[90] Falkus (1990, 304).
[91] Miller (2012, 90–91).
[92] Note by Alexander, 10 October 1958, OA/JLA/22/1.
[93] Jose (2012, 39–40).

fell to Filipino interests in 1959.[94] The transfer of the Smith Bell agency to another local firm in 1970 led to loss of the valuable hemp trade.[95] The retreat of the expatriate merchants in the Philippines coalesced with the emergence of a national line. The Maritime Company of the Philippines was admitted to the Europe-Philippines conference in 1969; combined with import restrictions, this was blamed for a downturn in OSSCo carryings to the islands during 1970.[96]

Investing in containerization and developing OCL, therefore, provided an opportunity for Holts to focus a greater share of its activity upon the lower risk trades of Australasia. Indeed, 'in view of the current political situation in Asia', it was decided in 1965 to redeploy two of OSSCo's eight ships in its general-cargo building programme from Asia to Australia.[97] Chairman Nicholson admitted to shareholders in May 1966 that: 'Given the political uncertainty which pervades so many parts of Asia it is impossible to foretell the course of development of our Eastern trades'. Prospects in Ghana and Nigeria might be improved by regime changes but 'the difficulty of prediction remained'.[98] As Nicholson pointed out after a visit to West Africa in February 1967: 'In these waters there are no dependable sailing directions and any observations must be treated with distrust, remembering that not even the most experienced local pilots foresaw the political "coups" of 1966'.[99]

Moreover, risks in developing countries could be offset by growth potential elsewhere. Containerization provided an opportunity to redeploy resources towards the global growth triangle of North America, Western Europe and East Asia, with an offshoot to Australasia. To the 1980s, at least, containerization proved a driver for growth primarily in North–North not developed–developing world trade.[100] That reflected Hopkins's reconfigured globalization after 1945 which encompassed 'shifts in the world

---

[94] Carter (2002, 157).
[95] BFL Minutes, 29 June 1970, OA/1772/4.
[96] *AR&A/Cs 1970*, 5–8.
[97] Note by MacTier, 18 January 1965 attached to note for the board by Nicholson, 18 January 1965, OA/JLA/20/1.
[98] *AR&A/Cs 1965*, 13–15.
[99] Note by Nicholson, 27 February 1967, OA/JLA/20/1.
[100] Ditto (2002, 45) and Bernhofen et al. (2016, 46–47).

economy', especially the tendency for increased exchanges between industrialized countries.[101] OCL's first containerized service was UK–Australia followed by Europe–East Asia during 1972 and 1973 where the principal attraction was the high value manufactures of Japan and Hong Kong, not the primary products of Southeast Asia, the hangovers of colonial globalization.[102] Even without unpredictable 'further political upheavals' in West Africa, Nicholson in 1967 saw little prospect for increases in profitability because 'the traffic consists almost entirely of cheap primary products', whose 'naturally low rates' were 'held down by political pressure reinforced by national poverty, dissension within the Conference, and the incursion of numerous outsiders'.[103]

Non-European Agency in Containerization

The lure of Australia, however, also needs to be set within the wider context of the decolonization of the former 'White' Dominions. As Hopkins stresses, during the 1950s and 1960s there was an 'almost unnoticed decolonisation, as the old dominions began to look to themselves rather to the "mother country"'. Exacerbated by Britain's groping towards the EEC after 1961, '[c]ommercial ties with Britain weakened'; these were the material 'symptoms of imperial dissolution' which matched those simultaneously taking place in the Afro-Asian world.[104] Moreover, as St. Johnston noted, the tendency by the early 1960s for rates to lag behind costs was not helped by independent Commonwealth governments, in Australia, New Zealand, South Africa and India, which increasingly oversaw rate-making.[105]

By the mid-1960s, the proverbial 'Sword of Damocles hung over [Blue Funnel's] heads', reflected Alexander, because the Canberra government 'realise[d] that cargo handling costs in Australia were very high' and 'the

---

[101] Hopkins (2017, 730).
[102] I am indebted again to Nicholas Barber for this observation. Email communication, 18 February 2013.
[103] Note by Nicholson, 27 February 1967, OA/JLA/20/1.
[104] Hopkins (2008, 229, 237–239; 2017, 734–736).
[105] 'Six Year Revolution'.

consequential rates of freight would…hamper Australian overseas trade'. Through 'moral and legal pressure', and with virtually no deep-seas flag tonnage, the Australians insisted that the Europe–Australia services be rationalized. In no uncertain terms, Canberra also wished to 'cut out the recalcitrant Australian docker' via containerization. If the British lines wouldn't containerize, the Australians 'would try to find somebody else' (Sea-Land being the obvious choice because of Atlantic over-tonnaging, and also Sea-Land was 'poised in the vicinity of Australia' through supplying huge quantities of stores to Vietnam).[106] Nicholson concurred in 1977: 'we decided under the threat of intervention by the Commonwealth Government that the trade between Europe and Australia had to be containerised quickly'.[107] In May 1966, the senior civil servant in Australia's Department of Trade, Sir Alan Westerman, called a conference on containerization in Canberra. Sir Alan emphasized that 'only if there is a rational and evolutionary approach in the question of relationships [between shippers and shipowners] will the kind of stability of service that we need be assured'.[108] Given the annual friction between New Zealand's Meat and Dairy Boards and British shipping during freight-rate negotiations, the containerization of the refrigerated trades after 1969 relied upon strong support from the top government brass in Wellington, including Sir John Marshall (deputy premier with responsibility for commerce and industry).[109]

In this regard, the OCL project need not be seen as a new departure. Containerization was an attempt to prevent further dissipation of established Commonwealth (including South African) trade links, threatened by the assertive and reorienting ex-Dominions. Nicholson regarded Furness Withy and B&C as essential partners in OCL because 'the South African trade [where B&C was particularly strong] should provide important and early throughput for OCL'; the 'South African services might combine conveniently with West Africa and/or Australia'; while Shaw, Savill & Albion, of Furness Withy, had 'a large stake in the Australasian

---

[106] 'Liner Shipping'.
[107] Note in Nicholson to Alexander, 21 October 1977, OA/1582.
[108] Bott (2009, 43).
[109] Bott (2009, 158–159).

4 Thinking Outside 'The Box': Decolonization and Containerization 89

trades'.[110] The containerization of the Europe–West Africa route was eventually rejected by OCL.[111] But West Africa was originally intended as a link in the global containerization chain since Elder Dempster experimented with the use of ten-ton boxes from the end of 1964. This proved unsuccessful. With the amalgamation of OSSCo and Elder Dempster during 1965, however, Elders was strongly encouraged not to abandon containers.[112] Lane's legitimization of the Elders-OSSCo merger, discussed above, was clearly in this context of providing capital and know-how to support the technological shift. This grand, post-imperial vision in intra-Commonwealth trade (which, in Asia, would encompass Singapore and Hong Kong) very likely explains the support of the Labour Government of 1964–1970 for OCL. Minister of Transport Barbara Castle was especially encouraging, making investment grants available not only for vessel construction, but also for the containers they would carry.[113] Notwithstanding Britain's second application to join the EEC in 1967, Harold Wilson's government remained remarkably pro-Commonwealth.[114]

Equally, however, British shipowners wished to secure a slice of burgeoning intra-Pacific exchanges, typical of the decentring of global trade that accompanied decolonization. Since the mid-1960s, 'the engine of growth in [Australasia's] international trade has been driven by links with Japan and the countries in the Association of Southeast Asian Nations…By the mid-1960s trade between Australia and Japan alone already exceeded the value of trade between Australia and Britain'.[115]

OCL partnered with CNC, in which OSSCo enjoyed a half-share, in the containerization of the Australia-Japan trade.[116] This was not merely to reduce labour costs. As in the European trade, there was 'continued pressure' from the Australian authorities, wishing to encourage routes linking

---

[110] Nicholson to Anderson, 13 December 1965, OA/JLA/20/1.
[111] Bott (2009, 34).
[112] Managers' Meeting Minutes, 14 September 1964; 30 November 1964; 22 August 1966, OA/1060/1/3.
[113] Bott (2009, 25–26).
[114] Catterall (2018, 838–839).
[115] Hopkins (2008, 239).
[116] Broeze (2002, 50).

Australia with markets in Japan and North America alongside Europe.[117] Australia-Japan's containerization was also spurred on by the ambitions of the government-controlled Australian National Line (ANL). Subsequently, ANL entered into 'all trades between Australia and South East Asian countries as consortium members within the conferences alongside OCL'.[118] Expelled from mainland China in the 1950s, Swires/CNC was obviously seeking new outlets. But, as Sir Adrian Swire, deputy-chairman of the parent company, recalled: 'an extra dimension…was the strident noises emanating from Canberra and ANL that the time had come for Australian-owned, Australian-flagged and Australian-crewed ships'. The original two Australia Japan Container Line (AJCL) vessels were devoid of Australian equity participation, while being British-flagged and Chinese-crewed. Yet, AJCL did employ Australian officers and the ships were built with 'magnificent crew accommodation' should fuller localization be required.[119] As Nicholson informed his opposite number at P&O in December 1965, it was not only Sea-Land and the Swedish Wallenius Lines, but also ANL which would capture business should the British companies not 'establish an effective organisation'.[120]

That the nature and pace of containerization was often determined by the exigent ex-Dominions is confirmed in the South African experience. There was a growing maritime nationalism on the part of Pretoria through the formation of Safmarine as the national line in 1946, a 'proprietorial interest…in keeping northbound rates of freight as depressed as possible', and a trend towards self-sufficiency with the official adoption of Apartheid in 1948 (and even more so after South Africa's Commonwealth exit in 1961).[121] But containerization was not contemplated until 1975 given plentiful supplies of cheap and quiescent labour plus ample port capacity. The advent of containerization in 1977 was largely determined by the nationalized South African Railways and Harbours. Given Safmarine's dominance of the South African Conference, five of the ten North Europe–South Africa ships and one of the three Mediterranean-South

---

[117] Bott (2009, 90–91).
[118] Bott (2009, 94).
[119] Bott (2009, 96–97).
[120] Nicholson to Anderson, 13 December 1965, OA/JLA/20/1.
[121] Bott (2009, 166–167).

4 Thinking Outside 'The Box': Decolonization and Containerization 91

Africa vessels were provided by the national carrier. The joint service was also forced into adopting a particular specification of insulated container, suspected as a ruse to prevent British consortia entering South Africa with their Australasian ships.[122]

Yet, the initiative of ex-British colonies in the take-up of containers needs to also encompass the non-Dominions. Singapore and Malaysia were the exemplars where container port development was embraced by pragmatic governments. As Levinson recognized, 'no government anywhere was as aggressive in preparing for the container age as Singapore's'.[123] Nor is the link between decolonization and containerization any less obvious: independent through ejection from Malaysia in 1965, and facing a rapid rundown of Britain's defence complex by 1968, Lee Kuan Yew's government built a container port in its strategies for economic survival—to become the commercial hub of Southeast Asia and to foster export-oriented industrialization.[124] Singapore's first container facility opened in June 1972, and OCL's new route to the 'Far East' encompassed Singapore with Hong Kong and Japan.[125] In the subsequent development of intra-Pacific services, it was not only ANL, but also Singapore's government-owned and largest line, NOL, which was 'waiting in the wings to participate'.[126] By 1978, Singapore possessed the second largest merchant fleet in Asia, and in 1982 fifteen of NOL's 33 ships were container vessels.[127] By the 1990s, Singapore was the world's largest container port.[128]

Anxious to be economically independent of the port-city nation, Malaysia followed suit. The government in Kuala Lumpur studied containerization, and Port Klang was decided upon as the main container terminal (Penang's approaches were too shallow and Klang was nearer to

---

[122] Bott (2009, 167–168).
[123] Levinson (2006, 209).
[124] Levinson (2006, 209–211).
[125] *AR&ACs 1971*, 5–6; Meek (2003 163–167).
[126] Bott (2009, 175). A container service between Australia and Southeast Asia was being seriously considered by the end of 1969. As Blue Funnel directors appreciated, in these cross trades the respective governments would want their own national flags operating and an approach to a Singapore/Malaysian interest as well as ANL was proposed, alongside P&O. Note in Swayne to Alexander, 12 December 1969, OA/JLA/5/1.
[127] Broeze (1987, 85, 88).
[128] Huff (1994, 306).

industrializing 'Greater Kuala Lumpur'). The first phase of Klang's expansion was completed in July 1973. OCL's *Tokyo Bay* was the first container vessel to dock at Klang.[129] British shipping agents in Malaysia found that containerization fit a particular government-led development agenda in the positive discrimination of the New Economic Policy (officially launched in 1971). The handling and inland distribution of containers was a new growth area which could be reserved for enterprises representing the economically disadvantaged Bumiputeras (Malays and other indigenous groups) and so reduce ongoing Malaysian Chinese and foreign (primarily British) domination of the economy.[130] Blue Funnel managers came to realise, too, that MISC spied an opportunity to expand through road haulage from Klang to Kuala Lumpur. Kontena Nasional, the forwarder established in 1973, involved a 25% shareholding by Malaysia's national line.[131] As Alexander of Blue Funnel appreciated in 1968, containerization of intra-Southeast Asian services would be 'popular with both Malaysian and Singapore governments', especially if reductions in rates were likely and part of OSSCo's holding in the Straits Steamship Company could be sold to them.[132]

The agency of post-colonial states is additionally brought out in the case of Sri Lanka. As Dharmasena argued, the economic decolonization inherent in the formation of the Ceylon Shipping Corporation (CSC) in 1969 (and nationalized in 1971) spurred on Colombo's containerization. The American President Lines may have been the innovator at Colombo, but 'as a relative newcomer CSC … had no particular reason to cling to the older technology'. From 1980, in partnership with NOL significantly, CSC commenced a service to Felixstowe, Hamburg, Rotterdam and Bombay. Reversing previous dependence, CSC quickly monopolized tea exports to Britain. Further collaboration followed with Singapore, linking West Germany, the Red Sea, Colombo and Singapore, as well as the European newcomer Maersk on the Colombo–Singapore–US–Canada

---

[129] Port Klang (2011, 64, 69); BFL Minutes, 28 April 1972, OA/1773; Bott (2009, 130–131).
[130] Kuala Lumpur to London, 29 September 1970; Annesley to London, 22 August 1974 and attached extract from *Sunday Times* (Malaysia), 4 August 1974, H&C/37600.
[131] BFL Minutes, 28 April 1972, OA/1773; 'Changes at the Top in Kontena Nasional', *New Straits Times*, 12 September 1981.
[132] Note by Alexander, 28 February 1968, OA/JLA/20/1.

route. Independently, CSC ran East Asian services.¹³³ By the mid-1980s, CSC's containerized services also encompassed the Middle East and Australia, and a Colombo–Bombay–Mangalore shuttle.¹³⁴ Eight of the eleven-strong CSC fleet by 1985 were container ships.¹³⁵ Shipping modernization reflected Sri Lanka's shift from an inward-looking development policy towards an export-oriented growth strategy emulating the East and Southeast Asian model.¹³⁶ That entailed upgrades in Colombo's infrastructure, with Japanese assistance. By the mid-1980s, Colombo eclipsed its foremost rival, Bombay, in container throughput and emerged as South Asia's top port.¹³⁷

Conclusion: Contextualizing Containerization

On the surface, the adoption of containerization by European shipping companies represented the usual business imperatives of cutting costs and meeting competition. But, as St. Johnston appreciated, the variables had been greatly influenced by the deeper post-war global phenomenon of decolonization:

> New nations, new aspirations, new fleets, new attitudes to trade with a … bias towards bilateralism, bred action and re-action, much of which had to be absorbed by … the conferences, whose memberships were then almost exclusively made up of 'haves' but whose future success and survival was now to depend on … finding a means of accommodating the 'have nots'.¹³⁸

As Furness Withy was being lured into the OCL consortium, its chairman, Sir Errington Keville, made an after-dinner speech in which he stressed that: 'The British shipping industry [had] to rationalise' because 'too many ships [were] chasing too many cargoes, despite the fact that world trade

---

¹³³ Dharmasena (1989, 107–108).
¹³⁴ Dharmasena (1989, 108).
¹³⁵ Dharmasena (1998, 241).
¹³⁶ Dharmasena (1998, 136–137).
¹³⁷ Dharmasena (1998, 238–239, 255).
¹³⁸ 'Six Year Revolution'.

had doubled in the [previous] ten years'.[139] But this wasn't just about the arrival of new national shipping lines. Political and economic instability and uncertainty, labour troubles, port inefficiency and pilferage, which also accompanied decolonization in the developing world and pushed up shipping costs, should be factored into the containerization equation as well.

Seen in this context, for all the talk of a 'container revolution' containerization was not that revolutionary. The strategic lead taken by British shipping companies post-1965 was primarily to save core business. Britain's second box business, Associated Container Transportation, also began its operations in Australia where three of the major partners, Cunard, Blue Star and Ellerman, had significant interests.[140] Redeployment and rationalization through containerization was in large part concerned with preserving Commonwealth links which were threatened by post-colonial globalization (including the UK's move towards Europe and the emergence of the US as a global shipping power). Defending intra-Commonwealth trade worked both ways, however. The decolonized ex-Dominions wanted to use the box to diversify their trade links, but also to reduce costs when the EEC threatened the loss of Commonwealth preference. Long-distance UK trade was still viable in containers suggesting that economic disengagement between Britain and the ex-Dominions during the 1960s was not as complete as Hopkins suggests. The UK took just 19% of New Zealand's exports in 1976 compared to 53% in 1960. Nevertheless, as Sir John Marshall encouraged containerization, he also sought guarantees for New Zealand's exports to Britain as the latter bid to join the EEC, and during the 1970s the UK remained the largest market for New Zealand's dairy products.[141] OCL claimed in 1981 that the oil price hikes of the mid-1970s nullified the freight-rate and speed efficiency savings of container vis-à-vis conventional vessels. But eventualities don't detract from the original perceptions that drove strategy in the 1960s, and 'visibly dramatic improvements' in 'losses from damage or pilferage' were

---

[139] *Fairplay*, 4 November 1965, cited in Forrester (2014, 215).
[140] Bott (2009, 34–35, 67).
[141] Lodge (1978, 303).

still achieved.¹⁴² Interlocking again with Tenold's chapter, the agency of Asian members of the Commonwealth should not be overlooked either; they containerized as part of their post-colonial development strategies. Decolonization and containerization went hand-in-hand in the mercurial mix of nationalizing and internationalizing tendencies that characterized the transition to post-colonial globalization. As Davies observed for West Africa, the 'prime factor' distinguishing the post-1945 era was 'political and then economic independence', but decolonization was 'closely allied to the greatly accelerated pace of technological progress'.¹⁴³

References

Archival Sources

H&C Harrisons & Crosfield Archive. Clerkenwell: London Metropolitan Archive.
LSSOA Liverpool Steam Ship Owners' Association Archive. Liverpool: Merseyside Maritime Museum.
OA Ocean Group Archive. Liverpool: Merseyside Maritime Museum.

Published Sources

Bernhofen, D. M., El-Sahli, Z., & Kneller, R. (2016). Estimating the Effects of the Container Revolution on World Trade. *Journal of International Economics*, *98*, 36–50.
Bott, A. (Ed.). (2009). *British Box Business: A History of OCL*. Britain: SCARA.
Broeze, F. (1987). From Imperialism to Independence: The Decline and Re-emergence of Asian Shipping. *The Great Circle*, *9*, 73–95.

---

[142] Sinclair (2010, 279). Hummels argues that savings in shipping costs were 'trumped in the 1970s by sharp increases in fuel and port costs' (2007, 152). Yet, as Kaukiainen has responded, while 'quality is much more difficult to measure than price', 'shippers gained indirectly from better, more predictable and secure services – a better value for money' (2014, 64, 77).

[143] Davies (2000, 297).

Broeze, F. (2002). *The Globalization of the Oceans: Containerization from the 1950s to the Present.* St. John's, Newfoundland: International Maritime Economic History Association.

Cafruny, A. W. (1987). *Ruling the Waves: The Political Economy of International Shipping.* Berkeley: University of California Press.

Carter, L. (2002). *Chronicles of British Business in Asia, 1850–1960.* New Delhi: Manohar.

Catterall, P. (2018). The Plural Society: Labour and the Commonwealth Idea, 1900–1964. *Journal of Imperial and Commonwealth History, 46,* 821–844.

Cooper, F. (1987). *On the African Waterfront: Urban Disorder and the Transformation of Work in Colonial Mombasa.* New Haven: Yale University Press.

Cooper, F. (1996). *Decolonization and African Society.* Cambridge: Cambridge University Press.

D'Eramo, M. (2015). Dock Life. *New Left Review, 96,* 85–99.

Davies, P. N. (2000). *The Trade Makers: Elder Dempster in West Africa, 1852–1972, 1973–1989* (2nd ed.). St. John's, Newfoundland: International Maritime History Association.

Dharmasena, K. (1985). The Port and Dock Workers of Colombo, 1860–1960. *The Great Circle, 7,* 100–115.

Dharmasena, K. (1989). The Entry of Developing Countries into World Shipping. *International Journal of Maritime History, 1,* 85–112.

Dharmasena, K. (1998). *The Port of Colombo, 1940–1995. Volume II.* Tokyo: Japan Overseas Ports Cooperation Association.

Ditto, A. G. (2002). *Ebb Tide in the British Maritime Industries.* Exeter: University of Exeter Press.

Evans, B. (2012). *A Semi-state Archipelago Without Ships* (Working Papers in History and Policy No. 6). School of History and Archives, University College Dublin. http://historyhub.ie/wp-content/files_mf/1366537718Evans_Marine_Final.pdf. Accessed 14 February 2019.

Falkus, M. (1990). *The Blue Funnel Legend.* Houndmills: Macmillan.

Fieldhouse, D. K. (1978). *Unilever Overseas: The Anatomy of a Multinational, 1895–1965.* London: Croom Helm.

Forrester, R. E. (2014). *British Mail Steamers to South America, 1851–1965: A History of the Royal Mail Steam Packet Company and Royal Mail Lines.* Farnham: Ashgate.

Hirachand, W. (1944). Why India Wants Her Own Shipping. *Annals of the American Academy of Political and Social Science, 233,* 193–199.

Hopkins, A. G. (2008). Rethinking Decolonization. *Past & Present, 200,* 211–247.

Hopkins, A. G. (2017). Globalisation and Decolonisation. *Journal of Imperial and Commonwealth History, 45,* 729–745.

Howarth, D., & Howarth, S. (1986). *The Story of P&O.* London: Weidenfield & Nicholson.

Huff, W. G. (1994). *The Economic Growth of Singapore: Trade and Development in the Twentieth Century.* Cambridge: Cambridge University Press.

Hummels, D. (2007). Transportation Costs and International Trade in the Second Era of Globalization. *Journal of Economic Perspectives, 21,* 131–154.

Iheduru, O. C. (1992). Merchant Fleet Development by Legislation: Lessons from West and Central Africa. *Maritime Policy and Management, 19,* 297–317.

Jackson, A. (2006). *The British Empire and the Second World War.* London: Bloomsbury.

Jamieson, A. G. (1995). Facing the Rising Tide: British Attitudes to Asian National Shipping Lines, 1959–1964. *International Journal of Maritime History, 7,* 135–148.

Jose, R. G. (2012). The Philippines' Search for Security in the First Years of the Cold War, 1946–51. In A. Lau (Ed.), *Southeast Asia and the Cold War* (pp. 29–42). London: Routledge.

Kaukiainen, Y. (2014). The Role of Shipping in the 'Second Stage of Globalisation'. *International Journal of Maritime History, 26,* 64–81.

Kleiman, E. (1976). Trade and the Decline of Colonialism. *Economic Journal, 86,* 459–480.

Kuok, R. with Tanzer, A. (2017). *A Memoir.* Singapore: Landmark Books.

Levinson, M. (2006). *The Box: How the Shipping Container Made the World Smaller and the World Economy Bigger.* Princeton: Princeton University Press.

Lindblad, J. T. (2008). *Bridges to New Business: The Economic Decolonization of Indonesia.* Leiden: KITLV.

Low, D. A. (1991). *Eclipse of Empire.* Cambridge: Cambridge University Press.

Meek, M. (2003). *There Go the Ships.* Spennymoor, County Durham: The Memoir Club.

Lodge, J. (1978). New Zealand and the Community. *The World Today, 34,* 303–310.

Miller, M. B. (2012). *Europe and the Maritime World: A Twentieth-Century History.* Cambridge: Cambridge University Press.

Port Klang Authority. (2011). *Port Klang: Malaysia's Maritime Marvel.* https://issuu.com/wildage/docs/coffee_book_20110303_. Accessed 18 December 2018.

Poulsen, R. T. (2010). The Emergence of New Organisational Forms in Liner Shipping: Swedish Liner Shipping and International Consortia, 1960–75. *Journal of Transport History, 31,* 69–88.

Robinson, R. (1984). Imperial Theory and the Question of Imperialism After Empire. *Journal of Imperial and Commonwealth History, 12,* 42–54.

Schler, L. (2016). *Nation on Board: Becoming Nigerian at Sea.* Athens: Ohio University Press.

Sinclair, D. (2010). *Uncharted Waters: The Cayzer Family Firm (1916–1987).* London: Cayzer Trust.

Sturmey, S. G. (1986). The Code of Conduct for Liner Conferences: A 1985 View. *Maritime Policy & Management, 13,* 185–221.

Turner, G. (1971). *Business in Britain.* Harmondsworth, Middlesex: Pelican.

White, N. J. (2011). 'Ferry off the Mersey': The Business and the Impact of Decolonisation in Liverpool. *History, 96,* 188–204.

White, N. J. (2012). Surviving Sukarno: British Business in Post-colonial Indonesia, 1950–1967. *Modern Asian Studies, 46,* 1277–1315.

White, N. J., & Evans, C. (2015). Holding Back the Tide: Liverpool Shipping, Gentlemanly Capitalism and Intra-Asian Trade in the Twentieth Century. In U. Bosma & A. Webster (Eds.), *Commodities, Ports and Asian Maritime Trade since 1750* (pp. 218–240). Basingstoke: Palgrave Macmillan.

Woodman, R. (2010). *Fiddler's Green: The Great Squandering: 1921–2010.* Stroud, Gloucestershire: History Press.

4 Thinking Outside 'The Box': Decolonization and Containerization

Open Access This chapter is licensed under the terms of the Creative Commons Attribution-NonCommercial-NoDerivatives 4.0 International License (http://creativecommons.org/licenses/by-nc-nd/4.0/), which permits any noncommercial use, sharing, distribution and reproduction in any medium or format, as long as you give appropriate credit to the original author(s) and the source, provide a link to the Creative Commons license and indicate if you modified the licensed material. You do not have permission under this license to share adapted material derived from this chapter or parts of it.

The images or other third party material in this chapter are included in the chapter's Creative Commons license, unless indicated otherwise in a credit line to the material. If material is not included in the chapter's Creative Commons license and your intended use is not permitted by statutory regulation or exceeds the permitted use, you will need to obtain permission directly from the copyright holder.

Part II

Companies

5

'Containerization in Globalization': A Case Study of How Maersk Line Became a Transnational Company

Henrik Sornn-Friese

Introduction[1]

Studies on the role of containerization in globalization have centred either broadly on the history of the liner shipping industry,[2] or more narrowly on strategic alliances[3] and global maritime networks.[4] Most of these studies in addition have been carried out at the industry level and have

---

[1] This chapter is generally based on and extends an earlier article, written in Danish, Sornn-Friese (2017).
[2] Broeze (2002), Donovan and Bonney (2006), Levinson (2006), Slack and Frémont (2009), and van Ham and Rijsenbrij (2012).
[3] Rimmer (1998), Ryoo and Thanapoulou (1999), Broeze (2002), and Slack et al. (2002).
[4] Frémont (2007, 2010), Gadhia et al. (2011), Ducruet and Notteboom (2012), and Ducruet (2016).

H. Sornn-Friese (✉)
Department of Strategy and Innovation, Copenhagen Business School, Frederiksberg, Denmark
e-mail: Hs.si@cbs.dk

largely neglected the strategic dynamics associated with identifying business opportunities at home and abroad, the mobilization of resources, and efforts to continually adjust company strategy and organization. This chapter adds to the literature in two ways. Firstly, by shifting the unit of analysis from that of industry to that of the firm and, secondly, by focusing on the process of a company's transnationalization, which entails the establishment of a global network of subsidiaries orchestrated by a central corporate headquarters.[5]

The chapter uses a historical case study of Maersk Line, the world's leading container carrier. Maersk Line's global leadership was achieved within a relatively short time period and was the result of Mærsk McKinney Møllers decision in 1973 to enter container shipping—the biggest investment in the history of the AP Moller companies. Maersk Line has since grown into the world's largest container ship operator with almost 33,000 employees in 130 countries, a fleet of 639 container ships serving 59,000 customers around the globe, more than 300 own company offices in 121 countries, global service centres in Denmark, the Philippines, India and China, and access to 343 port terminals and inland transport facilities in 61 countries, partly through its sister company APM terminals.

Why did Maersk Line decide to become a global company, and how did it manage so quickly to achieve leadership in an industry dominated by a small number of consortia organized in cartel-like liner conferences? The major features in the company's development are well documented, but the story of how Maersk Line became a transnational corporation is an overlooked chapter.[6] The replacement of long-established third-party agency agreements with own offices after 1974 was a decision of great importance that enabled superior services globally. The motto 'service all the way' was the hallmark and a major driving force for the company. In a rare interview, the person in charge of the new container initiative, Mr Ib Kruse, explained how the company's competitiveness rested on a service 'second to none', realized through the combination of modern and effective company-owned ships with sophisticated equipment developed

---

[5] Bartlett (1986).
[6] Hornby (1988) and Jephson and Morgen (2014).

in-house, a global network of own company offices and high-level communication, and sophisticated documentation and control systems.[7] This chapter examines the development of these elements.

Through interviews with current and former employees of the AP Moller-Maersk Group, documents from the company's private archives and various secondary sources, the transnationalization of Maersk Line is studied as an 'extended era', limited in time and focusing on the substitution of third-party agents abroad with own country offices. With inspiration from the theory of dynamic capabilities the chapter seeks to explain how Maersk Line created an efficient global organization while adapting its services to local market needs in the countries where it operates.[8] The chapter demonstrates strategic change by examining the company's ability to capture and understand new business opportunities, seize them and change the company's core competencies. The study of such dynamic capabilities provides new perspectives for the understanding of transnational corporations.[9]

The analysis focuses largely on the period from 1974 to 1999, during which the establishment of the company's global network of own overseas offices was particularly pronounced. In this period, the company's many country managers had, as 'entrepreneurs and kings', the responsibility to create profits in their own country, and there were many local investments in container shipping and related services.[10] The Copenhagen headquarters decided on the overall strategy for Maersk Line and had a direct role in local development, but country offices were run as profit centres. Towards the end of the period, culminating in the acquisition of Safmarine and Sea-Land in 1999, the organization changed gradually, with the multifarious activities increasingly organized into independent product lines.

---

[7] Ikeda (1980).
[8] Teece et al. (1997) and Eisenhardt and Martin (2000).
[9] Teece (2014).
[10] Jensen (2014).

A Transnational Company

Unlike the global companies of the eighteenth and nineteenth centuries, primarily plantation, mining and international trade, which were typically state-supported monopolies on specific trades within the European colonies, modern transnational companies such as Maersk Line are characterized by their involvement in direct business activities abroad and their ability to profit from cooperation and international division of labour.[11]

The decision in 1973 to enter into container shipping was the start of Maersk Line's deep internationalization, developing as a genuine transnational corporation. Not only is Maersk Line today a huge and diverse company that serves customers around the globe with different needs and expectations, its activities are also managed so as to provide economies of scale through a global organization while the company can concurrently handle various conditions in different regions of the world and differentiate its services to local needs.

Several factors differentiate the transnational company from other international companies.[12] Transnational companies are able to plan, organize, coordinate and control their business activities across countries—typically from a central headquarters and through the setting of common goals and strategies. Characteristically, they promote multiple internal management perspectives, through which they can decode and respond to the diversity of external demands and opportunities; their interdependent physical assets and management capabilities are distributed internationally; and they have a strong unifying management approach.[13] The latter is characterized by top management's ability to synchronously manage context, processes and content. Context management is the task of providing a structure for delegated decision-making based on clear goals and priorities, career development for leaders with a global mindset, and established decision-making procedures. Top management's direct intervention in organizational processes may include minor modifications, typically handled through continuous monitoring and additional decision

---

[11] Hymer (1971) and Heaver (2010).
[12] Bartlett and Ghoshal (1989).
[13] Bartlett (1986).

support, as well as major interventions (such as establishing temporary working groups and task forces) in larger or more complex situations. Through content management, top management intervenes directly in local decision-making situations, if an issue remains unresolved, or if a previously selected solution proves unsatisfactory.

Soon after World War II Maersk Line had established a handful of offices abroad, and these became important for the subsequent container endeavour and for the building of the company's transnational organization from the middle of the 1970s. The latter followed the expansion of the trade network, where new regions were gradually added. In each region, Maersk Line established key country offices, while in individual ports and certain mainland hubs it opened up small branch offices. In the few locations that did not offer enough business volume to form a true profit centre, the company continued to be represented by third party agents.

Only Taiwan's Evergreen matched Maersk Line's approach in scope and dedication, and the two became the first real transnational companies in international container shipping. Although there was strategic awareness of the importance of strong representation locally, Maersk Line's global organization was not the result of a conscious transnational strategy, but rather of a long process of change in which the company reacted to business opportunities as they arose and dismissed the elements it found not to work. It is true, however, that container shipping, at least initially, required proximity to the customers, that certain economies of scale to some extent justified strong local country offices, and that the strength of the company's distinct entrepreneurial culture, where it 'was better to get forgiveness than to get permission', made it desirable to have a functioning internal sharing of knowledge and information.[14] All this contributed to the transnationalization of Maersk Line through a period when container shipping—driven by the transition from general cargo traffic to standard containers and the relocation of production from the West to low-wage countries in Southeast Asia—was a high-growth market.

---

[14]Jensen (2014).

The Establishment of the First Maersk Line Offices Abroad

Shortly after World War I Arnold Peter Møller started tramp shipping services in the US freight market, from where he soon also served the Far East. In 1919 he and his cousin, Hans Isbrandtsen, who had immigrated to the United States in 1915, together founded the Isbrandtsen-Moller Company (ISMOLCO) in New York. The international activities of the AP Moller-companies thus early on included ownership and strategic management control across borders. In 1928 ISMOLCO went into the liner business of shipping cargo from the US East Coast via the Panama Canal to the Far East, and hence Maersk Line was born. The Panama line was successful, and in 1931 Maersk Line had three ships in regular services on the route.

Like most liner companies Maersk Line employed local agents in the ports where the company's ships were calling. ISMOLCO was an agent for Maersk Line in the United States, and a few years after the establishment of the Panama line Mr Møller had built a network of third-party agents in Asia. The network comprised of the shipping departments of large industrial companies, such as Mitsubishi of Japan and Compañía General de Tabacos de Filipinas ('Tabacalera') in the Philippines,[15] and international trading houses specialized in liner shipping, such as, Melchers & Co in Shanghai (1931–1946), Jebsen & Co in Hong Kong (1946–1975) and in Shanghai (1946–1969), and Tait & Co in Taiwan.[16] The latter were typically larger companies each with their portfolio of agencies and with their own teams dedicated to each customer. During 1973–1976 Chris Jephson was employed by Tait & Co in Taiwan and responsible for their Maersk Line team, a group of 15–16 people focused exclusively on servicing Maersk Line. Tait & Co was agent for more than 70 shipping

---

[15] During his visit to Manila in 1930, Mr Møller had urged Tabacalera, one of the largest sugar producers in the Philippines, to establish its own shipping department, which subsequently became Maersk Line's General Agent in the country. Please see, Hornby (1988).

[16] Tait & Co was a subsidiary of the British-owned Harrisons & Crosfield Ltd, an international trading company that would later serve as agents for Maersk Line in several districts of India and, from 1953 to the outbreak of the Civil War in 1958, in Indonesia.

companies from around the world, several of which were Maersk Line's direct competitors.[17]

WWII put a temporary halt to Maersk Lines' activities, but from 1946 the Panama line was reopened. In the post-war years, Maersk Line established country offices in Thailand, Indonesia, the United States and Japan. The four offices proved important for the development of Maersk Line's global organization after 1974. Moreover, in 1951 Maersk Company Limited was established in London as an independent company that could operate the AP Moller fleet under the British flag in the event of a new war in Europe. Similarly, during the Cold War, Maersk Inc. in New York (see below) developed as a separate shadow headquarters that could take over the Maersk Line fleet in the event of a new war in Europe.

The first country office had been established in New York, where Mærsk Mc-Kinney Møller stayed during WWII. Along with Thorkil Høst, the former head of the AP Moller liner department in Copenhagen, he founded the Interseas Shipping Company. The new company, which in 1943 changed its name to Moller Steamship Company, was set to replace ISMOLCO as agent for Maersk Line in the United States, as A. P. Møller had decided to break with his cousin. When Mærsk Mc-Kinney Møller in 1947 moved back to Denmark, the Moller Steamship Company was fully staffed and operational and busy rebuilding the Panama line. Under Høst's leadership from 1947 to 1967, the Moller Steamship Company grew into a large and successful company with autonomous top management and Board of Directors. In 1955 the company established its own office in Los Angeles and in 1973 extended with an office in San Francisco. After the containerization of Maersk Line the company quickly built an extensive network of own offices in the United States and Canada.

From early spring 1946 the ships were once again fully loaded travelling from the United States to the Far East, and many of the customers from before the war returned to Maersk Line.[18] It was, however, difficult to generate backhaul from the Far East to the United States, and Maersk Line was working keenly to adapt its agent network in Asia to generate homegoing cargoes. Cooperation with the agents in Hong Kong, Manila and

---

[17]Personal interview with Chris Jephson, 11 November, 2016.
[18]Hornby (1988).

Taiwan were strengthened, but to access the lucrative Japan traffic, which in the post-war years was reserved for American tonnage, the company had to make a detour.[19] In 1947, Mærsk Mc-Kinney Møller therefore established Maersk Line Ltd (MLL) in Delaware, which gave access to the Asian countries managed by the Americans under General Douglas MacArthur, the Supreme Commander of the Allied Powers. In 1948, MLL opened up its own country office in Yokohama south of Tokyo and branch offices in Kobe and Osaka, and in 1958 it expanded with a branch office in Jakarta, replacing the existing agency agreement with Harrisons & Crosfield in Indonesia. MLL was mainly an administrative unit and it played no direct commercial role for Maersk Line until 1983 when it got a contract with the US Defense Department.

The branches in Japan and Indonesia developed in a short time to become important country offices for Maersk Line in the Far East, and Japan became a bridgehead to Thailand. In September 1949, the first Maersk Line ship called on Bangkok with the supply of railway equipment from Japan to the Thai State Railways. The new Japan-Thailand route, which in the following year was extended to the Persian Gulf, provided safe and regular cargo, and already in 1951 Maersk Line established an office in Bangkok, which soon was as important as the country offices in Japan and Indonesia.

Maersk Line expanded dramatically during the post-war period with the establishment of new routes. In addition to Japan-Thailand and Japan-Persian Gulf, it established a transatlantic line in 1947 (which was closed down again in 1954), a Suez line in 1949, a Japan-Indonesia line in 1952, a Gulf of Mexico-West Africa line in 1958 and a Japan-West Africa line in 1959.

Table 5.1 shows Maersk Line's coverage through third-party agents and own offices in 1958. With continuous network expansion, the company's agent network grew significantly in the post-war years, and there was an increased need for coordination and information exchange. From 1956 there would be regular meetings between the Principal Agents and the liner department in Copenhagen. The first Principal Agents' Meeting was held North of Copenhagen and lasted two days, and the meetings were then

---

[19] Hornby (1988).

Table 5.1 Maersk Line's Agency Network in 1958

AP Moller (Copenhagen)	Moller Steamship Company (New York)	
Alleppey Harrisons & Crosfield, Ltd	**Baltimore** Robert C. Herd & Co, Inc.	**Montreal** The Robert Reford Co, Ltd
Assab Gellatly, Hankey & Co (Sudan) Ltd	**Boston** Sprague Steamship Company	**New York** [a]Moller Steamship Company, Inc.
Bangkok [a]Maersk Line, Bangkok Branch (Ltd)	**Charleston** Southern Shipping Company, Inc.	**Philadelphia** B. H. Sobelman & Co, Inc.
Calicut Harrisons & Crosfield, Ltd	**Chicago** F. C. MacFarlane Steamship Agency, Inc.	**Pittsburgh** Lamark Shipping Agency
Cochin Harrisons & Crosfield, Ltd	**Detroit** F. C. MacFarlane Steamship Agency, Inc.	**San Francisco** Fred. Olsen Line Agency, Ltd
Colombo Carson Cumberbath & Co, Ltd	**Hampton Roads** Dichmann, Wright & Pugh, Inc.	**Savannah** Smith & Kelly Co
Jakarta [a]Maersk Line, Djakarta Branch	**Jacksonville** Southern Shipping Company	**Southern New England** Timm Steamship Agency West Redding, Connecticut
Djibouti Gellatly, Hankey & Co (Sudan) Ltd	**Los Angeles** [b]Maersk Line Agency	**Toronto** The Robert Reford Co, Ltd
Hong Kong Jebsen & Company	**Memphis** O. L. (Ollie) Stevens	**Washington, DC** William J. Spurrier
Keelung Tait & Co, Ltd		
Manila Compañía General de Tabacos de Filipinas		
Massawa Gellatly, Hankey & Co (Sudan) Ltd		
Medan N. V. Macba		
Penang J. H. Vavasseur & Co (M) Ltd		
Saigon Plantations des Terres Rouges		
Singapore Anglo-American Corporation, Ltd		
Tokyo [a]Maersk Line Ltd, Japan Branch		
Tuticorin Harrisons & Crosfield, Ltd		

[a]Own country offices; [b]Own representation
Source AP Moller-Maersk, Main Archive, Box 286321

repeated at 2–3 year intervals.[20] When Maersk Line almost two decades later went into container shipping, the agent meetings had become weeklong events with executives from Copenhagen and the principal agents from around the world. Although they were indeed autonomous and legally independent companies, the principal agents were considered an integral part of Maersk Line, as made apparent by A. P. Møller in his welcoming speech during the second Principal Agents' Meeting in 1958: 'You are now all in the Maersk family, and we are happy to have you as members thereof. You have all done a good job to serve as a member of that family, and I hope that you will all continue to make the Maersk name honoured, respected, and still growing. I thank you, Gentlemen!'.[21]

Developments 1974–1999

Maersk Line's international organization proved to be an important prerequisite for the company's success in container shipping. The country managers in the United States, Japan, Thailand and Indonesia (so-called 'Maersk Top') were part of the 'crash committee' established by Mærsk Mc-Kinney Møller in early 1970 with the task to investigate whether the Panama line should be containerized.[22] Prior to this there had been a cautious attempt to initiate a containerized service between Asia and Europe in cooperation with Japanese 'K' Line, but the Japanese had terminated the partnership and Maersk Line's first container ship had instead been chartered out. The four-country managers were deeply involved in the decision to containerize the line and their country offices were important building blocks in the unfolding of this new venture globally.[23] Local presence along the Panama line was crucial for success as the ultimate goal was a worldwide door-to-door service in which the company would control the customer's transport task from supplier to final destination.[24] The

---

[20] Hornby (1988).
[21] AP Moller-Maersk, Main Archive, Box 161332.
[22] Jephson and Morgen (2014).
[23] Pedersen and Sornn-Friese (2015).
[24] Jephson and Morgen (2014).

country managers contributed international knowledge and experience as well as an organizational platform for the containerization of the line.

'Maersk Container Line' was initially shielded from AP Moller's conventional liner business and was a small unit in Copenhagen with only five employees: Ib Kruse (managing director), Flemming Jacobs (marketing and sales), Niels Jørgen Iversen (ship operations), Birger Riisager (finance and IT) and Erik Holtegaard (conference matters). Globally the unit had only about 30 employees. The recommendations from the crash committee to the organization were: 'Develop the essential management organization, taking account of both the new skills that will be necessary and the quality of staff required in each location'.[25] In 1974 it was decided to establish country offices in Hong Kong and Singapore, and from that time onwards there was rapid establishment of offices in Asia, Europe and North America and later in the rest of the world, as illustrated in Fig. 5.1.

The establishment of country offices were each international episodes of great importance and can be described as revolutionary steps towards the transnationalization of Maersk Line, whereas the creation of smaller, local offices were gradual extensions in an ongoing, evolutionary internationalization process.[26] Each country office was established as a profit centre—an independent, and in the country legally domiciled, company with its own board and management. Each establishment had thus a long-term perspective; they were 'good citizens' locally and not temporary structures aimed at 'looting'.[27] Country managers were typically expat Danes sent from the Copenhagen headquarters, while the other employees in the offices were well-qualified locals recruited from the shipping and freight forwarding industry. The focus on own country offices was on building a global agency network, with emphasis on the word 'network': although the offices were established as profit centres, there was a strong central management from Copenhagen in the form of advanced IT systems and behavioural incentives, and effective socialization mechanisms worked to interconnect the organization across countries and companies.

---

[25] AP Moller-Maersk, Main Archive, Box 151747.
[26] For the distinction between evolutionary and revolutionary internationalization processes, please see Kutschker et al. (1997).
[27] Personal interview with Flemming Jacobs, 10 March, 2017.

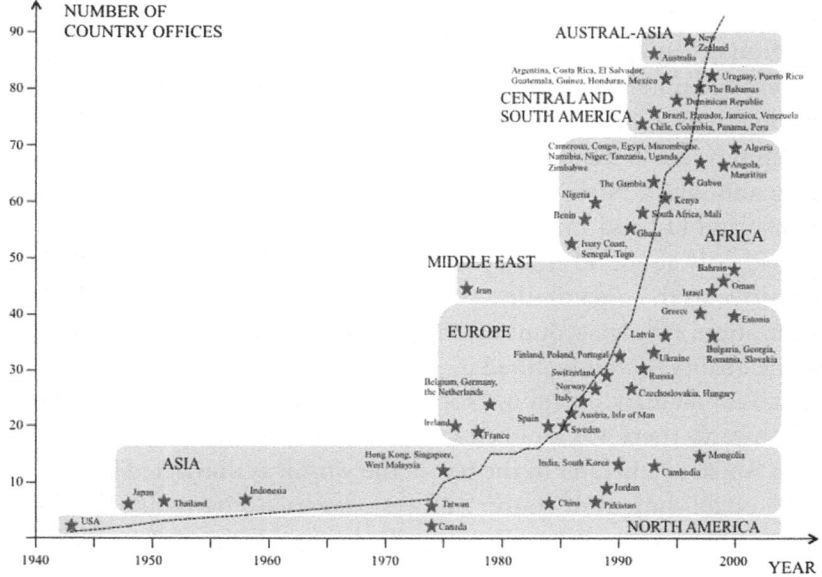

Fig. 5.1 The establishment of Maersk Line country offices (*Source* AP Moller-Maersk, Main Archive, various boxes)

- Employees were carefully selected and tested. Already in the 1960s McKinney-Møller had introduced a so-called Predictive Index (PI) system for staff assessment, where employees were measured on intellect and personality. From this system was drawn a global inventory of talents that could be called upon whenever the organization lacked 'the right person at the right time and place'.
- Employees were stationed in a country for a number of years and then either sent on to another country for an additional time period or back to the head office in Copenhagen. In that way, employees developed actual country experience and international perspective, and they forged strong ties to other Maersk people, essentially forming a 'Maersk-blue brotherhood'.
- Marketing and Sales was a primary management philosophy. A comprehensive and detailed marketing manual had been developed for use in the conventional liner business in 1974, the distribution of which

was restricted to Maersk Line personnel and agencies. The manual specified the Maersk Line logo, which consisted of two elements: 'a Maersk blue square with rounded corners containing a white seven-pointed star ("standing on two points"), and the name Maersk Line'.[28] It also specified in great detail how the logo should be applied in communication (e.g., transportation documents, cover letters, envelopes, name badges, and business cards), on the company's ships and vehicles, and in other advertisement (match boxes, playing cards, pencils and pens, memo pads, calculators, alarm clocks, LEGO ship models, and more). All overseas offices would use the manual to ensure that sales and marketing was handled properly.

- Similarly, there was a written manual for the design of Maersk Line offices, narrowly specifying the choice of colours, furniture and office wall art (the offices should always have pictures of A. P. Møller and Mærsk Mc-Kinney Møller as well as the Danish Royal family). The manual also promoted a strict dress code, however allowing for smaller deviations to accommodate to local customs in the different countries.
- There was outspoken focus on training and education, particularly in sales. The company's global sales training program was managed from Copenhagen, but performed and adapted locally. With the rapidly expanding global organization the company's training efforts were vigorously developed, and from 1993 firmly established in the M.I.S.E. program ('Maersk International Shipping Education'), which annually attracted more than 85,000 applicants worldwide to around 500 trainees positions.[29]

In 1967, Poul Rasmussen replaced Thorkil Høst as country manager in the United States, and after the decision to containerize the Panama line in 1973 he replaced the company's third-party agents in the United States with own offices in the most important ports. These typically focused on sales and customer services, but in major ports such as Baltimore and Charleston they would also carry out ship operations. In 1978, Alfred B. ('Ted') Ruhly took over after Rasmussen. Among many other initiatives,

---

[28] Maersk Line Communication Manual, Issued 1 August 1974.
[29] Sornn-Friese et al. (2012).

Ruhly introduced quality circles in the organization, based on the principle that 'what gets measured, gets done'. Quality Control subsequently spread to Maersk Line globally as a key underpinning in being 'second to none'.

When Moller Steamship Company in 1988 changed its name to Maersk Inc. and moved to larger premises in New Jersey, it had more than 30 own offices in the United States and Canada. The name change was a result of increased marketing of the Maersk brand, but the company's function was unchanged. Maersk Inc. had a high degree of autonomy from Copenhagen, partly due to the business volume based on the remarkable Post-WWII expansion of the US economy and the importance of the Panama service to Maersk Line, and partly due to the role the organization got with Mc-Kinney Møller's residence in the United States during WWII. In the 1990s, the culture to some extent was a reflection of the culture in Copenhagen but mixed with strong elements of American leadership.[30] When Maersk Line acquired Sea-Land in 1999 Maersk Inc. played a major role, both in the dialogue with the US authorities and in the work to get the two companies integrated. With the acquisition of Sea-Land, Maersk Inc. more than doubled in size and was now by far the largest shipping company in the Americas with more than 100 offices in the United States, Canada, South America, Central America, and the Caribbean.[31]

Until the mid-1990s the establishment of new country offices followed in a steady stream and anchored Maersk Line in Eastern Europe as well as in Africa, China and the Middle East. In the locations where Maersk Line, due to local institutional conditions, could not be established with wholly-owned subsidiaries, the company would set up exclusive Maersk Line units in the organizations of its third-party agents. Having own employees stationed was considered as a key issue, partly with the aim to inject the right dose of 'Maersk blue blood' in the organization and partly to provide own people with specific country experiences and an international outlook.

In 1993, Maersk Line went into nine new countries and 24 overseas Maersk Line offices were added to the organization. Particularly interesting

---

[30] Benson and Lambek (2000) and Jensen (2014).
[31] Nissen (2000).

was the establishment in Australia and the continuation of containerization of routes within Asia. These included the acquisition of EAC's Far East Line and certain of their offices in the area. This all happened before the intra-Asia container market became the world's largest. Included in the acquisition of EAC's Far East Line was an Eastern Australian service between Melbourne, Sydney, Brisbane and two ports in Japan and Korea, as well as a Western Australian service between Fremantle, Singapore, Malaysia, Hong Kong and Taiwan. The EAC's intra-Asia services were also included in the deal and were continued from Singapore through Maersk Line's new subsidiary MCC Transport.

Containerization of the Europe/Asia Route

In the late 1970s it was decided to containerize the important Suez line running between Europe and Asia. The Suez line had originally been established in 1946, when the company experimentally let the ships that had sailed out on the Panama line return to the United States via South and Southeast Asia and the Red Sea.[32] With the decision to start a weekly independent container service between Asia and Europe ten new large container ships were ordered, and the organization in Western Europe was considerably strengthened. Long-held agency agreements were replaced with own country offices: Dublin in 1976, Paris in 1978 and Hamburg, Rotterdam and Antwerp in 1979. In addition, the company established its own local branch offices in Bremen, Düsseldorf, Nürnberg, Stuttgart, Frankfurt, Munich and Amsterdam. The European focus was gradually extended first to Scandinavia in 1985 with an owned office, Maersk Line (Sverige) AB, in Gothenburg and smaller, local branch offices in Stockholm and Helsingborg and then to Eastern Europe. With the continued expansion of Maersk Line in Europe new agency agreements were made with third-party providers in new countries, only to be replaced with own Maersk Line offices later on. In Helsinki, for example, an agreement was entered with OY Jacobsen Shipping Ltd in 1976 and replaced with an owned office in 1990. This stepping-stone approach was a means for

---

[32]Hornby (1988).

Maersk Line to build up country experience in new markets that would later be used as lever for an own establishment.

Various documents related to the company's Europe Project show that Belgium, The Netherlands and Germany formed the core of containerization of the Suez line.[33] Experienced Maersk employees were installed as Board of Directors and together with the newly appointed country managers were directly involved in hiring high-calibre senior people to lead the main functions of the three offices. The offices were also linked to the company's new electronic systems that Maersk Data had developed in collaboration with Cable & Wireless in London for container management and documentation on the Panama line.

On Saturday, 28 June 1980, the country managers and senior people from the Europe offices together with the third-party agents in Switzerland, Denmark, Norway and Sweden were invited to a full-day information session in Copenhagen. Senior managers from Copenhagen and top officials from the advertising company Young & Rubicam also joined the meeting. On the program were the key elements in Maersk Line's management philosophy: ships and operations, marketing and sales, financial management and the unique IT systems. Sales philosophy was a significant strategic directive for the company: Maersk Line should offer a superior service and be known as the prime alternative to the three large container consortia Trio, Scan Dutch and ACE Group, which controlled more than 90% of container shipping on Asia-Europe through the cartel-like Far Eastern Freight Conference (FEFC). Maersk Line's partnership with Young & Rubicam was important and close. It was an integral part of getting the new container concept rolled out and marketed. Young & Rubicam had its own team of employees living and breathing for Maersk Line.

---

[33] AP Moller-Maersk, Main Archive, Box 151957 and Box 151963.

The World's Most Profitable Container Shipping Line

In 1985, it was decided that Maersk Line should become 'the most profitable international container transportation company in the world'.[34] This objective was to be achieved through first-class services, global coverage, and door-to-door services—three elements that from the beginning were captured in the motto 'service all the way'. To achieve the objective required outstanding ships and equipment, well-trained and highly motivated employees, maximum cost-effectiveness, tailor-made customer services, and investments in specialized tonnage and equipment for niche markets. With the objective followed a genuine growth strategy to be pursued through a combination of increased transport frequency in existing markets and entry into new geographic markets. The growth would be based on the experiences with the containerization of the Panama line, and should preferably be organic.

The establishment of own offices in key locations were formalized in the company's new growth strategy: 'Maersk Line must have as an objective to be represented by their own agencies, where this is feasible'. The strategy included detailed plans for the establishment of new offices in Europe, Asia and Africa, and for each country a short comment was attached.[35] For Italy it was noted, for example, that the previously used agent was 'owned and managed by aging Italians with no apparent dynamic crown princes'. For West Africa the note was more comprehensive: 'The ongoing study by the Line Department is expected to lead to a positive conclusion on the establishment of own companies in Ivory Coast, Togo and maybe Senegal to achieve overall control and undertake direct sales, customer service, documentation and container control—possibly leaving vessels' operations sub-contracted to existing agencies'.

In 1986, the remaining conventional liner services were merged with the container business in Maersk Line as a separate business unit and expanded with a new container line between Europe, the Middle East and West Africa. It was also somewhat of a stroke of genius to build a private

---

[34] AP Moller Maersk, Archive of Mr Ib Kruse, Box 122118.
[35] AP Moller Maersk, Archive of Mr Ib Kruse, Box 122118.

container terminal in what had hitherto been a fishing port in Algeciras in southern Spain. The project was simply called CPS—to keep it secret, which Maersk Line had the habit of, also regarding the current capacity of its container vessels.[36] CPS stood for 'Connecting Point Spain'. The basic idea of the concept included serving main lines by large container vessels avoiding 'convoy sailings', serving feeder legs by a flexible fleet easily adjustable in time with even short-term market fluctuations, and the availability of efficient berthing and operation facilities at the connecting point.[37] This involved replacing the 10–12 general cargo vessels on the existing conventional route from Asia to West Africa with only four major feeder ships of the line between Algeciras and West African ports. This hit two birds with one stone: first, utilizing capacity on ships from Asia to North Europe by stopping in Algeciras, and second, delivering the goods in West Africa much faster than had been the case on the longer way with general cargo vessels, and thus provide even better customer service. It would also save Maersk Line huge shipping costs.

A Deeper Reflection: The Establishment in Southeast Asia in 1975

Press releases brought in a number of Hong Kong, Singapore and Malaysian newspapers in the second half of 1974 showed that Maersk Line, with effect from 1 January 1975, would end the longstanding collaborations with third-party agents in Hong Kong and Singapore and set up its own offices.[38] As reasons were stated the company's new and large exposures in the container era. Strategically the decision was founded in the desire to establish Maersk Line as a strong brand and provide 'service all the way', but the timing was prompted by inadequate services from the existing agents. Maersk Line had already opened an own office in Taipei the year before. Even at the commencement of containerization in

---

[36] Personal interview with Flemming Jacobs, 10 March, 2017.
[37] AP Moller-Maersk, Main Archive, Box 285835.
[38] AP Moller-Maersk, Line Management Archive, Box 220732 and Box 220730.

1975 Taiwan was a very important market for Maersk Line, so a smoothly functioning and tightly controlled local operation was deemed crucial.

With the containerization of the Panama line the company decided to relinquish its 'serving Japan first' approach and instead focus on Southeast Asia, and there were careful considerations behind this choice.[39] Importers in Southeast Asia had begun to avoid lines that passed via Japan, and while Japan's imports from the United States were expected to considerably increase at the time, such increase would be in value rather than in tonnage. Moreover, Japan was the area in the Far East with the toughest liner competition and consequent over-tonnage. Tariff rates between the United States and Japan on general cargo were also lower than to Southeast Asia, and rebating more prevalent.

Even more important, however, was the decision to continue serving the markets that Maersk Line had built up long before the container era—mainly niche exports from the United States to Southeast Asia, where especially Hong Kong, Singapore and Taiwan were important destinations.[40] A major customer was Caterpillar, one of the world's leading manufacturers of construction machinery, but Maersk Line also carried frozen food, fresh fruit and much more. Not only did the dedication to existing customers imply that Maersk Line had to be strongly represented locally in Southeast Asia, but also that the bet on containerization required investments in flexible vessels and equipment. For example, with specially-built 'artificial tween-decks', which were portable 'three container cells wide' platforms that could be inserted into the stow of mainline container vessels as well as feeder vessels at any depth and in any hold,[41] Maersk Line could continue transporting heavy loads of non-standard size and shape. The tween-decks enabled heavy loads to be handled by shore container cranes without interrupting the flow of units. Containers were furthermore developed for niche requirements. With the transport of fresh fruit and frozen chicken it was important that the temperature in the containers could be adjusted as needed, and hence Maersk Line developed the refrigerated container with the cooling unit located on the container.

---

[39]AP Moller-Maersk, Main Archive, Box 151747.
[40]Personal interview with Flemming Jacobs, 10 March, 2017.
[41]Grey (1975).

During that period, the major ports in Southeast Asia were gradually switching to container shipping.[42] In 1966 the authorities in Hong Kong and Singapore had independently appointed committees to assess the implications of containerization and make recommendations on the establishment of container terminals, and in 1967 Malaysia had also initiated a major investigation. Through private investments, Hong Kong had opened its first container terminals between 1970 and 1973, and Singapore, which had achieved independence from first the United Kingdom in 1963 and subsequently from Malaysia in 1965, had also moved quickly to maintain its importance as a regional hub and inaugurated its first container terminal in 1972.[43] Finally, in 1973 the container activities had developed in Malaysia's main port, Port Klang. The changing requirements of containerization were formidable and eventually would completely transform the ports in Southeast Asia. In the middle of the 1990s a walk around the Hong Kong container terminals was a 'walk around a ghost town populated only by tall machines' as containerization had 'moved the traditional godown and warehouse away from its historic home at the edge of the sea' and moved depots and freight stations to 'the hinterland away from dock thieves, salt water, and sometimes maritime expertise'.[44]

Maersk Line's competitors provided shuttles between Northeast Asia and the United States, but Maersk Line's focus on existing customers led to a different business model. Rather than concentrate traffic to the Pacific mainline the company chose to continue to serve destinations, which at that time did not even have container facilities in their ports nor a well-functioning inland transport infrastructure. In some of the places the transport conditions on land were very simple and land transportation was by truck only. This meant that Maersk Line's containerization objectives required the development of extensive areas for storing containers and suitable transport infrastructure in the countries, another good reason for being strongly established with own offices locally.

---

[42] Trace (1997).
[43] Levinson (2006).
[44] Ignarski (1995, 95).

For the containerization of its Panama line the company therefore chose a weekly service from the United States directly and deeply into Southeast Asia and then returning to the United States via Japan, as evident from Maersk Line's Master Plan shown in Table 5.2. At a speed of 25 knots per

Table 5.2 The Master Plan for the containerization of the Panama line

Service: U.S.A./Far East			Schedule				Speed: 25 knots	
	Distances		Schedule					
			Arrivals		Departures			
	Miles	Lost time factor%	Date (1972)	Hours	Date (1972)	Hours	Sailing day	Comment
New York					7/10	1800	Sat	
Baltimore	410	6	8/10	1200	8/10	2400		
Charleston	552	6	9/10	2400	10/10	1800		
Panama	1560	6	13/10	1800	14/10	1800		
Oakland	3290	8	20/10	1800	21/10	1200	Sat	
Hong Kong	6044	11	2/11	1800	3/11	1800		Feeder to Manila and Kaohsiung
Singapore	1460	6	6/11	0600	8/11	1800	Wed	Feeder to/from Bangkok, Jakarta and Port Klang
Hong Kong	1460	6	11/11	0600	11/11	1800	Sat	Feeder from Manila
Kaohsiung	342	6	12/11	0600	12/11	1800	Sun	
Kobe	1121	6	14/11	1800				Feeder to/from Busan
Tokyo	365	6			17/11	2400	Fri	
Oakland	4559	9	25/11	0600	25/11	1800		
Panama	3290	8	1/12	1800	2/12	1800		
New York	1972	6	6/12	0600	9/12	1800		
Total Miles	26,425	8						
Total Time			54½ days					
Contingency Allowance			8½ days					
Time per Voyage			63 days					

Steaming	44	days
Sea margin (8%)	3½	days
Cargo handling time	8½	days
Canal passing	2	days
Contingency allowance	5	days
Total round voyage	63	days

Source AP Moller-Maersk, Main Archive, Box 151747

hour a reliable weekly service could be maintained with the company's nine newly built 1200 TEU mainline vessels in the A-series (the vessels were given names starting with the letter A), which was crucial for the new business model. As a novelty in international container shipping at the time, Maersk Line established a fixed schedule with port calls at certain weekdays. None of Maersk Line's competitors were geared for such an operation.[45] The new advertising slogan 'You can set your watch by Maersk' served to visualize the business model.[46]

Execution

The venture into containerization was essentially different from conventional liner shipping, and especially Maersk Line's business model put great demands on service and customer experience. It was vital to provide consistent service to all shippers and receivers anywhere on the planet, and the company could not build a successful business if it had to rely on the various routines and systems of its many third-party agents. A strong local presence in the Southeast Asian countries was therefore considered crucial to the new business model.

Minor adjustments were made to the containerization master plan. The Master Plan had stipulated a direct service to Kaohsiung in the south of Taiwan to commence in 1975. The Port of Kaohsiung had expanded greatly in the period after WWII culminating in 1975 with the completion of 'the Second Harbour', built to accommodate modern container vessels. During the following decades, the Port of Kaohsiung would develop into a regional hub port, or 'load centre' on a par with Hong Kong and Singapore.[47] The Master Plan however was implemented with the big ships calling from Hong Kong directly to Keelung in the north of Taiwan and then onwards to Japan, and at least initially Maersk Line would instead serve Kaohsiung by feeder. In the mid-1970s, nearly all the high-value exports from Taiwan were concentrated in the north of Taiwan, in the area around Taipei,

---

[45] Pedersen and Sornn-Friese (2015).
[46] Jephson and Morgen (2014).
[47] Trace (1997).

with some along a corridor towards Taichung in the centre West Coast of Taiwan, the latter of which was also the area for high-value imports (e.g., machinery, weaving equipment). Because the transport infrastructure on land was quite primitive at the time, Maersk Line decided to maintain its longstanding focus on the much closer Keelung, and while the main competitors, particularly Sea-Land and American President Lines, did call Kaohsiung directly, this decision gave Maersk Line a 1–2 days competitive advantage on top of its fast transit to the United States' West Coast.[48] Only years later did Maersk Line's big ships call directly at Kaohsiung.

Frictions in the relationship with the existing agents also provided an occasion to move fast in Hong Kong, Singapore and Malaysia. Maersk Line's principal agent for Hong Kong and Macao through 43 years was Jebsen & Company, a respected Danish-owned company domiciled in Hong Kong. In Jebsen's shipping department 25 employees worked exclusively for Maersk Line, and they had always provided a quality service for Maersk Line's conventional liner traffic. In the early 1970s, the Head of the AP Moller liner department in Copenhagen, Christian Lund, however, noted challenges with Jebsen & Company and after having vainly tried to place one of his own people at Jebsen's offices Maersk Line decided to terminate the agency agreement and instead establish its own office.[49]

In Singapore and West Malaysia there was also an experience of inadequate service from the Anglo-American Corporation, Maersk Line's principal agent for the two countries since 1953, and again it was decided to terminate the agreement and establish own offices. In a letter to Ib Kruse the recently appointed owner-representative of Maersk Line in the area, Niels Lillelund Jørgensen, claimed 'the urgent need of a solution', and to Christian Lund he stressed the need to establish a strong own organization in the area: 'with the start of the new container line Singapore will become so important that it will be necessary to have a strong organization. (…) An own office will also be able to develop business opportunities in Maersk

---

[48] Personal e-mail correspondence with Chris Jephson, 7–9 August 2017.
[49] AP Moller-Maersk, Line Management Archive, Box 220732.

Supply Service, Maersk Air, Sales & Purchasing, Chartering and Brokerage, Financial operations (incl. Asian Dollar), Industry, Maersk Drilling (incl. Aquadril), and so on'.[50]

After the decision was made to establish own offices in Hong Kong and Singapore the company moved fast with the registration of the new companies, obtaining work and residence permits, staffing, preparation of internal manuals and furnishing office space. The latter was considered important for cultivating employees and maintaining a strong corporate culture.[51] Country managers were appointed among experienced Maersk people who would hit the ground running, while senior staff and other employees were recruited locally, most of them directly from Jebsen and Anglo-American, respectively. Half a year later, Maersk Line also established its own organization in Malaysia with a large office in Port Klang and small offices in Kuala Lumpur and Penang, with 'Danish supervision as needed from Singapore'.[52]

The new offices were given the important task to organize port facilities throughout Southeast Asia and to secure Maersk Line vessels reliable access to the terminals. They were also involved in the roll-out of new advanced IT systems developed by Maersk Data. It was particularly important to get a handle on documentation so that customers at any time could track their cargo, and so that the conclusion of tasks could proceed smoothly. The new A-series of container vessels sailed so fast that it was not possible for the necessary documents to keep up with the normal way of transfer, but with the new IT systems the necessary information could quickly be transmitted from one end of the world to the other and printed locally. This was something that greatly differentiated Maersk Line from its competitors in Southeast Asia. Finally, the two offices were heavily involved in launching the company's first global sales training programme with the aim to professionalize the sales function in Maersk Line and ensure that the company could deliver consistent service globally.

---

[50] AP Moller-Maersk, Line Management Archive, Box 220730.
[51] Jensen (2014).
[52] AP Moller-Maersk, Line Management Archive, Box 220730.

The new country offices were hugely important for subsequent developments. They were crucial for the ability to detect and respond to unexpected changes in the market, and they established Maersk Line as an important name in Asia and founded the network to the major shippers and other important players. Local presence enabled not only superior and consistent service and the establishment of the necessary infrastructure and complementary assets locally, but also a good feel for the market and its development. It was thus Maersk Line offices locally in Asia and North America, which put the company in a position soon to perceive and quickly respond to the significant growth and development of the Asian economies, which really took off with 'exports in the opposite direction' in the late 1970s and helped making the Panama line profitable.[53]

The offices' local status and the strong network later proved crucial for getting access to Vietnam, the Bay of Bengal and China, among others. In 1984 the Hong Kong office established its first representation in Guangzhou in Mainland China, and from here the number of Maersk employees in the People's Republic of China over ten years increased to more than 100 people across 12 offices. Since the Chinese authorities would only allow foreign companies to operate in China via local agents, the offices were in the beginning run in joint venture with Chinese interests, but in 1994 Maersk Line was the first foreign shipping company authorized to establish a private, wholly-owned company with business activities everywhere in China. With this development the number of Maersk Line employees in China quadrupled in just one year.[54]

Conclusion

Maersk Line has always been an international company, but with the transition to container shipping in the early 1970s the company chose to focus globally in the sense that its many work processes were spread to locations across the globe, often with a high degree of autonomy locally but integrated in a way that accommodated Maersk Line's overall goals. The

---

[53] Jephson and Morgen (2014).
[54] Simonsen (1994).

goal was to deliver a worldwide, door-to-door container transport based on superior and consistent service. This chapter has shown how Maersk Line approached the task, including how the company established a global organization with strong local representation.

The internationalization of Maersk Line was a learning process in which the company reacted to business opportunities as they arose. Although there was a desire to have local representation in profitable markets, the transnationalization of the company can best be described as emergent rather than following a strategic plan. The initiative to own overseas offices, which were established as independent companies with their own management and board of directors, as a rule came from the head office in Copenhagen, but the further strategic development for individual countries were then left largely to the 'Maersk Top' in each country. The process was guided by some more or less well-defined management tools including explicit 'fundamental company objectives', a logic of operational independence, value-based decision heuristics, a focus on the importance of 'Maersk-blue blood' that resulted in a special 'man on the ground' philosophy, and customized training programs overseen by the Copenhagen headquarter; as well as special global information and communication systems developed specifically for Maersk Line.

When considering how Maersk Line managed to achieve global leadership in a period of just about 25 years, the chapter has pointed to the importance of the company's own country offices that allowed the interconnection of three types of networks: The *physical network* of ships and routes, the *digital network* of information and communication systems, and the *human network* of Maersk employees. The interaction between the vessels, the systems and the people is still at the core of the company today and central to its continued development.

References

Bartlett, C. A. (1986). Building and Managing the Transnational: The New Organizational Challenge. In M. E. Porter (Ed.), *Competition in Global Industries* (pp. 367–401). Boston: Harvard Business School Press.

Bartlett, C. A., & Ghoshal, S. (1989). *Managing Across Borders: the Transnational Solution*. Boston: Harvard Business School Press.
Benson, P. S., & Lambek, B. (2000, August 23). United Maersk of America. *Politiken*. Section 3, 1; Jensen, *Culture Shock in Maersk Line*.
Broeze, F. (2002). *The Globalisation of the Oceans: Containerisation from the 1950s to the Present*. St. John's: IMEHA.
Donovan, A., & Bonney, J. (2006). *The Box That Changed the World: Fifty Years of Container Shipping—An Illustrated History*. East Windsor: Commonwealth Business Media.
Ducruet, C. (2016). *Maritime Networks: Spatial Structures and Time Dynamics*. Milton Park: Routledge.
Ducruet, C., & Notteboom, T. (2012). The Worldwide Maritime Network of Container Shipping: Spatial Structure and Regional Dynamics. *Global Networks, 12*(3), 395–423.
Eisenhardt, K. M., & Martin, J. A. (2000). Dynamic Capabilities: What Are They? *Strategic Management Journal, 21*(10/11), 1105–1121.
Frémont, A. (2007). 'Global Maritime Networks: The Case of Maersk. *Journal of Transport Geography, 15*(6), 431–442.
Frémont, A. (2010). Maritime Networks: A Source of Competitiveness for Shipping Lines. In K. Cullinane (Ed.), *International Handbook of Maritime Business*. Cheltenham: Edward Elgar.
Gadhia, H. K., Kotzab, H., & Prockl, G. (2011). Levels of Internationalization in the Container Shipping Industry: An Assessment of the Port Networks of the Large Container Shipping Companies. *Journal of Transport Geography, 19*(6), 1431–1442.
Grey, M. (1975, October 2). Maersk Begins Its Trans-Pacific Container Challenge. *Fairplay International Shipping Weekly*, pp. 7–9.
Heaver, T. D. (2010). The Dynamic Role of International Shipping in Business Structures and Relationships. In E. van de Voorde & T. Vanelslander (Eds.), *Applied Transport Economics: A Management and Policy Perspective*. Antwerp: Antwerpen De Boeck.
Hornby, O. (1988). *'With Constant Care…'. A.P. Møller: Shipowner 1876–1965*. Copenhagen: J. H. Schultz.
Hymer, S. H. (1971). The Multinational Corporation and the Law of Uneven Development. In J. N. Bhagwati (Ed.), *Economics and World Order* (pp. 113–140). London: Macmillan.
Ignarski, S. (1995). *The Box: An Anthology Celebrating 25 Years of Containerisation and the TT Club*. London: TT Club.

Ikeda, M. (1980, October 29). Maersk's Containerization Plan in F.E./Europe Trade Explained. *Shipping and Trade News.*

Jensen, L. (2014). *Culture Shock in Maersk Line: From Entrepreneurs and Kings to Modern Efficiency.* Copenhagen: Vespucci Maritime Publishing.

Jephson, C., & Morgen, H. (2014). *Creating Global Opportunities: Maersk Line in Containerisation 1973–2013.* Cambridge: Cambridge University Press.

Kutschker, M., Bäurle, I., & Schmid, S. (1997). International Evolution, International Episodes, and International Epochs—Implications for Managing Internationalization. *Management International Review, 37*(2), 101–124.

Levinson, M. (2006). *The Box: How the Shipping Container made the World Smaller and the World Economy Bigger.* Princeton and Oxford: Princeton University Press.

Nissen, A. (2000, December 6). Mærsk Inc.: Trimmet til vækst. *Jyllands-Posten.* Section 4, 8.

Pedersen, T., & Sornn-Friese, H. (2015). A Business Model Innovation by an Incumbent Late Mover: Containerization in Maersk Line. In N. J. Foss & T. Saebi (Eds.), *Business Model Innovation: The Organizational Dimension* (pp. 217–239). Oxford: Oxford University Press.

Rimmer, P. J. (1998). Ocean Liner Shipping Services: Corporate Restructuring and Port Selection/Competition. *Asia Pacific Viewpoint, 39*(2), 193–208.

Ryoo, D. K., & Thanapoulou, H. A. (1999). Liner Alliances in the Globalization Era: A Strategic Tool for Asian Container Carriers. *Maritime Policy and Management, 26*(4), 349–367.

Simonsen, J. D. (1994, May 17). Mærsk udvider kraftigt i hele Kina. *Berlingske Tidende.* Section 3, 5.

Slack, B., Comtois, C., & McCalla, R. J. (2002). Strategic Alliances in the Container Shipping Industry: A Global Perspective. *Maritime Policy and Management, 29*(1), 65–76.

Slack, B. J., & Frémont, A. (2009). Fifty Years of Organizational Change in Container Shipping: Regional Shift and the Role of Family Firms. *GeoJournal, 74*(1), 23–34.

Sornn-Friese, H. (2017). Transnationaliseringen af Maersk Line: fra tredjepartsagenter til egne kontorer i udlandet. *Økonomi & Politik, 90*(2), 46–58.

Sornn-Friese, H., Poulsen, R. T., & Iversen, M. J. (2012). "Knowing the Ropes": Capability Reconfiguration and Restructuring of the Danish Shipping Industry. In S. Tenold, E. Lange, & M. J. Iversen (Eds.), *Global Shipping in Small Nations: Nordic Experiences After 1960.* London: Macmillan.

Teece, D. J. (2014). A Dynamic Capabilities-Based Entrepreneurial Theory of the Multinational Enterprise. *Journal of International Business Studies, 45*(1), 8–37.

Teece, D. J., Pisano, G., & Shuen, A. (1997). Dynamic Capabilities and Strategic Management. *Strategic Management Journal, 18*(7), 509–533.

Trace, K. (1997). ASEAN Ports Since 1945: Maritime Change and Port Rivalry. In F. Broeze (Ed.), *Gateways of Asia: Port Cities of Asia in the 13th–20th Centuries* (pp. 318–338). London: Kegan Paul.

van Ham, H., & Rijsenbrij, J. (2012). *Development of Containerization: Success Through Vision, Drive and Technology.* Amsterdam: IOS Press.

Open Access This chapter is licensed under the terms of the Creative Commons Attribution-NonCommercial-NoDerivatives 4.0 International License (http://creativecommons.org/licenses/by-nc-nd/4.0/), which permits any noncommercial use, sharing, distribution and reproduction in any medium or format, as long as you give appropriate credit to the original author(s) and the source, provide a link to the Creative Commons license and indicate if you modified the licensed material. You do not have permission under this license to share adapted material derived from this chapter or parts of it.

The images or other third party material in this chapter are included in the chapter's Creative Commons license, unless indicated otherwise in a credit line to the material. If material is not included in the chapter's Creative Commons license and your intended use is not permitted by statutory regulation or exceeds the permitted use, you will need to obtain permission directly from the copyright holder.

6

East Asiatic Company's Difficult Experiences with Containerization

Martin Jes Iversen

Introduction

On 9 January 1997, the remaining shipping activities of the Danish trading conglomerate East Asiatic Company (EAC) were sold to the Norwegian shipping company Tschudi & Eitzen A/S. EAC was out of business—at least out of maritime business. Thirty years earlier, in 1967, EAC had been the second-largest Danish shipowner, with 35 vessels and a total of 396,000 DWT. The largest Danish shipping company at that time, A. P. Møller, owned 86 vessels with 1482 million DWT.[1] In contrast to Norway, Danish shipping has traditionally been marked by a stable corporate structure in which old well-established shipping companies such as DFDS (founded in 1866), D/S Norden (founded in 1871), D/S TORM (founded in 1889)

---

[1] Iversen (2016, 359).

M. J. Iversen (✉)
Copenhagen Business School, Frederiksberg, Denmark
e-mail: mji.si@cbs.dk

and A. P. Møller (founded in 1904) survived upheavals and continued to dominate the sector.[2] EAC, founded in March 1897, was considered one of the corporate pillars in Danish shipping and a pioneer in at least two important respects: First, in December 1897 and as the first Scandinavian shipping company, EAC was recognized by the British dominated liner conference 'Agreement for the Working of the China and Japan Trade, Outward and Homewards', thanks to personal contacts at the Danish and British royal courts. Second, EAC was the first shipping company in the world to introduce an ocean-going diesel driven vessel, M/S *Selandia* built in 1912.[3]

How and why, then, did EAC lose its position as a leading international shipping company? This chapter focuses on three factors which contributed to the decline of EAC: (1) The internal disputes of the 1980s within ScanDutch, EAC's hitherto most profitable and successful shipping business operating liner shipping between South East Asia and Northern Europe; (2) the fatal investment in a completely new type of vessel, the Liner Replacement Vessels (LRV), in 1975–1977; and (3) EAC's view of itself as a political force rather than an ordinary business enterprise as symbolized by the extensive knowledge transfer concerning containerization from EAC to Chinese COSCO in 1978.

Taken together, these three factors constitute a pattern which can help understand EAC's maritime decline.

ScanDutch and EAC's Initial Containerization

In spring 1966, when EAC was still the second-largest shipping company in Denmark, the container ship *American Racer* left New York on its way to Europe. The ship was owned by United States Lines (USL), which thus initiated the first intercontinental container service. Companies such as USL and the American competitor Sea-Land, owned by the inventor and businessman Malcom P. McLean, had introduced a new mode of transport in international shipping that allowed to offer safe, quick and

---

[2]Tenold et al. (2012).
[3]Iversen (2016, 64).

cheap door-to-door transport. It was based on standardized freight boxes which could easily be moved from ship to truck through efficient cranes. The economic benefits were obvious. Loading and unloading of traditional cargo ships was a labour-intensive process which kept ships at quayside for weeks. Goods were often lost or damaged in this time-consuming and expensive process. In the early 1960s, Trans World Airlines was able to transport 300 kilograms of freight from Chicago to Zurich in 15 hours for USD 208. Sending the same freight by sea took 20 days for a price of USD 267. Liner shipping faced major challenges.[4]

At a meeting on 15 December 1965, four months before *American Racer*'s departure from New York, Mogens Pagh, the CEO and chairman of the largest Danish company at the time, the conglomerate EAC, raised the issue of containerization. Pagh stated that EAC's shipping department faced an 'almost explosive' technological development.[5] The size of tankers had been doubling within a few years, and now the liner segment would probably undergo a similar transformation. The relatively small cargo ships which EAC built after 1945 cost DKK 5–6 million per ship and the ships of the early 1960s about DKK 25 million. The cost of the newest, significantly larger and more advanced semi-container ships for the Pacific line amounted to up to DKK 45 million. In addition, if EAC adopted the container technology, investments also had to be made in containers, port facilities and land-based transportation.[6]

Mogens Pagh was appointed CEO of EAC in 1960, and his vision was to change the old trading house founded in 1897 into a more industrial direction including further investments in manufacturing activities. Initially, he had no vision for the Company's shipping activities. It was noted at the headquarters in Holbergsgade in Copenhagen that the revenue from shipping rose only slightly from DKK 259.8 million in 1961 to DKK 267.3 million in 1963, while shipping costs rose sharply—by DKK 15 million from 218.7 to 233.8 million in just two years.[7] The background to this depressing development was structural. EAC's traditional

---

[4]Levinson (2006) and Bruce (2014).
[5]The EAC Archive, Board Minutes, 15 December 1965.
[6]Iversen (2016).
[7]Ibid.

services were hit by competition from so-called outsiders, shipowners who had a surplus of tonnage and put these—primarily older—ships into the tramp trade, picking up cargo on the spot rather than sailing on a fixed route. In particular, customers who were more concerned with the price than with the frequency and speed of shipping used the new competitors. The problem was most severe on EAC's main service to East Asia. This service connected the important ports in Northern Europe with Southeast Asia through, among other destinations, Bangkok, Singapore and Shanghai. As a response to these challenges, Pagh and EAC's deputy director of the shipping department Storm-Jørgensen decided in June 1963 to strengthen EAC's organization by setting up a new specialized shipping office in Singapore.

So far, all ships had been commercially operated in a decentralized manner through EAC's local branches, but Pagh and Storm-Jørgensen concluded that the lines in the East faced such fierce competition that special coordination across the branches was required. For the management of the new office in Singapore, Pagh selected 34-year-old Henning H. Sparsø, one of the Company's younger, skilled shipping people who until then had led EAC's shipping department in Bangkok. Sparsø and his two employees Holger Castenskiold and Finn Ollendorff took on their task with great energy. Their first initiative was a new express route from Japan via Hong Kong and Singapore to Northern Europe. The route opened in October 1963 with EAC's fastest ships. By omitting a number of ports, the duration of the round trip was reduced from 169 days to 146. As a result, EAC became the only shipping company to offer a transit time from the last port of Japan to the first port of Northern Europe (Hamburg) of 37 days, against the usual duration of 59 days. 'Hurtigruten' (the fast route) produced encouraging results in 1964, helped by Japan's ever-increasing industrial exports to Europe. EAC's most modern ships—the A-Fleet with a speed of over 20 knots, delivered from 1964 to 1968—were put on the route. Thanks to the new route, EAC's shipping department managed to raise its revenue by DKK 84.2 million from DKK 267.3 million in 1963 to DKK 351.5 million in 1966, while costs rose by DKK

50.1 million. The profit margin increased—and so did satisfaction with Sparsø's work in Singapore.[8]

EAC's advantage was that the shipping routes to East Asia, India and Indonesia were unlikely to be affected by container shipping, at least in the short to medium term. On the other hand, renewed competition would soon emerge on the Pacific route which connected Europe to Japan via the American west coast. At the same time, the US shipping company Sea-Land was preparing to introduce container transport from the North American east coast to Europe. In EAC's shipping department, the development at the end of 1965 'gave rise to a major headache as it was difficult to foresee the course of the coming years'.[9] The question was how, when and how much to commit to the new technology. Everyone knew that these were critical decisions. The markets were in rapid motion. New alliances were concluded. On the North Atlantic, USL and Sea-Land in 1967 were joined by a new consortium, Atlantic Container Line (ACL), consisting of six leading European shipping companies: Cunard, Holland-America, Compagnie Générale Transatlantique, Swedish American, Wallenius and Rederi AB Transatlantic. While the Americans entered the market one shipping company at a time, the common European approach became the creation of consortia or alliances which could jointly shoulder the large investments. Such partnerships suited EAC which had sailed in alliances with other northern European shipping companies since the turn of the century. The question was who EAC should work with, under which terms and when.

In spring 1968, Henning H. Sparsø was ordered home to the headquarters in Copenhagen in order to address these challenges. As head of the Planning and Development Department, Sparsø would prepare EAC strategically for a future in the container industry. The first task was to start cooperation negotiations with two Nordic partners, the Norwegian shipping company Wilhelm Wilhelmsen and the Swedish East Asian Company. The three Nordic shipping companies had for years sailed together on three routes from Europe to Australia, Indonesia and Pakistan–India. None of these was a candidate for an immediate introduction of container

---
[8]Iversen (2016); EAC Archive, Annual Reports, 1963–1967.
[9]EAC Archive, Board Minutes, 15 December 1965.

shipping. The idea was to initiate cooperation on EAC's main route, that to East Asia.

At the end of 1968 rumours in shipping circles said that Japanese shipping companies were 'just about' to contract fast and large container ships for the Japan-Europe trade.[10] In addition, the British OCL alliance and US Sea-Land also considered introducing containers on the Japanese routes. In response to these specific threats, in autumn 1968 Sparsø negotiated an agreement with Wilhelm Wilhelmsen and the Swedish Ostasiatiska Kompaniet. It was an ambitious and crucial alliance containing four points[11]: (1) A fully coordinated Scandinavian service on the East Asia route with a total of eight departures per month, starting approximately 1 April 1969; (2) an operating office in Copenhagen with the top position occupied by an EAC manager; (3) joint agents in all ports in Europe as well as in Asia, based on EAC's existing shipping offices with the exception of Manila; (4) an ownership pool, in which EAC's share was 46.87%, with Wilhelm Wilhelmsen and the Swedish East Asian Company sharing the rest.

The Dutch shipping company Royal Netherlands Lloyd joined this alliance in autumn 1971. This agreement, which became known as ScanDutch, was of major importance to EAC's shipping department in the 1970s. With the partnership, EAC managed the critical introduction of container operations. Moreover, the ScanDutch operating office in Copenhagen had a major impact on the general development of Danish shipping as it led to the formation of special skills in operating ships on behalf of other shipping companies within pool agreements. As Sornn-Friese, Taudal Poulsen and Iversen have argued, 'EAC's co-operative capabilities would, in the development phase of Danish shipping, spread into the whole Danish shipping industry and form an important basis for the development of Copenhagen as an international centre for the commercial management of, in particular, pools of product tankers'.[12]

The head office of the new Scandinavian Joint Shipping Service—usually abbreviated to ScanService—was established in the famous shipbroker C. K. Hansen's old offices in Amaliegade in Copenhagen. The three

---

[10] EAC Archive, Board Minutes, 18 December 1968.
[11] Ibid.
[12] Sornn-Friese et al. (2012a).

Scandinavian shipping companies now offered barges on container ships from a number of selected ports. The service began on 1 April 1969 with a total of 51 ships, and on 2 September that year, the management concluded that provisional results were 'extremely satisfactory', despite fierce competition.[13] On the other hand, profits on EAC's four other routes were now hit hard by increasingly intense competition, especially on the Pacific route from Northern Europe via the American west coast to Japan. The conclusion was that these services should either be closed down or restructured and modernized. With this in mind, the planning and development department was now working intensely on a major strategy and investment plan.

On 2 September 1969, 40-year-old Sparsø was given the opportunity to present the shipbuilding programme to EAC's Board of Directors. It was quite unusual for a young middle manager to be in the boardroom, but Pagh had a great deal of confidence in the young shipping man. This was the most daring and biggest investment plan in the company's history.[14] For ScanService in East Asia, two new 2272 TEU container ships were to be contracted from the Danish shipyard B&W for delivery in the third and fourth quarters of 1972. The price for these two vessels was DKK 156.8 million. The ships, which received the classic EAC names *Selandia* and *Jutlandia*, were designed as the world's fastest ocean-going cargo ships with an operating speed of 28 knots (about 50 km/h) and a top speed of 31.5 knots. For the Pacific route, two container ships of 1200 TEU were to be contracted from the Danish EAC owned Nakskov Shipyard. The price for the two container ships was DKK 68.5 million, and they were to be delivered in the third quarter of 1971 and the second quarter of 1972 and were named *Falstria* and *Meonia*. *Falstria* was the first Danish-built container ship. In addition, EAC was negotiating an alliance with the British Blue Star Line and the Swedish Johnson Line, the latter being particularly strong on the Pacific Ocean. The alliance, named Johnson ScanStar, had a total of nine container ships in the Pacific from May 1972. Finally, one roll-on-roll-off would be contracted to the Australian line. The ship would cost NOK 75.7 million and was to be

---

[13] EAC Archive, Board Minutes, 9 September 1969.
[14] Ibid.

built at the Swedish shipyard Eriksberg. In autumn 1969, EAC signed the third cooperation agreement with Norwegian Wilhelm Wilhelmsen and Swedish Rederi AB Transatlantic, using 16 vessels. This alliance was named ScanAustral Carriers Ltd.

All in all, the plan Sparsø presented at the meeting of 2 September 1969 was extremely bold. Investing around DKK 520 million, EAC would become a main actor in the global container business as partner of three major alliances. The East Asia line was of particular importance. The two ships for this service were among the world's most expensive and most advanced cargo vessels. Their names, *Selandia* and *Jutlandia*, referred to EAC's history of bold innovation which included the world's first ocean-going diesel-powered vessel, *Selandia*, launched in 1912.

The cooperation within ScanDutch was coordinated from Amaliegade in Copenhagen with the participation of four leading shipping companies: Swedish Broströms, Norwegian Wilhelm Wilhelmsen, Dutch Nedlloyd Lijnen and French Compagnie Générale Maritime (CGM). ScanDutch was ground-breaking. The seven newly built container ships were supplemented with 22 conventional cargo liners, which allowed departures every ten days from all major ports between Europe and East Asia—EAC's original service started by the Danish company in 1899. On the eve of the 1973 oil crisis, ScanDutch's market share on the route from Northern Europe to East Asia was above 25%.

In the 1970s and 1980s, EAC enjoyed high and stable earnings of about DKK 100 million a year from ScanDutch. 1988 seemed to be an exceedingly profitable year. It was therefore extremely surprising—and unpleasant—when the Norwegian shipowner Niels Werring Jr. appeared at Sparsø's office on 19 August 1988 to tell him that the two Nordic partners, Swedish Transocean and Norwegian Wilhelmsen, had sold their 15% stakes in ScanDutch to Dutch Nedlloyd. The Dutch were already in possession of almost 30% of the company and they would thus own a majority of the alliance and consequently take control.[15] The immediate explanation of the sale was that Wilhelmsen was in desperate need of liquidity. Sparsø was furious about the message. In the original agreement, the Scandinavian partners had promised each other a right of first

---

[15] Iversen (2016, 462).

refusal in the event of sale. Niels Werring Jr. left Holbergsgade with a sharp message stating that EAC's lawyers would be involved, 'unless the transactions mentioned [were] immediately reversed'.[16] As a consequence, EAC entered into an agreement with the two Scandinavian partners regarding the acquisition of their pool and conference rights as well as two container vessels, *Toyama* and *Nihon*. EAC would be 100% owner of the Scandinavian branch of ScanDutch—ScanService—as of 1 January 1993. The price paid was USD 10 million for each partner's rights and USD 17.3 million for each of the two ships—in total, an investment of USD 54.6 million.[17]

ScanDutch thus changed from a joint venture between a number of different shipping companies to a partnership between EAC (*c*. 55%), Nedlloyd (*c*. 30%) and CGM (*c*. 15%). The Dutch partner was obviously not satisfied with the reversal of the agreement, and tensions appeared, but the two partners had to enter into a close dialogue. Despite tensions the commercial start was good. 1988 was a record year for the subsidiary due to more cargo and higher rates as well as lower crew costs, the result of the transfer of the two largest EAC vessels, *Selandia* and *Jutlandia*, to the newly created Danish International Ship Register (DIS). But competition was increasing in the international container market of the late 1980s. EAC therefore wanted to expand the cooperation and proposed that the two partners should invest in new, larger container ships and a modernized organization. Nedlloyd, however, did not share these views. On the contrary, the Dutch were upset by the acquisition of the Norwegian and Swedish interests by EAC. Their response was the promotion of an alternative line in their own name at the expense of ScanDutch. The situation was untenable—and it was made worse by the decline in the freight rates between South East Asia and Northern Europe in early 1989. At the beginning of August 1989, the three remaining partners held a crisis meeting in EAC's headquarters at Holbergsgade in Copenhagen. Sparsø, who was known to be a domineering manager, had personal difficulties with the Dutch and French colleagues. On a symbolic level, the climate between the two companies was poisoned when the Danish manager decided to

---

[16] EAC Archive, Board Minutes, 15 September 1988.
[17] Iversen (2016, 465).

return an official birthday gift from Nedlloyd. In early May 1990, the situation had become so difficult that the partners did not want to continue with ScanDutch. At about the same time, the two British shipping companies P&O and Ben Line Containers Ltd. informed the public that they would leave the TRIO consortium, ScanDutch's main competitor. EAC therefore initiated negotiations with Ben Line about a new cooperation on the important Europe–Asia route. The EAC-BenLine became a reality during the early 1990s and ScanDutch was discontinued. EAC was to contribute with six major container ships—including two new builds, *Arosia* and *Alsia*. The cooperation with Ben Line, a relatively small family-owned company with an old fleet, proved to be a disaster as it was launched in a difficult and competitive market. The service was unprofitable from the beginning, and in 1992 the partnership lost DKK 260 million. EAC sold its liner vessels to Maersk Line in March 1993 due to the combination of the depressed results from EAC-Ben Line and the additional problems in its shipping department resulting from the expensive investment in a new, but troublesome category of ships—the LRVs.[18]

The Liner Replacement Vessels: A Fatal Investment

On 2 October 1974, EAC's Board of Directors decided to promote Henning Sparsø to deputy CEO. Sparsø led the EAC's ship department and reported directly to Pagh, occupying what was traditionally the second most prestigious position in the Company. It was always the ships' results which were presented first at board meetings, and the department's development was placed at the beginning of the annual reports ever since the founding of the company in 1897. It was from a strong position that Sparsø on 24 September 1975 presented the Board of Directors with perhaps the most fatal initiative in the history of the EAC—an initiative which, according to insightful observers, would eventually destroy the entire company.[19]

---

[18] Iversen (2016, 503).
[19] Bjerrum (1991) and Højbo (1993).

The EAC board meeting on 24 September 1975 began at 9.30 AM with a review of the positive results of three shipping alliances: ScanDutch on the Southeast Asia route, Johnson ScanStar on the American West Coast and ScanAustral on the Australia route. After about two hours of a general review of the company's development, Sparsø was asked to round off the meeting with a review of EAC's shipbuilding programme.[20] Sparsø initially stated that the ship department had conducted in-depth analysis for a whole year in order to determine EAC's need for new ships. The conclusion was that the Company should contract a whole new type of ship to be called 'neo-bulk'. A relatively small and flexible ship—neither a traditional bulk carrier nor a container ship—of about 20,000 tonnes dwt, as against *Selandia* and *Jutlandia*'s 34,730 dwt. In fact, these ships went in the opposite direction to that taken with the recent container ship orders. Their service speed would be a modest 15.5 knots, and the energy-saving engine would only provide 11,600 hp against the two fast containerships' record-breaking performance of 82,000 hp. It was an ambitious plan of a series of eight modern ships. Such a series had not been contracted since the much smaller—and significantly cheaper—conventional liner ships of the 1950s and 1960s. Pagh presented an interesting argument for the contracting of the new vessels. Where ship orders so far had reflected EAC's specific strategic needs, what was sought now was 'the most commercially useful and economical ship that would be a good asset for future sale'. The ship was to be regarded as a financial asset.

The success of the new ship type was crucial for EAC, as it should, in Sparsø's cryptic words, 'fill the need beyond what conventional bulk carriers can accommodate and, on the other hand, make the modern container ships' facilities redundant'.[21] What kind of cargo Sparsø specifically had in mind was not clear at the meeting, but the philosophy behind the new ship was *flexibility*. The ship should be able to transport containers, specialized cargo and traditional dry cargo such as timber or grain. However, the price for flexibility was the loss of economies of scale, and at the same time the small engines and low top speed prevented another type of flexibility namely the capability to catch up in case of delays. In October

---

[20] EAC Archive, Board Minutes, 24 September 1975.
[21] EAC Archive, Board Minutes, 24 September 1975.

1975, the initial two ships, called the LRV, were contracted with the Mitsui Shipyard in Japan. There was an option for delivery of two more ships, and delivery would take place between 1 May and 31 December 1977. With this order, there was maximum pressure on EAC's own shipyard in Nakskov in Denmark. The prerequisite for placing an order for another six, maybe eight, ships was a competitive price. In this connection, it was crucial whether the shipyard management could achieve a pay-limiting agreement with the workers.[22] On 4 February 1976, negotiations with Nakskov Shipyard ended with a positive outcome. Six LRVs were contracted with an option for two more vessels. For Nakskov Shipyard, it was the first serial order of such a large scale. The prize was held low due to the purchase of steel, engines (four out of six) and cranes in Japan. In addition, shipyard workers had agreed to limit wage increases until the last ship was delivered. On the other hand, the shipyard would pay a bonus to the workers for each ship that was delivered on time and according to the agreed specifications. Mogens Pagh, like many others, was deeply concerned with labour market conditions in the 1970s. As the first Danish company, EAC had introduced employee shares in 1971. The chairman was particularly proud of the agreement with the shipyard workers. To the Board of Directors, he expressed the hope that the agreement 'might seem like a model for other industries'.[23] With this pious hope, the happy circumstances surrounding the LRVs ended—even before the first ship was built.

At the same Board meeting on 5 March 1976, it was stated that the Company's newbuilding programme now comprised 14 vessels with a total contract value of DKK 1.6 billion. The ships were contracted for delivery over four years from 1972 to 1976. During that period, conditions in international shipping changed profoundly. With the oil crisis, demand for transport decreased, and the re-opening of the Suez Canal in 1975 led to the bottom falling out of the tanker market. International shipping faced a ten-year crisis around 1975–1985. In particular, the years 1978–1980

---

[22] EAC Archive, Board Minutes, 3 December 1975.
[23] EAC Archive, Board Minutes, 5 March 1976.

were bloody as the total amount of transported goods fell for the first time since 1945.[24]

Between 70 and 80% of EAC's DKK 1.6 billion investment was financed by long-term loans over seven to eight years. There was thus no danger of an acute liquidity crisis. The problem for EAC was rather that the asset value of the ships dropped in line with the worsening market conditions. Thus, the value of the ships had to be written off faster—but could EAC afford that? Also on 5 March 1976, it was stated at the board meeting that even before delivery, the market value of the ships was 'significantly' below the value of the debt taken on to finance them. An attentive board of directors would of course have asked about the obvious risks of the large series contract for a completely new and untested ship type under these market conditions. But instead of this debate, management was congratulated on the wage restraint agreement at Nakskov Shipyard. The lack of debate and concern about EAC's indebtedness was particularly striking because the board was neither presented with an in-depth review of any specific market demand for the new ship type, nor with any analysis of the financial consequences of the investment. Such superficial scrutiny by the board of directors was in stark contrast to former large serial orders of ships under the previous chairman Hakon Christiansen in the 1950s and under the founder H. N. Andersen before and during World War I. At that time, decisions on major vessel contracts were discussed in detail—especially the financing, which often required the expansion of the share capital or new loan agreements. To make matters worse, the ship investments of the 1970s were relatively larger due to the increased size of the ships and more advanced technology. In March 1976, Pagh closed any possible debate with the claim that the ships were to be regarded as a 'financial commodity' created for the second-hand market rather than the company's own specific needs. The problem with this logic was twofold. First, the general shipping market turned out to be in free fall just in the years from 1977 to 1979 when the ships were delivered. Second and more important, it was uncertain whether there was any interest in a completely new type of vessel in the second-hand vessel market, whether depressed or not.

---

[24]Tenold (2006).

On 10 December 1976, one year and three months after the first board discussion concerning the LRVs, Sparsø reported that it had been decided to deploy the ships in a new Pacific liner shipping trade between the west coast of the United States and East Asia.[25] EAC had served this route from 1932 to 1954, when the service was discontinued due to increasing competition and poor results. The Pacific route was particularly difficult to service for three reasons: First, the liner shipping conference agreements in the Pacific were open to free participation in contrast to the closed conferences to Asia. Thus there were more, and less disciplined, players in the Pacific. Second, long distances across the world's largest ocean caused challenges in relation to regularity. In case of a storm or accident, there was a high risk of expensive delays. In this respect, the low engine power of the LRVs was completely unsuitable for sailing on the Pacific as the ships would not be able to make up any delays. Last but not least, the service was characterized by an imbalance in cargo volumes: In the 1970s, there was a significant need for transportation from East Asia to the United States, while there was only a slight demand for goods from the United States which was in the midst of a deep industrial crisis.[26]

The first report on the Pacific experience came in June 1977, when the first LRV ship in service had a 'reasonable' start.[27] This message was moderated in September that year to 'slightly slower start than expected'.[28] In December of the same year it was announced that two major shipping companies, German Hapag-Lloyd and Singaporean Neptune Orient Lines, were about to enter the Pacific route, which was already characterized by fierce competition and unbalanced trade patterns.[29] In March 1978, the message concerning the first two LRV ships, *Sumbawa* and *Songkhla* was clear: tough competition combined with the lack of appropriate cargo for the rather small and slow vessels. By the autumn of 1978, the situation had become so serious that the leader of the shipping department, Wøldike Schmith, decided to travel to Vancouver to investigate the situation. Since the spring of 1977, five new competitors had entered

---

[25] EAC Archive, Board Minutes, 10 December 1976.
[26] Bjerrum (1991).
[27] EAC Archive, Board Minutes, 3 June 1977.
[28] EAC Archive, Board Minutes, 6 September 1977.
[29] EAC Archive, Board Minutes, 5 December 1977.

the Pacific trade. It was therefore not surprising that 1978 showed 'a significant loss' for the new EAC line. No specific amount was recorded to the Board on this loss. When the newly elected Member of the Board, L. Beckvard, at a board meeting in December 1978, asked for these figures, Sparsø replied 'that the final number would appear in the March 1979 financial statement'.[30]

EAC's annual accounts for 1978 were depressing, for three reasons in particular: (1) the difficult conditions of shipping, particularly on the Pacific; (2) the high debt resulting from the new tonnage contracted in the mid-1970s; and (3) the industrial crisis in Western Europe and North America. EAC's total revenues dropped markedly from DKK 23.12 billion in 1977 to DKK 18.46 billion in 1978. EAC's earnings halved from DKK 100.4 to DKK 50.63 million. Most seriously, long-term debt increased by approximately DKK 470 million in just one year from DKK 2.47 billion in 1977 to DKK 2.9 billion in 1978. EAC was on an unsustainable financial course and the LRVs contributed to the problems until the mid-1980s, both through the increased debt EAC took on to build them and through annual operating deficits from 1978 to the mid-1980s when they were withdrawn from the Pacific trade and subsequently sold.[31]

From EAC to COSCO—A Difficult Case of Knowledge Transfer

After Mao Zedong's death in September 1976, Hua Guofeng was appointed President of the Communist Party and China's Prime Minister. In February 1978, Hua announced an ambitious ten-year plan, aiming to increase China's industrial output by 10% a year and agricultural production by 4–5%. The plan was based on the Four Modernizations, that is, in agriculture, industry, defence and science/technology. The following month, at a major science conference in Beijing, Deputy Prime Minister Deng Xiaoping announced a training programme for 800,000 researchers in China. The goal was to promote development in a number

---

[30] EAC Archive, Board Minutes, 12 December 1978.
[31] EAC Archive, Annual Report, 1978.

of high-priority areas, including energy resources, computers, laser and space technology.[32]

Mogens Pagh visited China a few weeks after Deng Xiaoping's groundbreaking speech and, on his arrival, received a spectacular invitation for a meeting with China's Minister of Transport.[33] The Minister initiated the meeting by introducing the ambitious goals for China's development over the following eight to ten years. The Chinese government was aware that this development could only take place through foreign technology and know-how. EAC was therefore requested officially to assist the Chinese government in the development of its external transport system. At the meeting, it was agreed that EAC would send a delegation to China in order to be able to draw up a more detailed programme. Pagh immediately saw almost unlimited potential in the official request. Later on the journey, his assumptions were confirmed, as he was asked to meet with the Deputy Prime Minister who proved to be well informed about the transport minister's proposal. Not since Andersen's days around 1900, when the company's founder established the first EAC office in Shanghai, had EAC worked at such a high political level in China.

Immediately after his return to Copenhagen, Pagh decided to send a delegation of senior EAC employees and experts to China, headed by CEO Henning Sparsø and EAC's China expert Holger Hansen. Their initial meetings with the ministry's officials showed that the Chinese wanted something very specific from EAC, namely support for initiating containerization. This was to include[34]:

- plans for the physical lay-out, equipment, workflow and administration for the first two container terminals in China, Tianjin and Shanghai;
- suggestions for streamlining workflow and administration of the conventional shipping sector in Tianjin and Shanghai;
- proposals for the harmonization and streamlining of inland transport, which was under the responsibility of three different ministries. In this connection, verification and documentation procedures for land-based

---

[32] Spence (1991, 668–671).
[33] EAC Archive, Board Minutes, 14 June 1978.
[34] Ibid.

transport of containers (road transport had not yet been completed) would also have to be developed.
- EAC assistance with the implementation of these plans in the longer term.

EAC's board of directors became acquainted with the Chinese plans at a meeting on 14 June 1978. Mogens Pagh was obviously excited about the perspectives: 'we have had our relations with China for a very long time and this gives us a big chance'. So far, it was not something that had made a financial surplus of significance, explained Pagh, but now there was hope of 'an opportunity for really great chances for us'.[35] The last remark made the 68-year-old board member Prince Georg raise the question of fees for such large-scale work. Pagh replied quite thoughtfully that the Chinese were the most skilled business people in the world. Regarding the fee, the chairman stated that it was nothing at all that he had wanted to speak about yet. 'We have expressed our satisfaction with the tasks that the Chinese are giving us, and we have to look at a suitable fee later on'. 'Surely', continued Pagh, 'the Chinese will never forget us if we do something like this for them now'.[36]

By the end of 1978, Pagh considered the development in China as the true bright spot in an otherwise dark picture concerning the future of EAC. As stated above, the debt issues related to the liner business in the Pacific grew significantly during this period, and industrial plants in Western Europe and North America suffered significant losses. But at the same time, EAC's trading activities accelerated in Beijing. During 1978, agency import contracts to China amounted to DKK 230 million in total.[37] Representation in Beijing was increased from two to four men, and the office, as the first foreign company, was authorized to install a telex machine in 1978.[38] EAC was a Western pioneer in Deng Xiaoping's reforming China and the most promising project was containerization. EAC sent ten of the company's best shipping people to China in July

---

[35] Ibid.
[36] Ibid.
[37] EAC Archive, Board Minutes, 12 December 1978.
[38] Ibid.

1978. In the following months, the Danish staff prepared a whole new design of quays and warehouses in Tianjin, the largest port city in North China and the main port of Beijing. Specifications for and positioning of crane systems were established and the EAC experts provided a detailed manual for the management and documentation procedures that had to be set up before the container traffic could be introduced. Once this work was completed in November 1978, the EAC experts moved on to Shanghai. Here, port facilities were planned to handle 10,000 and 50,000–60,000 containers per year in port districts nine and ten, respectively. In order to implement the plan, cranes, forklifts and other special equipment worth USD 15–20 million had to be imported. As part of the agreement, the Chinese would pay EAC a commission on these imports, but otherwise the work was free of charge.[39]

In addition to the work of reorganizing the Chinese port facilities in Tianjin and Shanghai, EAC staff also undertook a significant advisory task for the state-owned Chinese shipping company COSCO. The Danes conducted a complete review of the entire state-owned organization in China, covering all its functions. Marketing, management and control, repair and maintenance routines were reviewed, all for the purpose of introducing containerization. Concurrently with—and probably related to—the knowledge transfer from EAC COSCO established the first regular Chinese overseas container line.[40] On 26 September 1978, COSCO's first container ship, *Ping Xiang Cheng*, sailed from Shanghai bound for Sydney.[41] The chief architects behind this development were EAC staff and the task also included training of Chinese personnel. In January 1979, the first Chinese employees arrived at the EAC headquarters in Copenhagen, where they were trained in administration. At the same time, Chinese teams of navigators and engineers were posted on a number of EAC container ships. And as a third step, in February 1979, Chinese port officials received a thorough introduction to EAC's roll-on-roll-off terminals around the world.[42]

---

[39] Ibid.
[40] Ibid.
[41] For references to the history of COSCO, see http://www.cosfrexj.com/en/history.aspx.
[42] EAC Archive, Board Minutes, 30 March 1979.

Against this background, it was a shock to EAC that, in March 1979, the Chinese announced unexpectedly that the containerization cooperation had to be 'paused' with immediate effect. The Chinese officials underscored that the decision should not be known to the public. The unexpected suspension had nothing to do with the efforts of EAC. At a board meeting on 30 March 1979, Sparsø stated that China had suddenly decided to break off partnerships with all Western countries. EAC was affected relatively late and in a limited way—for example, the Dutch had been sent home and in other cases the Chinese had cancelled even relatively loose agreements. The background for the new Chinese policy was to be found in internal political conditions in China. On 18 December 1978, a small group of young Chinese held a demonstration for freedom and democracy in Beijing, and in January 1979 there were further demonstrations of up to 30,000 rural workers outside the capital. The Chinese government reacted by dropping its economic reform plans. The modernization process was not only politically risky, it was also costly. The trade deficit grew to USD 3.9 billion in 1979–1980. It was decided to emphasize modernization of agriculture over the three other parts of the Four Modernizations.[43] Against this background, EAC's modernization of container traffic was no longer urgent. The Chinese had time—plenty of time. And if nothing else, COSCO's first container line had been started, and the Beijing and Shanghai authorities had gained free access to valuable knowledge of how modern container lines, port facilities and ship management worked.

The suspension hit Pagh particularly hard. It had been his decision that the crisis-ridden company would allocate significant management and staff resources to the Chinese project for several months without charge. He had rejected Prince Georg's request for fees based on his understanding of *guanxi*—the importance of reciprocity and personal networks in China. Pagh was undoubtedly right that the Chinese would never forget the EAC's goodwill and generosity. On the other hand, Pagh at the same meeting described the Chinese as 'the best business people in the world'. The entire arrangement in 1978–1979 was costly for EAC and lucrative for China. Unfortunately for Pagh, neither he nor EAC could afford to wait for a

---

[43]Spence (1991, 678–687).

long, slow and difficult economic and political development in China. It was Sparsø, not Pagh himself, who informed the board of directors about the Chinese withdrawal, and only three months later, Pagh announced his departure as Chairman of EAC. His era was over—as was EAC's.

Conclusion

EAC was founded in 1897 based upon the first shipping line connecting Northern Europe and South East Asia. Exactly 100 years later the last shipping interests were sold, and what had been a leading Danish international shipping company in the 1970s was out of business. This chapter has focused on the ScanDutch partnership, the investment in the LRVs and finally the knowledge transfer to COSCO in 1978 to explain this trajectory. All three factors in their way contributed to the fall of EAC as a leading shipping company. The financial losses from the LRV investment and the failure to develop ScanDutch in the late 1980s had obvious financial consequences for EAC. It is more complicated to assess the financial and organizational consequences of knowledge transfer to COSCO in 1978. These consequences may be analysed at three levels, the management, the company and the national economy, and in relation to three chronological perspectives, the short, medium and long term.

The first level concerns Mogens Pagh, CEO from 1964 to 1980. In the short term, the knowledge transfer project cost him prestige internally in the board, which again contributed to a coup d'etat in 1980 in which Pagh lost his position as chairman. In the long term Pagh thus became irrelevant for EAC. At the level of EAC as a company, the knowledge transfer caused an immediate lack of man-power in 1978 due to the fact that key experts were transferred from various offices around the world to the Chinese project. It is difficult to measure the actual impact of this, but it is worth noting that EAC had a series of prosperous years in container shipping in the late 1970s and the early 1980s. The use of scarce manpower in China may well have prevented development of more promising opportunities at a critical time for containerization when, for instance, the competitor Maersk Line expanded rapidly. In the medium term, EAC's diplomatic relations with China were probably strengthened by the knowledge transfer and EAC managed to occupy and develop a rather unique position in the mid-1980s as agent for major Western companies in China and even in the 1990s, EAC still enjoyed remarkably close relations with the Chinese authorities. In the long term, however, EAC was unable to exploit these commercial opportunities. At the national level, other Danish companies were able to benefit from a special relationship between China and Denmark. The chairman of Maersk, Mærsk McKinney-Møller, was received personally by President Jiang Zemin in October 1998 when Maersk Line was the market leader in shipping between Northern Europe and South East Asia. This was partly thanks to Maersk's acquisition of EAC in 1993, and thus linked indirectly to the special relation created by Pagh's decision to promote containerization in China in 1978.

According to Geoffrey Jones, the modern globalization process could be divided in three phases: the first globalization from the 1870s to the 1910s, the de-globalization from the 1930s to the 1970s and finally the second globalization after the 1980s.[44] Paradoxically EAC, traditionally one of the most internationalized Danish companies, suffered in the 1980s and 1990s as markets were opened through trade agreements and new technologies. In fact, these developments devalued EAC's historic competence in navigating closed markets via personal and political connections applied in commercial transactions. As markets opened up and level playing fields were established, EAC's political competences gradually lost their value. In the 1980s, EAC was thus unable to reap the advantages on the Chinese market, sowed by the knowledge transfer to COSCO in the late 1970s.

Acknowledgments The article is been based on access to EAC's corporate archive and I would like to thank Jan Erlund (former chairman of EAC), Professor Even Lange for contributions to the research and Professor Niels P. Petersson for his comments on this article.

---

[44]Jones (2005).

References

Archival Sources

The EAC Archive, 1897–2005 located in Copenhagen at Asia House, the EAC Foundation.

Published Sources

Bjerrum, C. (1991). *ØK i uvejr – da ØK's aktiekapital sank i Stillehavet*. København: Børsen Bøger.
Bruce, P. (2014). *Danish Liners Around the World*. København: Nautilus.
Højbo, F. (1993). *Det sidste kompagni*. København: Schultz.
Iversen, M. J. (2016). *Udsyn, ØK, Danmark og verden*. København: Lindhardt & Ringhof.
Jones, G. (2005). *Multinationals and Global Capitalism: From the Nineteenth to the Twenty First Century*. Oxford: Oxford University Press.
Levinson, M. (2006). *The Box: How the Shipping Container Made the World Smaller and the World Economy Bigger*. Princeton: Princeton University Press.
Sornn-Friese, H., Poulsen, R. T., & Iversen, M. J. (2012a). Incentives, Capability and Opportunity: Exploring the Sources of Danish Maritime Leadership. *International Journal of Maritime History, 23*(1), 193–220.
Sornn-Friese, H., Poulsen, R. T., & Iversen, M. J. (2012b). "Knowing the Ropes": Capability Reconfiguration and Restructuring of the Danish Shipping Industry. In S. Tenold, M. J. Iversen, & E. Lange (Eds.), *Global Shipping in Small Nations-Nordic Experiences After 1960* (pp. 61–99). Basingstoke: Palgrave Macmillan.
Spence, A. (1991). *Kina, historien om de seneste 400 år*. København: Politiken.
Tenold, S. (2006). *Tankers in Trouble: Norwegian Shipping and the Crisis of the 1970s and 1980s*. St. Johns: International Maritime History Society.
Tenold, S., Lange, E., & Iversen, M. J. (2012). *Global Shipping in Small Nations: Nordic Experiences After 1960*. London: Palgrave Macmillan.

Open Access This chapter is licensed under the terms of the Creative Commons Attribution-NonCommercial-NoDerivatives 4.0 International License (http://creativecommons.org/licenses/by-nc-nd/4.0/), which permits any noncommercial use, sharing, distribution and reproduction in any medium or format, as long as you give appropriate credit to the original author(s) and the source, provide a link to the Creative Commons license and indicate if you modified the licensed material. You do not have permission under this license to share adapted material derived from this chapter or parts of it.

The images or other third party material in this chapter are included in the chapter's Creative Commons license, unless indicated otherwise in a credit line to the material. If material is not included in the chapter's Creative Commons license and your intended use is not permitted by statutory regulation or exceeds the permitted use, you will need to obtain permission directly from the copyright holder.

7

Shipping as a Knowledge Industry: Research and Strategic Planning at Ocean Group

Niels P. Petersson

Introduction

One of the most important transformations of the post-war world was the rise of what some contemporaries called the knowledge society. Knowledge created in the social and natural sciences now increasingly permeated society and with it the corporate world. This chapter approaches the question of how transformations in the world of shipping relate to wider trends in business and general history through the lens of knowledge. It will investigate how technological and managerial knowledge was created, developed and exploited as a corporate resource from the 1950s onwards in Ocean Transport and Trading, one of the UK's leading liner shipping firms. The chapter will, first, briefly discuss the resource-based view of the firm and the importance of knowledge as a corporate resource. It will then examine Ocean's use of technological and operational knowledge in the

---

N. P. Petersson (✉)
Sheffield Hallam University, Sheffield, UK
e-mail: n.p.petersson@shu.ac.uk

© The Author(s) 2019
N. P. Petersson et al. (eds.), *Shipping and Globalization in the Post-War Era*,
Palgrave Studies in Maritime Economics,
https://doi.org/10.1007/978-3-030-26002-6_7

post-war era. The following section examines the introduction of modern management concepts at Ocean from the late 1960s and their impact on corporate strategy. In conclusion, the chapter will argue that the introduction of managerial concepts of knowledge contributed to Ocean's gradual withdrawal from shipping and transformation into a provider of global logistics services and that analyzing shipping as a knowledge industry helps make sense of the transformation of the industry.

Knowledge as a Resource

The resource-based view of the firm was first developed by Edith Penrose in the 1950s. It has been widely adopted in management and organization studies since the 1980s to inform research into how firms can identify and develop their competitive advantage, enhance their performance and nurture 'dynamic capabilities' that allow them to adapt to changing market conditions.[1] The key assumption of the resource-based view is that the firm is best analyzed as a set of specific resources under the control of the management. One of the key resources identified by Penrose was knowledge. Later work has placed knowledge at the centre of an economic theory of the firm, regarding the firm as an organization concerned with integrating individuals' specialist knowledge for use in the production of goods and services.[2]

The literature distinguishes a number of types of knowledge and ways of using knowledge. Tacit knowledge is implicit, informal, personalised, and usually based on experience and skills rather than formal learning—qualities that would make it difficult to replicate and communicate, giving a firm controlling such knowledge a competitive advantage. At the same time, tacit knowledge does not easily feed into training, research, and discussion, making its systematic development and adaptation difficult. Explicit knowledge, on the other hand, is easily communicated, managed, stored, distributed, often actively created through research and reporting,

---

[1] Penrose (1959). For an overview of Penrose's impact, see Christos Pitelis's introduction in the 2009 edition of her work, ix–xlvii. Notable later contributions include Wernerfelt (1984, 1995) and Barney (1991, 2001) as well as Teece (2016).
[2] Grant (1996) and Spender (1996).

and ultimately also bought and sold. It is easier to use, but not necessarily a durable foundation of competitive advantage unless its use can be restricted, for example through patents.

The resource-based view emphasizes the crucial role of a firm's management, describing it as 'the primary task of management … to maximize value through the optimal deployment of existing resources and capabilities, while developing the firm's resource base for the future'.[3] Managers' capacity to do so under conditions of 'deep uncertainty' over the development of markets, inputs and outputs has been discussed under the heading of a firm's 'dynamic capabilities'.[4]

Scholars working within this framework have occasionally pointed to the benefits to be derived from historical research as 'the conditions under which resources are developed or acquired in one period have implications for the strategic advantages of firms in subsequent periods', and resources may lose their value if the market that determines their usefulness disappears.[5] 'Firm-level history' has been proposed as one way of finding out 'how firm resources and capabilities are accumulated and eroded' and 'how resources' relative values may be affected by market changes'.[6] At the same time, work on knowledge as a resource also suggests a number of questions that are potentially useful for business historians. On a basic level, these relate to the extent to which knowledge was recognized as a key resource by managers and entrepreneurs and to changes in the type of knowledge used, the personnel hired and the organizational structures created to develop or deploy such knowledge. More difficult, but also more interesting, are questions around the consequences of such changes in the use of knowledge—how did they affect corporate strategy and, ultimately, corporate success? Such questions provide a useful framework for analyzing the development of shipping in the post-war era. Like many other industries, shipping underwent profound and complex, internal and external transformations. As explained in Chapter 1 in this volume, the technology, business organization, and geographic focus of the industry changed,

---

[3] Grant (1996, 110).
[4] Teece (2016, 204). Jones et al. (2013) and Henrik Sornn-Friese in this volume analyse dynamic capabilities in a shipping context.
[5] Barney (2001, 51).
[6] Priem and Butler (2001, 35).

resulting in profound shifts in competitive advantage. How did managers make sense of such transformations, how did they respond, what role did knowledge play in their response, and which were the consequences of the knowledge they used and the way they used it? Over the rest of this chapter, a resource-based perspective will be used to explore the changing use of knowledge in the industry.

Technology and Operations

Improving Traditional Liner Shipping

In the 1950s, the technology of cargo shipping that had not seen much innovation for decades began to change, mainly due to two developments: rising volumes of trade and rising wages, in particular for manual labourers such as dockworkers and seafarers. Shipowners responded by running larger, faster ships with smaller crews and more automated systems. From the 1950s onwards, 'supertankers' and large bulk carriers increased efficiency and brought down costs. In liner shipping, Ocean's main business, such rationalization was impossible as long as cargoes were highly diverse and essentially had to be stowed by hand. By the mid-1960s, tanker size had increased by 82% and tramp and bulk carrier size by 52%, but cargo liner size only by 14%. Cargo liners spent 60% of their time in port, and freight handling could account for over one-third of the total annual cost, including depreciation, of running a cargo liner.[7]

Ocean's naval architects in the 1950s knew that their ships were outdated and initiated a programme of research into optimal ship design. Ocean was among the first shipping companies to research the performance of its ships under real-world conditions, using current data as well as company archives to construct data series. Even by the late 1960s, most shipping companies lacked trained technical staff and had done little research in areas that were crucial for their operations and profitability, while much of the research undertaken by public bodies and shipowner associations lacked relevance or studied technologies without looking at

---

[7] van den Burg (1969, 11).

their economic costs and benefits.[8] Research on operating costs had mostly focused on fuel economy, which however was not a major concern in times of cheap fuel. Ocean's research now allowed to quantify the disproportionate increase of stevedoring costs and of time lost in port. Sea time had fallen from 200 days per year in 1950 to 180 in 1962. Keeping stevedoring costs in check, speeding up loading and reducing crew size therefore became the key considerations in designing the last generation of Ocean's cargoliners to enter service before the container age.[9] The new ships, the *Priam* and *Glenlyon* classes, were designed with large and easily accessible cargo spaces. This made them more expensive to build as they were larger and heavier than strictly necessary to accommodate their cargo, but their spacious, more regularly shaped holds allowed savings where it mattered—the cost of time and labour when loading and unloading.[10] The newer ships also could sail with smaller crews than their predecessors. While officer numbers were unchanged, only 29 ratings were required, against over 60 on older ships. Reducing crew size was a concern as the share of wages had risen from 10% of voyage costs in 1930 to 26.7% in 1963 and a shortage of seafarers had begun to emerge.[11]

Naval architects praised Ocean's research-based approach to the design of new ships, highlighting 'the commercial advantages … which could accrue from proper investigation of the design aspects at the right time and not, as so frequently happens, after construction of the ship has commenced'.[12] However, these efforts had their drawbacks. With the *Priam* class ships, the 'thinking and designing period, combined with the building period, covered no less than 4½ years'.[13] Over these years, market conditions had changed substantially. The Suez crisis briefly dented growth and decolonization and political unrest in Malaysia, Singapore and Indonesia cast doubts over the economic development of key ports to be serviced

---

[8] Goss (1998), Goss (2011), and Committee of Inquiry into Shipping (1970, 199–204).
[9] Meek (1964, 243).
[10] Ibid., 242, 246.
[11] Falkus (1990, 310); see King (2000, 58–60) on the labour market for seafarers.
[12] Meek (1964, 279).
[13] Meek and Adams (1969, 271).

by the new ships.¹⁴ After a period of hesitation the ships were redesigned to make them faster and offer more refrigerated cargo space so that they could be used on different routes.¹⁵ The *Glenlyon* and *Priam* class ships were superseded almost as soon as they were delivered and eventually saw their service lives cut short by containerization.

Alongside technological change, operational improvements were constantly being made based on in-house research. Ocean created a dedicated research department in 1964, and a cargo superintendent was appointed to investigate the causes of the rise in cargo handling costs in various ports and suggest remedies.¹⁶ Yet, while substantial reductions in operating costs were achieved, these were far from game-changing and could not keep pace with the rapid increase in the costs of labour, credit, fuel etc. through the 70s. Even radical proposals such as the 1970s German study of the 'ship of the future' run by a minimal, versatile crew, and similar British studies of the 'Efficient Ship' undertaken in the 1980s were unable to fully compensate for such cost pressures.¹⁷

Overall, Ocean's experience with in-house research was mixed. Only limited potential for increased efficiency in traditional liner shipping was discovered. The main obstacles to increased efficiency and profitability in liner shipping were to be found not on board but in the way cargo and labour were organised in port. Meanwhile, the decision to design in-house and order purpose-built ships slowed down the introduction of technological innovation. Ships embodying state of the art 1950s operational and technological research were brought into service at a time when the fundamental break-through of containerization was already around the corner. Moreover, it was not necessarily rational for shipping companies to do their design and research in-house when such explicit and transferable knowledge could be bought off-the-shelf or developed by specialized outside organizations. Ocean's chairman himself came to realize that designing ships in-house had 'produced too many expensive mistakes'

---

[14] For the development of Ocean's main markets in these years, see Nick White's chapter in this volume.

[15] Falkus (1990, 323–328).

[16] Ibid., 310.

[17] For the Ship of the Future, see Ocean's summary 'A note on the V.D.R. experiment', 27 November 1974, 4.B.2328, for the Efficient Ship Daily Telegraph (2013).

and getting shipyards to build one-off designs had become prohibitively costly.[18] Finally, the application of knowledge remained patchy, and key economic factors such as the expected life of ships, their second-hand or scrap value, and the estimated distribution of revenues and operating costs over their service lives were not considered at all.[19] This had an effect on Ocean's profitability, its ability to finance fleet replacement, and ultimately the value of the company as a whole.

The Leap into Container Shipping

If innovation in conventional liner shipping was methodical but limited and slow, containerization represented a deliberate and abrupt leap into the dark, both in commercial and in technological terms. Initially, Ocean was sceptical about the potential of containerization. However, early studies had assumed that containers would be used alongside conventionally packed cargo in conventional ships.[20] Moreover, the problems that made containers attractive were only getting worse: port labour costs continued to rise, without any increase in productivity. In London, the real cost of loading cargo tripled during the 1960s. On the London-Sydney route, cargo handling costs represented 36% of round voyage costs in 1960 and 64% in 1970. Escalating stevedoring costs were aggravated by strikes. Liner ship owners saw the cost of cargo handling as the key reason for their lack of profitability and were looking for a long-term solution.[21] When American competitors Sea-Land began to plan the containerization of Australian traffic, Ocean was quick to realise that this required a response. Chairman Sir John Nicholson argued that containers were 'bound to present such cost advantages to shippers / receivers … as to be an inevitable development', and he concluded: 'If we (or other shipowners) don't provide such a service, someone else will, and eventually may be in a position to dominate liner conferences'.[22] P&O's chairman Sir

---

[18] Memo J. Nicholson, 31 May 1972, CA/JLA/box 7.
[19] Meek (2008, 136).
[20] Falkus (1990, 360).
[21] Gardner (1985, 195–197).
[22] Memo J. N. Nicholson, Container & Unit Load Service, 3 May 1965, OA/OCL box 61.

Donald Anderson shared this view. In his opinion, cargo handling costs were becoming 'unacceptable' to customers and mere 'improvements on the existing system' were insufficient. 'We believed that the liner trades were coming under such pressure that they must soon be revolutionised, and that containerisation was likely to be the most practical form which the revolution could take'.[23]

The outcome was the establishment of Overseas Containers Ltd. (OCL), a consortium consisting of Ocean, P&O, Furness Withy and British & Commonwealth.[24] OCL began its life in 1965 as 'a Research organisation set up to carry out a feasibility study', not surprising given that its task was to create a revolutionary transport system, starting with a 'clean slate'.[25] From mid-1966, when it was decided to go ahead with containerization on the UK–Australia route, OCL underwent a 'rapid transformation' into a proper shipping consortium. Within two years, OCL had to acquire 'hardware …particularly ships, containers and a new overall system of refrigeration'. A 'comprehensive control and information system', shore establishments in the UK and Australia, a trunk haulage system in the UK, a 'radically new system of documentation', and 'a radically new organisation for cargo procurement' had to be designed and implemented. Policy issues (industrial relations, personnel, pensions, PR) had to be resolved and a financial and accounting structure created.[26] Sales staff had to be trained or re-trained and customers had to be familiarized with the new way of shipping cargo, through measures including trial container shipments on traditional ships and advice on how best to load containers.[27]

Shipbuilders were faced with completely new challenges: 'When work first began early in 1966 on the design of these ships there was not a great deal of precedent to work on … the commercial planners who were endeavouring to match the number of containers and size and speed of ship to

---

[23] D. F. Anderson, Draft private & confidential: Containerisation, 13 September 1966, OA/OCL box 61.
[24] For the history of OCL, see Bott (2009).
[25] Circular to all senior staff, Organisation of O.C.L., 17 June 1966, OA/OCL box 61; ibid., 37; Miller (2012, 333, 339, 341).
[26] Circular to all senior staff, Organisation of O.C.L., 17 June 1966, OA/OCL box 61.
[27] Bott (2009, 106).

the likely trade were also starting from scratch'.[28] Research into container ship technology lagged behind the building of such ships. Knowledge of the required rigidity of container ships remained inconclusive well into the 1970s, 'long after these ships were first designed'. Experiments—such as setting up various configurations of cranes and mocked-up loading bays in an industrial yard to find the best way to get containers into the ship and hold them in place—had to be undertaken to inform design because neither theoretical models nor practical experience did yet exist.[29]

Under these circumstances, a number of measures had to be taken to mitigate commercial and technological risks. Ample safety margins were designed into these ships and, apart from the entirely new system for storing and fixing the containers, they were built to a deliberately conservative design, with a single-screw steam engine. They were also designed to allow conversion into bulk carriers in case containerization failed to take off. Many of these design choices had to be amended at a later date. Sometimes, this was fortunate: excessive safety margins allowed to increase cargo capacity by adding an extra layer of containers when demand turned out to be even larger than anticipated. On the other hand, the steam turbine engines were far too thirsty and powerful for the post-1973 era of high bunker costs and 'slow steaming'. They had to be replaced with diesel engines in the 1980s. The most conservative, 'safe' aspect of these ships' design was not necessarily commercially the most successful.[30]

Both technologically and commercially, containerization was begun under conditions of radical uncertainty—the new container ships' schedules, competition, loading times or the ports they were to call at were yet unknown when the naval architects got to work. However, 'for the first time in dry cargo ship design the nature of the cargo [was] known precisely. It [was] a predetermined number of boxes of standard size'.[31] Thus, containers changed the role of knowledge in cargo handling. Before containerization, officers, ratings and dockworkers had to draw on their

---

[28] Meek (1970, 1).
[29] Ibid., 40, 17–22. Mostert (1974, 70–75, 144–145) notes that supertankers likewise were experimental ships of unproven (and often dubious!) quality.
[30] Meek (1970, 35).
[31] Ibid., 4.

experience and specialized knowledge to solve ever-changing problems on the spot every time cargo—in the shape of bags, drums, boxes, cars, live animals for example—was moved into or out of the ship. With containers, handling and stowing could be automated and engineered with great precision. An enormous amount of knowledge was embodied in the design of interlocking systems, but once they were in place, little implicit knowledge or traditional craft was required to operate them. Such knowledge as was needed was of an explicit nature, easily recorded and taught, and largely the same on every ship and in every port.

Containers thus emancipated transport from 'the most costly, limited and disturbing factor in cargo handling, the unpredictable and rightly or wrongly pretentious human being'.[32] Standardization and routinization soon brought along computerization. Loading arrangements for Ocean's container ships were worked out by a computer and the data stored on disks that were transported by aeroplane to arrive before the ship. Operating ships changed from art to science and from craft to industry. One of Ocean's key resources, the knowledge of how to operate cargo liners economically and to high standards that had been developed and transmitted over decades, suddenly lost its value.[33] It was replaced by knowledge that was explicit, codified and easily transmitted. Such commodified knowledge transformed shipping from bottleneck to engine of global connectivity, but it was no longer a resource that could underpin a company's long-term competitive advantage. Indeed, as Nicholas White points out in this volume, by the 1980s, with infrastructure in place and knowledge readily available, newcomers from Asia's developing countries found it relatively easy to enter the industry.

Nonetheless, containerization was profitable. After a difficult start, OCL continuously outperformed other shipping companies as well as the 'average for UK industrial and commercial companies'.[34] More importantly, containers would soon change the way the world produced and consumed goods, and allow the emergence of present-day transcontinental supply chains and transnational corporations. Yet, the more shipping relied

---

[32]van den Burg (1969, 141); see also King (2000).
[33]This accumulated knowledge is described in Miller (2012, 95–103).
[34]Gardner (1985, 205 and Tables 4, 5).

on explicit knowledge and codified procedure rather than tacit knowledge and ad-hoc problem solving, the more it became commodified, favouring large-scale, low-cost operators and putting pressure on conference arrangements.[35] Finally, while shipping became cheaper, quicker and more predictable for shippers, for those involved in operating ships, it became routine and often boring.[36]

Management and Strategy

Introducing Strategic Planning

1965 marked not only the 100th anniversary of Ocean but also a number of momentous changes for the company, including the establishment of OCL as well as a reorganization of the fleet and flotation on the stock market. Flotation—undertaken to demonstrate a high share price before the introduction of capital gains tax in the UK—meant that Ocean became vulnerable to take-over by investors interested in the company's substantial cash reserves and unused tax allowances. To preserve its independence, Ocean had to make use of the resources it had accumulated.[37] Ocean was also aware that successful containerization of major routes would not only destroy the value of its accumulated operational knowledge but also make most of its traditional business obsolete, with a few container ships replacing the entire fleet of nearly a hundred liners. While the *Glenlyon* class ships spent 191 days at sea per year, the *Priams* managed 216 and the *Liverpool Bay* container ships 300, achieving six to seven times as many ton-miles per year as the *Priams*.[38] The pressure that had been building for the company to transform itself into something new now became irresistible. From the late 1960s onwards, Ocean adopted a new company structure, embarked on a diversification drive both within and outside shipping and eventually disengaged from all marine activities, including

---

[35] Barber (2003).
[36] See Lane (1986) and Gerstenberger and Welke (2002).
[37] Falkus (1990, 334–336).
[38] Meek (2008, 167).

container shipping. The direction of these changes, and no small part of the impulse behind them, came from the systematic introduction and implementation of the factual and conceptual knowledge that informs the development of explicit business strategies.

Transformation meant diversification—using the company's resources (people, capital, tax allowances and so on) for other, ideally profitable, purposes. To guide diversification, an explicit strategy was required. Around this time, a whole new body of knowledge dealing with corporate strategy emerged and was disseminated in business books, taught in business schools and promoted by consultancy firms.[39] Eventually, it became '*the* framework by which companies understand what they're doing and want to do', but this process took time.[40] In the UK, 'management thought remained the product of relatively few intellectuals' and no more than 3700 people were enrolled in management courses in 1966–1967.[41] Ocean and other shipping firms provided financial support for management courses at university level 'because … management education in general is so important to this country', even while deploring that universities focused on postgraduate degrees and neglected the shorter and part-time courses for mid-career managers industry demanded.[42]

Turning towards diversification, restructuring and explicit strategic plans, the shipping industry followed the lead of many other international businesses. At Ocean, the introduction of modern management thought was the work of Sir Lindsay Alexander, a director responsible for commercial development and then chairman from 1971 to 1980, and of Nicholas Barber. Barber joined Ocean in 1964 as one of the 'crown princes' or 'student princes', promising Oxbridge graduates the company recruited from time to time with a view to fast-tracking them into senior

---

[39] For these developments, see Wilson and Thomson (2006, 117–123, 165–166) and Toms and Wright (2002, 101–105).
[40] Kiechel (2010, 4). On the history of strategic management thought, see Freedman (2013, ch. 28–36) and Mintzberg (1994).
[41] Child (1969, 113–114).
[42] Memo H. B. Chrimes, 11 June 1970, OA/JLA/box 22.

management.[43] Back in Liverpool after two years in Singapore, he persuaded Alexander to send him on an 18-month MBA course at Columbia University in 1969–1971 and then stepped into a new role as the company's Strategic Planner.[44] His personal correspondence with Alexander sheds light on this crucial period in the company's development.[45]

Ocean's strategic planning systems were created from scratch, based on a review of how large US companies had introduced strategic planning. Priorities were quickly established: the emphasis was to be on identifying areas of development, because 'the whole need for strategic planning has arisen from our having to look for new business'; 'real support at the top' was considered necessary in order to get 'people interested in longer term problems which do not involve immediate operational pressures', and planning had to appear as Ocean's 'own activity rather than something done by people looking like management consultants'.[46]

The Barber-Alexander correspondence led to a briefing document for Ocean's board, accompanied by a fuller version with background and reflections added. It started from the assumption that '[a]ll companies have a strategy but not usually explicitly,' and that an explicit strategy was particularly important when branching out into new business. Strategic planning was to help the Board '[d]etermine *what kind of Company* Ocean wants to become, particularly what businesses we expect to be in, for what rewards / risks'. It was to be an annual process, seeking to make top and middle management '*planning minded* (including budget-minded), i.e. oriented to looking at the long term'. Planning was to become embedded in the company's processes and devolved from the Board and central departments downwards to senior and middle managers. The job of the Strategic Planning Division was 'to ask awkward questions / insist on

---

[43] On Ocean's recruitment strategies and the 'student princes', see Falkus (1990, 10, 18, 59, 283, 289).

[44] John Lindsay Alexander Papers, OA/JLA/box 7; personal communication, 25 October 2018.

[45] Barber to Alexander, 5 March 1970, 7 June 1970; Alexander to Barber, 9 March 1970, 18 June 1970; N. Barber, Basic approach to strategic planning, 30 March 1971, OA/JLA/box 7.

[46] Barber to Alexander, 23 August 1970, OA/JLA/box 7.

answers / encourage management to do its own planning ... It will (must) *not* write its own answers. Paradoxically, planners should not plan'.[47]

Barber's (and Alexander's) starting point was that 'O[cean]'s major problem concerns strategic direction'. Asking '*what kind of Company* Ocean wants to become' not only led to a 'master plan for the whole Company', but also to the setting of 'objectives for the future in terms of profit, return on investment and sales growth'.[48] Once up and running, the system of strategic planning and budgetary control would allow for the first time to work on company strategy on the basis of detailed information on what the individual divisions were doing, how they were performing and developing, and how efficient they were.[49] Along with strategic planning, a new company structure was introduced. While strategy was kept under the control of Ocean's managers, Boston Consulting Group was called in to help with development of the new structure. The result was a multi-divisional company structure that would free up resources for strategic decision-making at Group level, with an Executive Committee free from operational responsibility, while planning and decision-making would be devolved to the operating divisions.

It is easy to dismiss these changes as little more than new jargon, or an imitation of changes occurring in many companies at the time: diversification, bureaucratization and the creation of multi-divisional structures.[50] But the aims, and effects, of Ocean's strategic planning system were more far-reaching. The fact that the company's objectives were now stated in terms of profit, return on investment and growth should not be underestimated. So far, not making a loss and living up to self-set quality standards had been the only guidelines for company strategy. Now, economic performance indicators at least theoretically had gained primacy over other aims and unspoken assumptions. While fully implementing this new outlook would still take some considerable time, Ocean's managers now began to see themselves as business managers rather than shipowners.

---

[47] N. Barber, Brief for strategic planning, 9 March 1971, N. Barber, Strategic planning, 11 May 1971, OA/JLA/box 7. All quotations in this paragraph are from this document.
[48] Ibid.
[49] The operation of the system is described in the September 1972 Blue Book 'Strategic Planning and Budgetary Control' (photocopy in possession of the author, kindly provided by David Riddle).
[50] Channon (1973).

The dangers of a lack of explicit criteria and strategy are illustrated by some of the attempts at diversification that Ocean had already undertaken, for example a move into services and hotels in the Caribbean, and diversification into new areas of shipping such as tankers, bulkers and liquefied natural gas. The Caribbean ventures never became profitable and nobody could in the end make sense of how they fitted in with the rest of the company. The acquisition of the LNG tanker *Nestor*, ordered in 1970, nearly broke the company—it was built for a market that did not materialize, went straight from the dockyard into layup and was sold off in 1989, never having seen service. It later turned out that basic errors were made in assessing the viability of the project.[51]

Strategic planning was supposed to prevent such mistakes by reviewing the strengths and weaknesses of the company, the resources it had, the markets it might move into, and the resources it would need to succeed. Thorough analysis of Ocean's resources soon revealed important weaknesses alongside the company's acknowledged strengths. Ocean's knowledge was concentrated in a narrow, unfortunately increasingly irrelevant, area: the operation of cargo liners in cartelized markets. In many other areas, the company lacked knowledge and well-trained staff. To enable Ocean to diversify and seize opportunities in other markets, new expertise was required in areas such as finance, accounting, taxation, internal audit, and personnel. Management in general was seen as a weakness, with a shortage of general management skills and a lack of experience in marketing, retailing, and 'working to fine margins'. Accordingly, the first exercises in strategic planning resulted in 'mostly very poor' plans and gave 'no demonstration that the line manager really understands the business he is in'.[52] Falkus notes that before the early 1970s, Ocean's rigid management structure and lack of 'financial and accounting expertise … made the implementation of a coherent diversification plan well-nigh impossible'.[53] Ocean's people were good at operating ships but not at running a business. Like other shipping companies, or the trading houses active in disappearing colonial markets, Ocean had to accept that resources such as

---

[51] Falkus (1990, 342–344); Nicholas Barber, personal communication, 3 March 2016. Gardner (1985, 205) argues that it was diversification that held back liner shipping profits over the 1970s.
[52] Barber to Alexander, 15 May 1972, OA/JLA/box 35.
[53] Falkus (1990, 291).

accumulated skills and experience were being devalued by political change such as decolonization and technological change such as containerization, and were not easily transferable into other complex industries.[54]

Despite disappointment with the initial results, the strategic planning exercise paid off quickly. Conducting a thorough assessment of threats, aims and resources enabled Ocean to seize the opportunity when the services company Cory came up for sale in 1972. Ocean quickly identified Cory as a perfect match, Cory was bought and over the coming years, Ocean's shipping activities were gradually scaled down and Cory provided the basis for the company's transformation into an industrial services business. Many of the managers brought in with Cory or recruited from other non-shipping sectors at the same time would soon play leading roles in Ocean. The mission of OCL, initially defined as achieving a dominant position in container shipping, was redefined as providing the best possible return on the parent companies' investment.[55] By the end of the 1980s, Ocean, in Barber's words, resembled a 'Polo Mint'—a company formed around a shipping core that no longer existed.[56] Commercial knowledge, including a heightened awareness of resources, costs and profitability led to diversification away from the shipping industry—an activity Ocean was good at, but where the knowledge accumulated over more than a century was no longer relevant due to the commodification of operations bulk and container shipping had brought with them.

Implementing Strategic Planning

This brief big-picture summary should not distract from the considerable difficulties Ocean experienced trying to implement strategic thinking and budget-conscious management. By the mid-1970s, Ocean still used an 'amalgam of various accounting systems', consolidation of which remained a goal for the longer term.[57] Developing human resources policies and procedures aligned with overall Group strategy took many years.

---

[54] A point made by Jones (2002, 220, 680–682, 761).
[55] Bott (2009, 144).
[56] Personal communication, 3 March 2016.
[57] Ocean Group Finance Division, Strategic Plan 1976–1980, OA/OCL/box 9.

7 Shipping as a Knowledge Industry: Research and Strategic … 173

The transition out of liner shipping took much longer than expected, as diversification within shipping failed dramatically and the newly-acquired Cory businesses were slow to take off while traditional liner shipping business declined more slowly than anticipated. The Cory businesses seemed more responsive to planning than the old Ocean core. The shipping divisions and in particular OFL, the staffing and maintenance division, often adopted a defensive attitude, sensing that—even though they still contributed the bulk of Group earnings and profits—their importance and opportunities were declining. Far from implementing the strict focus on return on capital required in the strategic planning process, in day-to-day management, Ocean tried to keep up 'fleet morale' and shore up its 'marine base'. In the short run, it seemed very costly to wind down marine activities while maintaining the reputation and identity of a 'responsible employer', but in the longer run, opportunities to sell ships while they still commanded reasonable prices were lost, and staff had to be made redundant nonetheless, and in overall much worse labour market conditions.[58]

Elaborate strategic plans for all parts of the business had become part of Ocean's operational routines by the mid-1970s. These plans noted that the process of planning had made operations more efficient generally, but also that planning and forecasting had usually tended to 'over-react to the prevailing conditions at the time of planning'.[59] More importantly, while strategic planning could yield sharper insight into the nature of existing difficulties and deficiencies, it often was less successful in finding alternative uses for Ocean's resources. Mid-1970s strategic plans paint the picture of a company that had few strategic options and was trapped by laws and regulations in a declining sector and in an inflation-ridden economy controlled by trade unions and a socialist government. The Group Personnel Division's plan for 1977–1981 noted that the strategic planning system and its aim to allocate resources to the most promising markets was based on the assumption of free markets, in particular for labour, which was no longer correct. Even the basic notion of growth which was at the heart

---

[58] Marine Committee meetings, 28 November 1977, 24 June 1978, 7.A.1951-1. For further references, see Petersson (2018).
[59] Group Strategic Plan 1977–1981, 4.B.1860.

of both Ocean's internal planning and BCG's proposals had apparently become 'suspect' in much of public discourse.[60]

'The lack of indicated growth opportunities, combined with the capacity to invest, is a major planning gap', noted the 1976–1980 Group Strategic Plan. Probing questions were asked, but not answered: did Ocean need new businesses or a new 'product' 'to answer our longer term growth requirements, and to enable us to escape from the increasing likelihood of State interference and constraint in the service industries of transportation and distribution?' Could the answer be a move to overseas investment in familiar businesses? 'Or, does a new activity imply a new business altogether, such as manufacturing? leisure? mining? engineering? or what?'[61] These are the question the diversification literature at the time recommended asking, and strategic planning made sure that such questions were asked, the company's situation was analyzed and growth opportunities were sought.[62] Ocean had begun to function as a business seeking ways to achieve the best possible return on the capital employed. Yet, solutions were not easy to find. Plans continued to highlight the need to develop new activities in order to 'balance the preponderance of mature and declining businesses', and to affirm: 'We have very substantial capacity to invest and few identified growth opportunities to enable us to exploit these resources'. Asking entrepreneurial questions seemed easier than finding entrepreneurial answers.[63]

Management Development

There was a practical as well as a strategic side to the increased attention paid to management knowledge as a corporate resource at Ocean in the 1970s. Until then, training had been largely on-the-job, with no systematic, formal training of management staff for specific roles. Barber

---

[60] Group Personnel Division Strategic Plan 1977–1981, in Rees (1987), Appendix 61, 10.
[61] Group Strategic Plan 1977–1981, 4.B.1860.
[62] Rich (1978a, b).
[63] Group Strategic Plan 1977–1981, 4.B.1860.

bemoaned a lack of entrepreneurial spirit, along with an atmosphere characterized by amateurism and paternalism.[64] A systematic effort to train and empower managers was made alongside the introduction of strategic planning. Yet John D. Rees, who joined Ocean as management development adviser in 1973, claims that the devolution of responsibility and leadership too often was only a theoretical goal, whereas in practice the Board were reluctant to give up control[65]—perhaps understandably, given the deficiencies revealed by the first strategic plans. Rees saw the increased role of formal knowledge as the signature of modern business. He tried to get everyone on Ocean's management development programme to read Peter Drucker's *The Age of Discontinuity*—the main theme of which was the rise of the knowledge society—as well as Alvin Toffler's *Future Shock* which, he hoped, would 'shake complacent managers into an awareness of changes in their work environment and in the wider context of a post-industrial society'.[66] Rees's management development programmes focused on aspects that had become important under the new decentralized multidivisional structure. In particular, personnel management techniques and procedures were introduced, with all line managers becoming responsible for appraising their staff and setting objectives closely aligned with company and divisional strategic plans. Likewise, all managers had to brush up on finance and accountancy.[67]

It is not easy to assess the overall effect of these changes. The transformation Ocean managers described as one from 'family business style' to 'big business style'[68]—a development that mirrored the gradual engagement with management weaknesses throughout British industry at the time[69]—was more difficult to achieve in practice than to sketch out on paper. The impact of managers brought in through the Cory acquisition shows that it is often easier to acquire resources from outside than to develop them from

---

[64] Nicholas Barber, personal communication, 3 March 2016.
[65] Rees (1987, 33–35).
[66] Drucker (1969) and Toffler (1970). The quote is from Rees (1987, 87).
[67] Rees (1987) provides a narrative as well as detailed examples of the training courses introduced while he was at Ocean.
[68] Falkus (1990, 350).
[69] Wilson and Thomson (2006, 41–42).

scratch internally.[70] Yet it appears plausible that both personnel management and financial knowledge were essential to operating a business in the 1970s and beyond as labour relations were becoming more bureaucratic and the company was focusing on the financial 'bottom line'. What is clear is that the Ocean of the 1970s and onwards fully understood the necessity of systematically developing, distributing and applying modern management knowledge throughout its senior workforce, as well as of recruiting, nurturing and promoting skilled staff.

With strategic planning, diversification, management development and implementation of the multi-divisional structure, the days where the knowledge that underpinned Ocean's competitive advantage was about operating liner ships in a cartelized environment were gone. Systematic strategic planning processes were now governing both 'grand strategy' at a group level, and detailed mapping out and budgeting of individual divisions' development over the medium term. But did the adoption of strategic planning achieve its objectives and lead to a sustainable improvement in performance? David Riddle, Barber's successor as Ocean's strategic planner, argues that the 'successful development of a broadly based freight group [was] the result of the creation of business plans driven by long term profitability and the move away from basic ship operations. … I put it down to the introduction of planning and related reporting in the early 1970s'.[71] The literature on strategic planning is often much more sceptical about what could be achieved through the strict application of strategic planning methodology, arguing that its formalistic nature tended to prevent, rather than support, strategic thinking and suffocate entrepreneurialism.[72] Planning is described as designed for the stable growth conditions of the 1960s and unsuited to the radical uncertainty and heightened competition of the 1970s. Ocean's experience seems to lend qualified support to both sides of the argument. On the one hand, the most fundamental strategic decisions were taken either before strategic planning was fully in place or did not figure in the strategic plans (as with

---

[70] A point made by Wernerfelt (1984, 175).
[71] Personal communication, 1 August 2016, 30 November 2018.
[72] This is the main argument in Mintzberg (1994); see also Freedman (2013, 518).

the acquisition of Cory), and planning did not provide much help in identifying growth and investment opportunities in the 1970s. On the other hand, though, strategic planning seems to have provided the tools required to identify and assess strategic opportunities. Again, the Cory acquisition is a prime example because though it was clearly an opportunistic move it could not have been identified as a strategic opportunity without the work already undertaken in the context of the introduction of strategic planning. At the level of individual businesses, planning helped implement strategic decisions and keep a focus on commercial performance. Within the resource-based framework adopted in this chapter, it can be argued that strategic planning helped mobilize and apply knowledge about the company, its divisions, its customers, competitors and environment both in strategic decision-making and in day-to-day implementation. It thus seems to have fostered the systematic development of knowledge as a corporate resource. As such, planning underpinned and enabled strategic thinking and decision-making—what it could not, and at least in Ocean's case was not intended to, achieve was replace them.

Conclusion

Lutz Raphael highlights that all aspects of modern society are transfused with concepts and findings derived from research (calling this, in untranslatable German, 'Verwissenschaftlichung des Sozialen').[73] This chapter has examined the role of formalized, research-based technological, operational and conceptual managerial knowledge in Ocean's transformation. Many of the changes discussed above were initiated by managers who studied academic publications on technology, business and society, while academic researchers closely followed transformations in the corporate world.[74] At Ocean, knowledge was increasingly seen and nurtured as a key corporate resource and explicit strategy was embodied in rolling five-year strategic plans. Across all processes within the company, explicit and documented knowledge took the place of tacit, experience-based knowledge. From the

---

[73] Raphael (1996).
[74] The preface to Channon (1973) provides an example.

1950s, systematic research informed incremental changes in ship design and operations. However, its impact remained limited. Only containerization would eventually remove key bottlenecks in cargo liner shipping. Ocean was among the firms that pro-actively adopted and implemented containerization, developing an interlocking system of technological and operational innovations to make it work. This, however, had the effect of devaluing the largely implicit, ad-hoc knowledge that underpinned the competitive advantage of traditional liner shipping firms and replacing it with standardized, commodified knowledge—an example of 'how firm resources and capabilities are accumulated and eroded' and 'how resources' relative values may be affected by market changes'.[75]

While modern technology usually consists of explicit knowledge and thus is easily accessible to those able to study it or to pay for it, it is much more difficult to work out how or whether to use it. A resource-based perspective stresses the key role played by operational and strategic knowledge in shaping and reacting to wider transformations. Here, Ocean's focus shifted from nurturing the craft of shipping towards running a business. With the introduction of strategic planning, budgets, cost, profits and return on capital moved centre stage. This shift in perspective eventually transformed Ocean, but it was a gradual process involving change in personnel, large-scale training and cultural change as well as the change of procedures and explicit strategy. The implementation issues encountered along the way raise the question to what extent even companies operating with a large body of explicit knowledge and well-document procedures rely on tacit knowledge allowing employees to identify necessary shortcuts and work to the spirit, rather than the letter, of the rules. Another aspect that deserves to be highlighted is the effect of new types of knowledge on power within the corporation. The introduction of strategic management, performance planning and explicit targets for growth and profits served to assert and legitimate the power of managers, and bolstered the interests of shareholders.[76]

---

[75] Priem and Butler (2001).
[76] Child (1969, 22–23, 232–233) and Knights and Morgan (1991); see also Freedman (2013), Mintzberg (1994), and Bott (2009, 189, 205–207).

A focus on knowledge allows highlighting the agency of managers, as well as the limits on that agency and the complexity of their task under conditions of fundamental uncertainty. What they could not know, for example, was to what extent their initiatives would succeed, which transformations would unfold and which ones would falter, and how new knowledge would ultimately become embodied in new types of institutions and organizations. Containerization and diversification were initiatives dating back to the 1960s, a time of optimism and stable expansion, but had to be implemented in the 1970s, a period of depressed growth, high inflation and unpredictable structural change. The organizational transformations of the 1970s were the key factor that unlocked the potential of the technological changes made in the 1950s and 1960s, eventually transforming shipping into an engine of globalization and the key mechanism in global chains of production and consumption. However, the transformations the industry underwent along the way were largely unforeseen. In fact, applying business knowledge to the shipping industry changed the industry so much that it became unviable for many of the first movers to remain active in it.

Acknowledgements I would like to thank Nicholas Barber CBE and David Riddle (ex-Ocean) for sharing their ideas and answering my questions and Dr. Chris Corker and Prof. Stig Tenold for reading suggestions.

References

Archival Sources

All archival sources referred to are part of the Ocean Group papers located in the Merseyside Maritime Museum archives, Liverpool.

Published Sources

Barber, N. (2003). Ocean as a Liner Shipping Company. *Nestorian, 20,* 11.

Barney, J. B. (1991). Firm Resources and Sustained Competitive Advantage. *Journal of Management, 17,* 99–120.
Barney, J. B. (2001). Is the Resource-Based "View" a Useful Perspective for Strategic Management Research? Yes. *The Academy of Management Review, 26* (1), 41–56.
Bott, A. (Ed.). (2009). *British Box Business: A History of OCL.* SCARA.
Channon, D. F. (1973). *The Strategy and Structure of British Enterprise.* London: Macmillan.
Child, J. (1969). *British Management Thought: A Critical Analysis.* London: Allen & Unwin.
Drucker, P. (1969). *The Age of Discontinuity: Guideline to Our Changing Society.* London: Heinemann.
Falkus, M. (1990). *The Blue Funnel Legend: A History of the Ocean Steam Ship Company, 1865–1973.* London: Macmillan.
Freedman, L. (2013). *Strategy: A History.* New York: Oxford University Press.
Gardner, B. (1985). The Container Revolution and Its Effects on the Structure of Traditional UK Liner Shipping Companies. *Maritime Policy & Management, 12*(3), 195–208.
Gerstenberger, H., & Welke, U. (2002). *Seefahrt im Zeichen der Globalisierung.* Münster: Westfälisches Dampfboot.
Goss, R. O. (1998). Rochdale Remembered: A Personal Memoir. *Maritime Policy & Management, 25*(3), 213–233.
Goss, R. O. (2011). Strategies in British Shipping 1945–1970. *Mariner's Mirror, 97*(1), 243–258.
Grant, R. M. (1996). Toward a Knowledge-Based Theory of the Firm. *Strategic Management Journal, 17,* 109–122.
Jones, G. (2002). *Merchants to Multinationals: British Trading Companies in the Nineteenth and Twentieth Centuries.* Oxford: Oxford University Press.
Jones, O., Ghobadian, A., O'Regan, N., & Antcliff, V. (2013). Dynamic Capabilities in a Sixth-Generation Family Firm: Entrepreneurship and the Bibby Line. *Business History, 55*(6), 910–941.
Kiechel, W., III. (2010). *The Lords of Strategy: The Secret Intellectual History of the New Corporate World.* Boston: Harvard Business Review Press.
King, J. (2000). Technology and the Seafarer. *Journal for Maritime Research, 2*(1), 48–63.
Knights, D., & Morgan, G. (1991). Corporate Strategy, Organizations, and Subjectivity: A Critique. *Organization Studies, 12*(2), 251.
Lane, T. (1986). *Grey Dawn Breaking: British Seafarers in the Late Twentieth Century.* Manchester: Manchester University Press.

Meek, M. (1964). *Glenlyon* Class: Design and Operation of High-Powered Cargo Liners. *Royal Institution of Naval Architects: Quarterly Transactions, 106*(3), 241–285.

Meek, M. (1970). The First O.C.L. Container Ships. *Royal Institution of Naval Architects: Quarterly Transactions, 112*(1), 1–41.

Meek, M. (2008). *There Go the Ships*. County Durham: Memoir Club.

Meek, M., & Adams, R. (1969). "Priam" Class Cargo Liners—Design and Operation. *Royal Institution of Naval Architects: Quarterly Transactions, 111*(3), 271–298.

Miller, M. B. (2012). *Europe and the Maritime World: A Twentieth Century History*. Cambridge: Cambridge University Press.

Mintzberg, H. (1994). *The Rise and Fall of Strategic Planning*. London: Prentice Hall.

Mostert, N. (1974). *Supership*. London and Basingstoke: Macmillan.

Obituary: Marshall Meek. (2013, September 29). *The Daily Telegraph*.

Penrose, E. (1959). *Theory of the Growth of the Firm*. Oxford: Blackwell.

Petersson, N. P. (2018). Managing a "People Business" in Times of Uncertainty: Human Resources Strategy at Ocean Transport & Trading in the 1970s. *Enterprise & Society, 19*(1), 88–123.

Priem, R. L., & Butler, J. E. (2001). Is the Resource-Based "View" a Useful Perspective for Strategic Management Research? *The Academy of Management Review, 26*(1), 22–40.

Raphael, L. (1996). Die Verwissenschaftlichung des Sozialen als methodische und konzeptionelle Herausforderung für eine Sozialgeschichte des 20. Jahrhunderts. *Geschichte und Gesellschaft, 22*(2), 165–193.

Rees, J. D. (1987). *A Study of Management and Organization Development in a UK Shipping Transport and Trading Company, 1972–80* (MA thesis). Durham.

Report of the Committee of Inquiry into Shipping. (1970). London: H.M. Stationery Office.

Rich, C. A. (1978a). Corporate Planning in Shipping: Relating Theory to Practice, Pt. 1. *Maritime Policy & Management, 5*(1), 31–38.

Rich, C. A. (1978b). Corporate Planning in Shipping: Relating Theory to Practice, Pt. 2: Corporate Strategy. *Maritime Policy & Management, 5*(1), 39–50.

Spender, J. C. (1996). Making Knowledge the Basis of a Dynamic Theory of the Firm. *Strategic Management Journal, 17*, 45–62.

Teece, D. J. (2016). Dynamic Capabilities and Entrepreneurial Management in Large Organizations: Toward a Theory of the (Entrepreneurial) Firm. *European Economic Review, 86*, 202–216.

Toffler, A. (1970). *Future Shock*. New York: Bantam.

Toms, S., & Wright, M. (2002). Corporate Governance, Strategy and Structure in British Business History, 1950–2000. *Business History, 44*(3), 91–124.

van den Burg, G. (1969). *Containerisation: A Modern Transport System.* London: Hutchinson.

Wernerfelt, B. (1984). A Resource-Based View of the Firm. *Strategic Management Journal, 5*(2), 171–180.

Wernerfelt, B. (1995). The Resource-Based View of the Firm: Ten Years After. *Strategic Management Journal, 16*(3), 171–174.

Wilson, J. F., & Thomson, A. (2006). *The Making of Modern Management: British Management in Historical Perspective.* Oxford: Oxford University Press.

Open Access This chapter is licensed under the terms of the Creative Commons Attribution-NonCommercial-NoDerivatives 4.0 International License (http://creativecommons.org/licenses/by-nc-nd/4.0/), which permits any noncommercial use, sharing, distribution and reproduction in any medium or format, as long as you give appropriate credit to the original author(s) and the source, provide a link to the Creative Commons license and indicate if you modified the licensed material. You do not have permission under this license to share adapted material derived from this chapter or parts of it.

The images or other third party material in this chapter are included in the chapter's Creative Commons license, unless indicated otherwise in a credit line to the material. If material is not included in the chapter's Creative Commons license and your intended use is not permitted by statutory regulation or exceeds the permitted use, you will need to obtain permission directly from the copyright holder.

Part III

Connections

8

The Role of Greek Shipowners in the Revival of Northern European Shipyards in the 1950s

Gelina Harlaftis and Christos Tsakas

Introduction

Greece continues to be the largest shipowning country in terms of cargo-carrying capacity (309 million dwt), followed by Japan, China, Germany and Singapore. 'Together, these five countries control almost half of the world's tonnage'.[1] In the immediate post-World War II years Greek shipowners managed to become major players in world sea transport. By entering the oil shipping market they became leaders in the tanker business. Led by Aristotle Onassis, the first Greek to invest in newly-built tankers before the war, prominent shipowners like Stavros Niarchos,

---

[1] UNCTAD (2017, 28).

G. Harlaftis
Rethymnon, Greece

C. Tsakas (✉)
Princeton University, Princeton, NJ, USA

Stavros Livanos, the Kulukundis-brothers and the P. Goulandris-brothers became United States' main shipping partners, carrying much of its foreign trade. During the 1950s they all launched massive shipbuilding programmes and became catalysts for the revival of the war-torn European shipyards, and particularly of the West German and British ones along with those of Belgium, Sweden, France and the Netherlands. As shipping has always been important in geopolitics, this was as much about business as it was about politics.

The US policy-makers often attempted to take advantage of the Greeks' dominant position in the independent tanker industry, either using them as scapegoats for their internal policies or stressing the crucial role they could play in regional Cold War crises in their foreign policy. From accusing them of 'red trade' during the Korean war, fraud during the change of government from Democrats to Republicans in 1954, to imposing embargo on Cuba in the aftermath of Fidel Castro's revolution in 1960s, Greek shipowners occasionally became the focal point of US diplomatic efforts.[2] Seeking safe refuges in times of crisis, had been a constant objective for Greek shipowners since the early 1950s. After their dispute with the US authorities during the 1950s they all shifted their focus to Europe and ended their brief stay in New York.[3] Apart from Britain, one of their main maritime centres since the nineteenth century, the Federal Republic of Germany (FRG) became their new maritime entrepreneurial target, where they launched massive shipbuilding programmes that revived the war-torn German shipyards. Haakon Ikonomou and Christos Tsakas, by addressing the responses of Greece and Norway to the Common Shipping Policy efforts in the 1960s and the 1970s, have recently shown how two leading maritime nations from the outer periphery reacted to, and largely influenced, the integration dynamics of the shipping sector at the regional European level.[4] Our study will also give some insights on the potential contribution of business and maritime history into scholarly debates on

---

[2] *Foreign Relations of the United States* (hereafter *FRUS*), *1958–1960*, VI, 980–991 (545) and *FRUS*, *1964–1968*, XVI, 174–179 (82).
[3] Harlaftis (2014).
[4] Ikonomou and Tsakas (2019).

the role of pre-existing international business networks in the process of European integration.[5]

As this volume indicates, shipping was both an example and an engine of globalization and structural change in the post-war era. This chapter builds on the recent work of Michael Miller, who has highlighted how the Europeans ran the maritime business world in the twentieth century and has located shipping in the prevailing historical narrative of global business, and of Gelina Harlaftis, who has indicated how the Greeks created global shipping business in the twentieth century.[6] Harlaftis examines the choices of Greek shipowners, led by Aristotle Onassis, who were able to exploit the opportunities given by the oil companies in the United States in the 1940s and led the way in tanker shipping in Europe.[7] Greeks were able to establish the new institution of the global shipping company, a kind of multinational company, that was based in many countries and used Panamanian and Liberian companies and flags which meant that it was taxed under the law of these countries. They served the ever-increasing oil industry by contracting long-term charters with American oil companies and by using finance from American banking institutions to invest initially in American but later more in northern European shipyards.

Miller has largely focused on liner shipping, whereas the Greek shipowners were involved in tramp and bulk shipping.[8] Tramp and bulk shipping made possible a global supply line for basic resources like food, energy and raw materials for the industry. Greeks in the South of Europe, often under Flags of convenience, proved a prime example of the evolution of the regional European maritime businesses to serve the global economy. In fact, one could safely argue that the history of modern bulk and tramp shipping simply cannot be written without them. Miller's focus, however, on the shipping infrastructure as a key component of the industry's globalizing effect, points to an interesting direction for further research. Hamburg, one of the big European ports Miller studies, became synonymous for the German shipyards along with a few other shipbuilding hubs,

---

[5] Ramirez Perez (2010) and Rollings and Kipping (2008). For a recent account, see Tsakas (2018).
[6] Miller (2012) and Harlaftis (2019).
[7] Carlisle (1981).
[8] See Stopford (1997) for an introduction to the distinctions between the various segments.

such as Bremen and Kiel. These industrial hubs were targeted by Greek shipowners. Aristotle Onassis was the first to turn to the war-torn German shipyards and revive them, thus contributing to the 'German economic miracle', known as *Wirtschaftswunder*. Across the Channel the war-struck British shipbuilding industry built an even larger amount of tanker tonnage for leading Greek shipping companies like the Kulukundis brothers, Stavros Livanos and Stavros Niarchos.

The shipbuilding industry reflected wider transformations in shipping that led to the present-day globalized economy. We examine how Greek shipping entrepreneurship, American finance and northern European technical know-how triggered the revival of European shipyards and the continuation of European hegemony in global shipping in the 1950s and thereafter. Greek shipowners were able to promote technological advancements in European shipbuilding that were diffused globally and transformed the global tanker industry. This is the story of a rare twentieth century reversal of roles. In the post-World War II period in the case of shipping and shipbuilding, southern Europe helped revive not only northern European shipbuilding, but also became the mainstay of European shipping to the present day.

Why the Greeks?

Greek shipowners after World War II were able to take advantage of the major transformations that took place in the shipping markets and in world leadership. During this period, three important changes took place that changed the maritime world. The first was the shift from coal to oil as a main energy source, and as a main commodity to be carried. The second was the shift from the political hegemony of Great Britain to that of the United States. The third was the use of offshore companies and flags of convenience which Greeks were among the first to adopt and set the pace for the creation of the global shipping firm which was not connected to one nation.

If the history of the maritime transport of power in Europe in the first half of the twentieth century was written by coal and tramp ships, in the second half it was written by oil and tankers. The 1950s was the critical decade for this transition. In 1900 oil was an insignificant source of energy; world production of 20 million tons met only 2.5% of world energy consumption. Because production was so limited there was little need for specialized vessels; tankers, mostly owned by Europeans, accounted for a tiny 1.5% of world merchant tonnage. By 1938 oil production was 273 million tons per year and accounted for 26% of world energy consumption.[9] But it was after 1945 that oil became the primary energy source worldwide; by 1970 it had risen to a peak of 56%. Another very important change was that although before the Second World War the United States was the world's leading oil producer, by 1948 it became a net importer for the first time. In the 1950s Middle Eastern production surged and major US oil companies (Chevron, Esso, Gulf, Mobil and Texaco) and two European firms (Shell and BP) dominated production, distribution and sales around the world, except in the socialist countries. Between 1953 and 1973 the volume of seaborne oil increased by six times to almost two billion tons, amounting to about 60% of all maritime trade. This enormous increase went alongside an unprecedented demand for tanker tonnage.[10]

After the end of World War II the US possessed the largest fleet of merchant ships in the world, with 60% of world tonnage, compared with 1939 when it was about 14.5%.[11] Due to alarming ship losses during the war, the United States through the United States Maritime Commission (USMC) had launched a massive shipbuilding programme through which 4694 ships of all kinds, both commercial and military were built.[12] Despite the enormous fleet, the United States was not able to support this fleet as it had not been able to develop a maritime tradition equivalent to that of Britain or provide internationally competitive maritime services. After the war the American officials were thus faced with the huge problem of what to do with this enormous and costly fleet that was six times larger than needed, with ships that were mostly of a rather older technology and were too costly to be operated by American shipowners. In the end, American

---

[9] Eden et al. (1981).
[10] Ratcliffe (1985).
[11] Perry (1946).
[12] Achee-Thornton and Thomson (2001).

policymakers decided to sell two-thirds of the fleet and to form a reserve fleet with the rest. In March 1946 President Truman signed the Merchant Ship Sales Act which authorized USMC to sell government-owned vessels to domestic and foreign shipowners.[13] There were however, a number of restrictions on the types of vessels available to foreigners, for example tankers were not available for sale to foreigners, only in specific cases and limited numbers.[14]

The Greeks were among the first to purchase such ships, in particular the famous 'Liberty' type that were medium-sized cargo ships.[15] In 1939, the Greek merchant fleet consisted of 1.8 million grt but by 1946 only 500,000 grt remained. The sale of Liberty ships was a great opportunity for Greek shipowners to acquire new ships on highly favourable terms. On 9 April 1946, the Greek government guaranteed the purchase of 100 Liberties on behalf of its shipowners, with long-term loans from the American banks with the obligation to hoist the Greek flag. Another 300 vessels of the USMC merchant fleet were purchased by Greek shipowners in cash or with loans provided by American banks and under the condition that they would hoist the so-called 'flags-of-convenience'.[16]

The Flags of convenience as they came to be called in the 1950s became a key manifestation of American maritime policy led by American oil companies that needed low-cost transport. This came as a result of the shift of political power and influence from Britain to the United States after 1945 which ushered in a new era in world shipping. 'Flagging out' from traditional registers to Flags of convenience became a major feature of post-world war II international shipping. The Flags of convenience of Panama, Honduras and Liberia—known as the PanHoLib fleet—were part of the trend to turn to offshore companies. This solution not only provided an economic shelter, like cheap flags with low taxes, but also flexibility beyond state control in a global environment.[17] When a sealift was needed, the

---

[13] More on the review in Hutchins (1951).
[14] Marx (1948).
[15] Sawyer and Mitchell (1973).
[16] *Naftika Chronika*, 1 April 1946 and 15 April 1946; Harlaftis (1996, 2013) and Tzamtzis (1984).
[17] See Cafruny (1987); the fleets were also referred to as PanLibHon. For a classic on Flags of convenience, see Metaxas (1985). For the resort of the Greeks to Flags of convenience, see Harlaftis (1989).

PanHoLib would immediately become the United States' allies, and the American Navy could forcibly requisition this fleet. Thus in the second half of the twentieth century, the United States was able to 'rule the waves' by this tacit policy, that started in the interwar period and culminated in the 1940s and 1950s.[18] Consequently, 'America's hegemonic ascendancy was expressed not through supplanting the European powers and filling the oceans with American flag vessels but rather through constructing a system in which the European merchant fleets could flourish but in which core American interests were safeguarded'.[19]

Greek shipowners were able to exploit the opportunities offered in the United States better than did their main competitors, the Norwegians, who were handicapped by their state's decision to restrict and finally prohibit purchase of foreign vessels in 1949–1950. Norwegians were among the world's main tanker owners in the interwar period and the decision by their state handicapped their international business.[20] It was the Greeks that filled the space. They engaged the U.S., the world's new economic power, as their main trading partner, as they had done with Great Britain in an earlier period. This was the advantage of cross-traders and of tramp owners: By serving international trade rather than the needs of a particular nation, they were able to adjust to changes in the world environment.[21] They were able—and also encouraged by the American credit institutions that financed them—to take advantage of the situation serving simultaneously both American and their own interests.

Among the prime movers of this trend were Aristotle Onassis and a group of Greek shipowners established during World War II in New York. Onassis was among the first to (a) establish the new institution of the global shipping company, a kind of multinational company that was based in many countries and used Panamanian and Liberian companies and flags which meant that it was taxed under the law of these countries; (b) serve the ever-increasing oil industry by contracting long term charters; (c) provide finance from American banking institutions to invest

---

[18] A prime example of an American 'invisible billionaire', Daniel Ludwig. See Shields (1986). For the use of Flags of convenience by American shipowners, see de la Pedraja (1992).
[19] Cafruny (1987, 87).
[20] Tenold (2019, 150–151).
[21] Harlaftis (1993, 43–46).

in shipbuilding, and (d) turn from the American to European shipyards triggering development in the war-torn shipyards of Germany, Britain, France, Belgium, Netherlands and Sweden. Alan Cafruny has argued that 'in formal terms, Flags of convenience are the result of foreign direct investments by multinational companies or independent bulk carrier operators', citing Onassis among the prime examples of the latter category.[22] The use of Flags of convenience was very much frowned upon in the European traditional maritime nations even as late as the 1980s. This practice which paved the way to the global shipping company broke the so-called 'genuine link' between the ship's flag and the nationality of its owner. But this was part of the irreversible globalization trend. By the mid-1980s, however, a quarter of the fleet of the European Community's members were flying flags of convenience.[23] The next sections will reveal the foreign direct investments of Greek shipowners in the German, British and other European and non-European shipbuilding industry concentrating in tankers. In doing so, we contend that the Greek shipowners, acting as a bridge between global and local dynamics, transformed not only the maritime industry, but also the shipping infrastructure of the ports where they established offices, and, most importantly, networks.

Building Tankers in European, American and Asian Shipyards

Greeks were involved in both dry and liquid cargoes but it was the latter and particularly oil and the entrance in the tanker market that brought the apogee. During the decade 1950–1960 they were able to build an extraordinary tanker fleet of 268 tankers, almost 50% of which in the European shipyards. More specifically, as is evident in Table 8.1, Britain and Germany attracted 77% of the Greek shipowners' orders of tankers in European shipyards followed by those of Sweden, the Netherlands, Belgium, France and Yugoslavia. They built 127 tankers in Europe; to this number of ships, one has to add an equally large, and even larger, number of cargo

---

[22]Cafruny (1987, 91).
[23]Tenold et al. (2012, 11).

Table 8.1 Tankers built by Greek shipowners in European, American and Asian shipyards, 1948–1960

Place of shipyards	No. of ships	%	grt	%	nrt	%
Total Europe	127	47	1,945,537	39	3,029,817	37
Great Britain	60	47	831,581	43	1,278,028	42
Germany	38	30	641,536	33	1,019,441	34
Sweden	9	7	160,677	8	250,817	8
Netherlands	7	6	96,244	5	145,067	5
Belgium	5	4	81,581	4	128,638	4
France	4	3	74,644	4	117,786	4
Italy	3	2	45,939	2	70,069	2
Yugoslavia	1	1	13,335	1	19,971	1
Total America and Asia	141	53	3,007,496	61	5,108,663	63
Japan	92	65	1,967,679	65	3,205,102	63
USA	46	33	976,540	32	1,805,596	35
Canada	3	2	63,277	2	97,965	2
General total	268	100	4,953,033	100	8,138,480	100

Source Lloyd's Register of Shipping, 1948–1960; Ioannis Theotokas and Gelina Harlaftis, "Pontoporeia 1945–2000", unpublished database, see Theotokas & Harlaftis

ships. They thus revived the war-torn shipyards of northern Europe. The American shipyards that saw their heyday in the years immediately after the war until the beginning of the 1950s received less than one-eighth of the total orders of tankers. It was the Japanese shipyards that was the new rising Asian player indicating the trend that was to follow in the world shipbuilding industry. The European shipyards received more of their orders during the Korean war, in the first half of the 1950s whereas the Japanese shipyards thereafter.

As the British shipbuilding industry was the most important before World War II and Greek shipowners held representative shipping offices in London since the nineteenth century it was only natural that in Europe most of the orders would be placed with the British shipyards.[24] The shipyards of Furness Shipbuilding Co., Ltd., in Hartlepool, and of Vickers-Armstrongs Ltd., in Newcastle on the river Tyne in north-eastern England, provided more than half of the production of tankers. The rest were built in other eight British shipyards; in Scotts' Shipbuilding & Engineering Co.,

---

[24] Johnman and Murphy (2002).

Ltd., in Blythswood Shipbuilding Co. Ltd. and in Fairfield Shipbuilding & Engineering Co on the river Clyde in Scotland; in Sir James Laing and Sons Ltd., in William Doxford & Sons Ltd. and Bartram & Sons Ltd., in Sunderland, Smith's Dock Co. Ltd., in North Shields and W. Gray & Co. Ltd. in West Harlepool, all in northeastern England. In France in the Societé des Ateliers et Chantiers de France in Dunkirk and Chantiers & Ateliers de St. Nazaire-Penhoët, S.A. at St. Nazaire, in the Ateliers & Chantiers de la Seine Maritime (Worms & Cie) in Trait in north-western France, and in Chantiers Navals de La Ciotat in La Ciotat in southern Mediterranean France. In Sweden they built tankers in Kockums Mekaniska Verkstads Aktiebolag in Malmö and in Uddevallavarvet Aktiebolag in Uddevalla, both in southern Sweden. In the Netherlands, in Nederlandsche Dok & Sheepsbouw Maatschappij V.O.F. in Amsterdam and in N.V. Wilton Fijenoord Dok-en Werf Maats in Rotterdam. In Belgium in J. Boel & Fils and in the Societé Anonyme Cockerill-Ourge and in Italy in the Cantieri Riuniti dell' Adriatico in Trieste. In Germany the three big North Sea ports hosted the largest German shipyards Howaldtswerke A.G. in Hamburg and Kiel and A.G. Weser in Bremen. All the above were traditional long-term business establishments that had built most of the world's fleet carrying an established know-how and tens of thousands of workers. With a large number of shipyards almost destroyed during the war, the flow of orders for advanced technology vessels, backed up with American finance which Greeks secured, contributed to the northern European industrial development.

The 'big five' or the so-called 'golden' Greeks, were the ones that invested in more than 20 tankers each, namely Aristotle Onassis (35 tankers), Stavros Niarchos (40 tankers), Kulukundis brothers (32 tankers), Stavros Livanos (31 tankers) and Petros Goulandris' sons (24 tankers) (see Table 8.2). Other Greek shipowners that ordered about ten tankers each were C.M. Lemos (12 tankers), N.J. Goulandris' sons and Carras. Shipowners like Andreades, Vergottis, Embiricos, Nomicos, Chandris, Lykiardopulo, Papadakis invested in between five and seven tankers and another 18 shipowners in between one and three tankers. All Greek shipowners that ordered tankers were traditional shipowners, meaning that they were second, third or fourth generation into the shipping business. Their families hailed from the traditional Greek shipping islands of Andros

Table 8.2 Tankers built in European and non-European shipyards by Greek shipowners

Name	Total ships	British	German	Swedish	French	Dutch	Belgian	Italian	Yugoslavian	US	Canadian	Japanese
Niarchos	42	24%	17%	12%		5%				17%		24%
Onassis	35	63%	57%		9%					29%		6%
Kulukundis brothers	32		3%	6%		6%			3%	3%		16%
Livanos S.	31	23%	13%		3%	10%	6%			26%		16%
Goulandris P. sons	24									42%	8%	50%
Lemos C.M.	12									8%		92%
Goulandris N.J. sons	10											100%
Carras	10	10%								10%		80%
Andreadis	7	43%										57%
Vergottis	6											100%
Embiricos	6	17%					17%	17%				50%
Nomicos	6	33%										67%
Chandris	5	60%										40%
Lykiardopulo	5	60%	40%									
Papadakis	5	60%	12%	3%			6%	6%				
Other Greeks	33	21%								18%	3%	30%

Source As for Table 8.1

(Goulandris, Embiricos), Kasos (Kulukundis, Papadakis), Cephalonia (Vergottis, Lykiardopulo), Chios (Livanos, Chandris, Carras) and Santorini (Nomicos). The only newcomers in the business were in fact Aristotle Onassis and Stavros Niarchos.

Aristotle Onassis led the way. In the immediate post-World War II era, ensuring a large tanker fleet under the U.S. flag with second-hand vessels from the war-built American fleet, Aristotle Onassis proceeded at the same time into a large shipbuilding programme. For his newbuildings, he firstly turned to the American shipyards, which desperately needed clients after an intensive period of extraordinary shipbuilding during the war. The first tanker Onassis built after the war was in the American Sparrow Point Shipyards in Bethlehem. It was of 11,298 grt and 18,151 dwt, about 3000 dwt bigger than his three Swedish tankers, built almost ten years earlier. *Olympic Games*, delivered in 1948 launched his famous 'Olympic' fleet. Another five tankers were delivered in 1949 and 1950 by the same shipyard; these were much bigger, 28,000 dwt.

In 1951, Onassis turned to European shipyards. The main reason was that he saw an upcoming conflict with the United States government, which was not hospitable anymore to foreign shipowners.[25] In 1951, the FBI had started investigations into his shipping business in New York and his purchases of American tankers from the United States Maritime Commission. This culminated in February 1954, when he was sued by the United States government, for 'illegal purchases' of tankers from the United States Maritime Commission.[26] Stavros Niarchos and the Kulukundis brothers and others were equally accused and sued. As the American government could not make a case of illegal purchases and take to court the Greek shipowners, at the end, settlement agreements were arranged for all. As Rodney Carlisle has argued it was probably the case that Greeks were used as scapegoats by American politicians, a buffer for the internal problems caused by the American shipping businesses and seafarers that saw foreigners like the Greeks and foreign companies like offshore companies take over America's external trade.[27] This policy was

---

[25] Harlaftis (2014).
[26] Harlaftis (2014).
[27] Carlisle (1981) and Harlaftis (2019).

not at all in accordance with the interests of American shipyards. In fact, as Daniel D. Strohmeier, the vice-president of the American Bethlehem yard said to the press prophetically on the event of the launching of Niarchos' *World Glory*, 'Merchant shipbuilding in this country will be all finished by the end of this year. Our situation would be brighter if our public servants in Washington would devote as much energy in helping us to cultivate foreign shipbuilding as they do in driving it away through legal harassment'.[28]

The conflict between the U.S. government and Greek shipowners was a watershed. The Greeks, who were turning to New York as their new and rising entrepreneurial shipping base, all turned their back to the United States and the American shipyards. They proceeded to launch massive shipbuilding programmes in the European shipyards and the newly emerging Japanese ones. The four top Greek shipowners, Onassis, Niarchos, Kulukundis and Livanos, built more than two thirds of their tankers in northern European shipyards. The rest of the Greek shipowners built on average 38% of their fleet in Europe (see Table 8.2). The only exception was the group of companies of Petros Goulandris' sons who built half of their tanker fleet in the United States and the other half in Japan.

By building most of their tankers in British, Dutch, Swedish, French and Belgian shipyards, Greeks followed pre-existing business networks. What is interesting to see here is the turn to the German shipyards. Henry Burke Wend, addressing the early post-war US policy regarding the future of the West German shipbuilding industry, has detailed its shift from the politics of dismantling through reconstruction to prioritizing rearmament. This shift, made possible due to major Cold War considerations, largely contributed to making the shipyards one of the largest exporting industries in the Federal Republic of Germany. Wend's focus on US high politics, however, has left the role of business actors understudied. Who made this shift possible? Moreover, his investigation of the shipyards under US control (namely the shipyards in Bremen, including AG Weser, one of the biggest shipbuilding firms) has excluded the shipyards of the British-controlled ports in Hamburg and Kiel.[29] It was the German-Greek business networks that have been left out until now in the debate on the *Wirtschaftswunder*.

---

[28] Quincy launches largest tanker. 1954. *The New York Times*, 10 February 1954, 31.
[29] Wend (2001).

In 1954, with 963,114 dwt, the West German shipbuilding industry was a major contributor to the German economy, representing over 18% of the world shipbuilding production, second only to Great Britain.[30] The West German shipbuilding industry ranked second to none in terms of export intensity, as foreign contracts represented 54% of its total production.[31] Furthermore, two West German shipyards, Deutsche Werft and Kieler Howaldtswerke, were on the top of the list of the biggest shipyards of the world.[32]

This dynamic growth, which even came to threaten the British supremacy,[33] had not been the case for a long time. In 1952, with 520,172 dwt overall production, the West German shipyards ranked third in the world, representing 11.84%, just above the USA and Sweden (10.64 and 10.34% of world production respectively),[34] whereas in 1950 the shipbuilding production in the newborn Federal Republic of Germany barely exceeded 150,000 dwt.[35] Labelled as the 'forbidden industry', shipbuilding suffered strict restrictions under the Allied controls, and it was not before November 1949 that the Petersberg Agreement lifted most of them, paving the way for its development.[36] Still, German shipyards were in need of capital inflows and in search of contracts and German shipping was able to provide them neither the former nor the latter. Moreover, the war-devastated German shipyards faced not only market dominance from British, the US and Swedish shipyards, but also the French, Italian and Japanese competition.

It was Onassis that made the difference. When in 1951, Onassis turned his back to the American shipyards he targeted the German shipyards for tanker shipbuilding. He brought back to life the shipyards of Hamburg, Bremen and Kiel introducing an amazing shipbuilding programme financed by the New York City Bank of New York. In three years, the three

---

[30] *Schiff und Hafen*, 5, May 1955.
[31] *Schiff und Hafen*, 5, May 1955. *Jahresbericht des Bundesverbandes der Deutschen Industrie 1 Mai 1954–30.* April 1955, May 1955 and *Schiff und Hafen*, 2, February 1955.
[32] *Schiff und Hafen*, 4, April 1955.
[33] *The New York Times*, 19 July 1954.
[34] *Schiff und Hafen*, 5, May 1954.
[35] *Schiff und Hafen*, 9, September 1955.
[36] Boie (1993).

Western German shipyards, Howaldtswerke (Hamburg), Howaldtswerke (Kiel) and A.G. Weser (Bremen) built 18 tankers for him; these were mostly tankers of 21–22,000 dwt. Onassis' orders represented 85% of the Kieler Howaldtswerke tonnage, 62% of the AG Weser and 67.5% of the Howaldtswerke Hamburg tonnage delivered in 1954.[37] These shipyards ranked second, third and fifth respectively in the Federal Republic of Germany and were the second, ninth and 18th top shipyards in the world respectively regarding their production in 1954.[38] These figures show that Onassis's orders literally revived from ashes the war-torn German shipyards, boosting not only their building capacity and employment in the industry, but also technological innovation. The great technologic achievement of the German shipyards and Onassis's technical team received worldwide attention. The launching of the biggest tankers in the world at the time, signalled the transition to ship gigantism.

The size of tankers exploded between the late 1940s and the 1970s. The aim was to achieve economies of scale; the larger the tanker, the lower the cost of transport, the higher the profits. Such economies of scale would not have been possible without shipbuilding technological advancements. These also related to the speed of loading and discharging operations. There were further improvements in the engines, in the design of hull, in propulsion, in the introduction of the bulbous bow, in rudder, in navigation aids, and in hull paints, etc. Technical advances were made inside the hull too; gradually automation reduced the number of crew from over 50 to about 30 seamen. In an interaction of shipyard-shipping company, Greeks contributed to the advancement of tanker ship technology. Among them, Aristotle Onassis was a pioneer. He was the first Greek shipowner to invest in tanker newbuildings before World War I. He was a great believer in European shipbuilding. His first tanker was the *Ariston*, of 15,360 dwt, which was ordered from a Swedish shipyard; it was one of the biggest and technologically advanced tankers of its time.

---

[37] Our calculations include only ships over 4000 dwt. The relevant list published by *Schiff und Hafen*, 4, April 1955.
[38] Ibid.

Ownership of huge ships became a struggle of prestige among the large tanker owners. The tanker that Onassis built ten years later, in 1949, was almost double the size: *Olympic Flame*, 28,385 dwt in the USA. The newspapers in the 'new' and 'old' world were full of articles on shipbuilding in American and European shipyards. The 'invisible millionaire', the American Daniel Ludwig who owned the company National Bulk Carriers had built in the American shipyards five tankers of 30,000 dwt by 1948. In 1952 the *New York Times* presented a tanker 'champion' of 32,500 dwt, the *World Enterprise* built by Vickers-Armstrongs in Newcastle-upon-Tyne. But the reign of the new champion was doomed to be short-lived.[39] Two years later, the German shipyards of Hamburg were in all the news on 24 July 1953 when the largest tanker in the world, *Tina Onassis*, of 46,080 dwt, for which the term 'supertanker' was coined, was launched. The term introduced a new type of tanker that was between 50–70,000 dwt, at the time. It was only superseded by Onassis' *Al-Malik Saud Al Awal*, of his ill-fated *Saudi Arabian Tankers Co*; the supertanker that hoisted the Saudi Arabian flag for a few years was of 47,130 dwt.[40] It was 1104 feet long, high as twelve-storey building.[41]

Onassis continued building supertankers in the German shipyards and his *Olympic Challenger* built in 1960 was 64,750 dwt. As larger ships kept being built, the industry invented more superlatives like the 'mammoths' of 100,000 dwt[42]; Onassis' 'mammoth' *Olympic Fame* was built in 1965 in French Shipyards. When there were no other superlatives, the ships of above 200,000 dwt were called Very Large Crude Carriers (VLCCs) in the late 1960s.

Stavros Niarchos and Manolis Kulukundis tried to surpass Onassis' glory in the German shipyards and built new supertankers themselves. Other traditional Greek shipowners like Stavros Livanos, Diamantis Pateras, Lyras Bros and newcomers like Marchessini also ordered in the German shipyards. But most of the Greek shipowners, including Stavros Niarchos, ordered their ships in Great Britain and in order to fulfill the rapidly

---

[39] *The New York Times*, 27 September 1952.
[40] Harlaftis (2019, Chapter 7).
[41] *The New York Times*, 4 June, 1954.
[42] Ratcliffe (1985, 19–20).

Table 8.3 Loans from American banks for ships purchased, 1949–1959

Dates of purchase	Type of ship	Type of purchase	Number of ships	Loans ($Million)
1949–1954	Tankers	Newbuildings	30	46.6
1958–1959	Tankers	Newbuildings	6	17
Total loans			36	63.6

Source Harlaftis (2019, Table 7.6)

increasing demand for oil transport spread their shipbuilding activities to the Swedish, French, Dutch and Belgian shipyards.

The largest number of the tankers built in European shipyards hoisted the PanHoLib flags. After the international boycott of 1958 against flags of convenience and particularly Panamanian and Honduran flags, Onassis, like the rest of the Greeks, mainly used in his Olympic fleet of tankers the Liberian flag. From 1948 to 1960, he had built 35 tankers, 30 of which, of the latest technology, and of the largest size, were built in Europe.[43] He raised 64 million dollars from the American banks, most of which were channelled in Europe and particularly to Germany (Table 8.3). Equal amounts were drawn by the other leading Greek shipowners, like Stavros Niarchos, from American banks to be invested in the European shipyards.

According to moderate estimates, processing the data compiled by the West German journal *Schiff und Hafen* (which was based on diverse sources), Onassis's share in total orders in German shipyards (1,791,000 dwt) in January 1953 was 24.54%.[44] Onassis's contribution to the revival of West German shipyards is even more impressive in terms of his share in the shipbuilding production. In 1954 West German shipyards launched 11 tankers for Onassis's companies totalling to 250,635 dwt. That is to say that Onassis's share in the West German shipbuilding production that year (963,114 dwt) was 26%. Moreover, his share in the West German total production of tankers (444,000 dwt) was 56.46%, whereas his share in the West German production of tankers for foreign shipping companies (380,216 dwt) was 65.93%.[45]

---

[43] Table 8.3 is based on Harlaftis (2019, Table 7.6).
[44] *Schiff und Hafen*, 11, November 1955.
[45] *Schiff und Hafen*, 5, May 1955 and 9, September 1955.

Onassis' relationship with the German shipbuilding industry originated in the close contacts he had developed with Hamburg since late 1940s for his whaling fleet. It was then that he saw the war-devastated shipyards, the wasted know-how of thousands of workers and shipping engineers, and grabbed the opportunity. Before placing his first orders of tankers in Kieler Howaldtswerke in early 1951, this shipyard had delivered 15 converted whaling ships to Onassis in 1950 (see Table 8.4).[46] Those ships represented a substantial part of the first post-war orders in Howaldtswerke Kiel. Onassis had met Adolph Westphal, the director of Howaldtswerke, thanks to the Norwegian shipowner Anders Jahre,[47] but Onassis and Howaldtswerke seem to have forged an independent business alliance. Certain attributes typical of maritime business networks between shipowners and builders, such as mutual trust and preference at equal prices,[48] seem to apply in this case. The story of the twin supertankers Onassis ordered in Howaldtswerke is most telling: Celebrating the launching of some of his ships in the Kieler Howaldtswerke, Onassis asked Westphal about the costs of building one supertanker and the shipyards director gave a rough estimate. Shortly afterwards, Onassis ordered a twin supertanker, but Westphal asked an amount well above his initial estimate, claiming he had played down the costs in the first place. Though surprised, Onassis placed the second order as well, without further bargaining.[49]

Howaldtswerke were not the only shipyards Onassis maintained close links with. Dr. Kurt W. Reiter, a key figure in the Olympic Maritime, Onassis's agency in Hamburg, had been the first post-war director of AG Weser, Bremen. Furthermore, Onassis was not the only shipping tycoon of Greek origin enjoying a special relationship with West German shipyards. Stavros Niarchos, with orders totalling to 130,000 dwt in Kieler Howaldtswerke and 32,500 dwt in Howaldtswerke Hamburg in late 1952,[50] promised further orders in German shipyards in 1954,

---

[46] Boie (1993). Table 8.4 is based upon data from *Lloyd's Register of Shipping, 1950–1956*. Onassis Business Archive, Alexander S. Onassis Foundation, Minutes of Balleneros Ltd S.A., 1949–1951.
[47] Harlaftis (2014).
[48] See Boyce (2003).
[49] Boie (1993, 61–62).
[50] *Schiff und Hafen*, 11, November 1952.

Table 8.4 The Onassis whaling fleet

Name of ship	Flag	Type of vessel	grt	Date of built	Date of purchase
Olympic Arrow	Honduras	Whaling	702	1944	1950
Olympic Conqueror	Honduras	Whaling	714	1940	1950
Olympic Chaser	Honduras	Whaling	708	1941	1950
Olympic Cruiser	Panamanian	Whaling	699	1943	1950
Olympic Champion	Honduras	Whaling			
Olympic Explorer	Honduras	Whaling	699	1942	1950
Olympic Fighter	Honduras	Whaling	712		1950
Olympic Hunter	Honduras	Whaling	715	1941	1951
Olympic Lightning	Honduras	Whaling	702		
Olympic Rider	Honduras	Whaling	717	1940	1951
Olympic Promoter	Honduras	Whaling	699	1942	1950
Olympic Runner	Honduras	Whaling	715	1940	1950
Olympic Tracer	Honduras	Whaling	406	1949	1951
Olympic Victor	Honduras	Whaling	702	1944	1950
Olympic Winner	Honduras	Whaling	744	1942	1951

Source Gelina Harlaftis (2019). *Creating Global Shipping: Aristotle Onassis, the Vagliano Brothers and the Business of Shipping, c. 1820–1970*. Cambridge: Cambridge University Press Table 7.3; based on Lloyd's Register of Shipping, 1950–1956. Onassis Business Archive, Alexander S. Onassis Foundation, Minutes of *Balleneros Ltd S.A.*, 1949–1951

in case they offered equal prices with their Swedish rivals.[51] Niarchos's orders in the Federal Republic of Germany had not been on the same level with those of Onassis, but their concentration in Howaldtswerke and preference at equal prices imply the existence of network relations

---

[51] *Handelsblatt*, 41, 7 April 1954.

between shipowner and builder. One should note that Stavros Niarchos had a similar shipping business group to Aristotle Onassis. By 1950 they both owned more than 50 vessels each, mainly tankers of about half a million gross registered tonnage.[52]

Greek Shipowners, European Shipyards and International Politics

In Germany, Onassis and Niarchos attempted to extend this network alliance to an investment or ownership tie. As early as 1951, Onassis and Niarchos, participating in a consortium with German firms, bid for the state-owned Howaldtswerke.[53] The purchase of Howaldtswerke became a disputed issue within the federal government and a swift privatization proved impossible. Despite his meeting with Konrad Adenauer and considerable support from certain advisors of the Chancellor, Onassis failed to strike a deal due to opposition of the German finance minister, Fritz Schäffer.[54] Major concerns included the possibility of losing control to foreigners, cutting production capacity and the resulting unemployment in a labour-intensive industry.[55] Moreover, although taking over both Howaldtswerke Hamburg and Howaldtswerke Kiel would be very expensive, the viability of the next best option, their split and the purchase of the premises in Hamburg and Kiel separately, was questionable. After his failure to jointly buy the Kieler Howaldtswerke with Onassis, Niarchos offered a DM 15 million loan to the Kieler Howaldtswerke to take over

---

[52] For Onassis's fleet, see Harlaftis (2019, Appendix 2B). For Niarchos fleet, see The Career of Stavros Niarchos. 1952. *Naftika Chronika*, April 15.
[53] Scholz to Kattenstroth, Howaldtswerke AG, 4 December 1951 and the attachment Bundesministerium der Finanzen (BMF), Veräusserung der Aktien der Howaldtswerke AG, Hamburg, 29 November 1951, Bundesarchiv Koblenz, B102/15552.
[54] CIA to State, Efforts of Onassis to purchase German ship works, 5 August 1954, CIA, Nazi War Crimes Disclosure Act (FOIA)/ESDN (CREST): 519a2b7b993294098d50ffcd; *Hamburger Anzeiger*, 4 May 1954, Bundesarchiv Koblenz, B108/5149.
[55] BMF to Bundeskanzleramt, Verkauf der Howaldtswerke Hamburg AG Hamburg, 19 August 1954 and the attachment Verkauf der Howaldtswerke Hamburg AG Hamburg, undated, Bundesarchiv Koblenz, B108/5149.

Deutsche Werke Kiel, providing financial security to the whole project in exchange for participation in the governing board.[56]

The attempt by Onassis and Niarchos to purchase West German shipyards was an episode of a broader story with far-reaching implications. According to a CIA source, Robert Pferdmenges and Hermann Abs, top bankers close to Adenauer, intended to break the US-British control of oil and shipping fleets and influence Onassis projects with Arabs.[57] Aristotle Onassis had signed with the Minister of Finance of Saudi Arabia El Suleiman and the full consent of King Saud on 20 January 1954 an agreement that brought a global turmoil that brought him against all the oil industry and many states. According to the agreement, which would come into effect on the 9 April 1954, Onassis obtained the right to carry all Aramco (Arabian-American Oil Company) oil in excess of that carried by Aramco's own tankers. Aramco's tankers carried about 10–20% of the total production. The agreement would prohibit the shipment of oil in chartered tankers of other nations.[58]

Although this was a business agreement, it was to be perceived as a threat and a counter attack to the US government, and it did just do that. This agreement went against the agreement of Aramco, the consortium of four large American oil Companies, Standard Oil of New Jersey, Standard Oil of California, Texas Company and Socony-Vacuum Oil Company, with Saudi Arabia, which had provided a monopoly of mining, refining and distribution of oil from 1933 to 2000.[59]

In this context, the launching of *Al Malik Saud Al Awal* in the Howaldtswerke Hamburg, was not just a coincidence. Yet, it was the Aramco case and its far-reaching implications that might have caused this purchase to fail. Although a CIA report, in August 1954, implied an ongoing cooperation between the Onassis and Niarchos,[60] there was a falling

---

[56] Scholz to Graf, Kieler Hütte AG, 23 January 1953, Bundesarchiv Koblenz, B102/75949.

[57] CIA to State, Efforts of Onassis to purchase German ship works, 5 August 1954, CIA, Nazi War Crimes Disclosure Act (FOIA)/ESDN (CREST): 519a2b7b993294098c50ffcd.

[58] Harlaftis (2019, Chapter 7), based on 'Royal Government of Saudi Arabia. Memorial', Alexander S. Onassis Foundation, Onassis Archive, the Government of Saudi Arabia and the Arabian American Oil Company.

[59] FBI, 'Aristotle Onassis', part 4, Bufile 46-17783, Office Memorandum from A. H. Belmont to L. V. Boardman, 'Visit to Middle East and North Africa by Bureau's Army Liaison Representative', 16 June 1954. The Court at The Hague finally passed an agreement in 1958 in favour of Aramco.

[60] Ibid.

out between Onassis and Niarchos particularly in the role the latter had played in the case of the US government vs Aristotle Onassis during this period.[61]

After their split and failure to purchase a shipyard in the Federal Republic of Germany, Onassis and Niarchos, seeking a secure environment they could use as a refuge in times of crisis, decided to invest heavily in Greece. In 1956 Stavros Niarchos established the Hellenic Shipyards and in 1957, he earned a concession for the ten-year operation of a newly built oil refinery, the only such establishment in Greece. At the same time Onassis secured a contract for the operation of Greece's airlines and created Olympic Airways, the only other private airline company after TWA. In the meantime, Onassis and Niarchos had clashed over the concession for the establishment of a big shipyard near Athens. Niarchos won the concession in collaboration with shipbuilders in the Netherlands.[62] Although Onassis had placed emphasis on the Greek character of his investment in contrast with his rival's joint venture with a Dutch shipyard,[63] he also sought technical support from a foreign shipyard, namely Howaldtswerke Kiel.[64] Moreover, Onassis attempted to break Niarchos's alliance with the Dutch shipbuilders, using the previous network relations between him, Niarchos and the German shipbuilders, promoting a joint project with Niarchos's and Howaldtswerke's participation at the latter stage of the negotiations.[65]

Despite the failure of Onassis's project for the establishment of a shipyard in collaboration with Howaldtswerke in Greece, the importance of his proposal should not be neglected. The development of the Greek shipbuilding industry along with the development of other key industries such as the oil industry, chemicals and metallurgy was part of the industrialization and Europeanization strategy put forth by the Greek Prime Minister Constantinos Karamanlis for Greece's convergence with Europe's richest

---

[61] Harlaftis (2014).

[62] Ministry of Coordination, Chronicle of some major contracts, 7 April 1969, Nikolaos I. Makarezos Archive, Institute for Mediterranean Studies-Foundation for Research and Technology Hellas, Rethymno, F275/A; For relevant reportage, see *O Oikonomikos Tachydromos* (19 April, 17 May, 12 July, 2 August and 13 September 1956).

[63] *O Oikonomikos Tachydromos*, 17 May 1956.

[64] *The New York Times*, 16 May 1956.

[65] *O Oikonomikos Tachydromos*, 2 August 1956.

countries. In the formative years of European integration, German-Greek business relations and economic cooperation was a crucial factor that could enhance Greece's competitive advantages through industrial projects and joint ventures. From 1953 on, successive bilateral agreements had aimed at enhancing West German investments in Greek manufacturing and it was in 1958 with the Adenauer-Karamanlis agreement that this process was explicitly linked to Greece's European prospects. Furthermore, Greek shipping tycoons and their international business connections represented a potential source of capital of unique importance to a sluggish peripheral economy that had recently suffered a harsh Axis occupation and a devastating civil war.[66]

It is interesting to note that at the time that Niarchos purchased the Hellenic Shipyards Onassis turned to Britain. From 1957 onwards Aristotle Onassis started buying shares of the British shipyards in Ireland, Harland & Wolff. By 1965 he had reached a total of £1,180,032 out of £4,396,082 representing 26.8% holding of the shipyards' capital. He tried to purchase the whole of the shipyards in the early 1970s with no success; by 1975 he owned one-fourth of the shares.[67] Britain attracted more capital from Greek sources. The traditional shipowners Kulukundis brothers and their group of companies in 1957 purchased half of the shares of the Sunderland shipyards of Austin & Pickersgiel. In April 1948, the Kulukundis brothers had founded together with Basil Emmanuel Mavroleon in London, the *London and Overseas Freighters*, one of the first independent private tanker companies based in Britain in the post-war period. In 1957 *London and Overseas Freighters* owned 50% of the shares of Austin & Pickersgill, and took over the whole company in 1970.

Far from just an episode in their dispute with US authorities in the aftermath of the Korean War, Onassis's and Niarchos's move from the United States to Europe and their heavy investments in Europe had broader implications both on a global and a local European level. On the global level on the one hand, they had challenged and overtaken the main European shipping entrepreneurs until World War II, the British, and on the other they had become the main international carriers of the new hegemonic

---
[66]Harlaftis (2008).
[67]Moss and Hume (1986, 416).

power, the United States. On the European level, their primacy signalled the revival of the European shipyards. Their massive shipbuilding programmes brought Britain to the top of the list of export-intensive shipbuilding countries and second to the German shipbuilding industry, thus contributing to the German economic miracle. Moreover, they played a crucial role in the development of Greece's infant industries, establishing oil refineries, shipyards and airlines, that was an integral part of Karamanlis's industrialization strategy and *sine qua non* prerequisite for Greece's participation in European integration.

Conclusions

In the formative years of the immediate post-World War II period the European shipyards were in need of contracts and investment in order to increase their capacity and efficiency. The Greek shipowners offered them the American finance via the new global institutions they had adopted, offshore companies, and Flags of convenience. Almost all ships built were owned by Panamanian or Liberian companies. The flags hoisted on the vessels were Honduran, Panamanian or Liberian and ran by European crews. Their operating offices and agencies were in North and South America and in Europe. The choices they made were much talked about, frowned upon and at times received great animosity and slander. They chose to create their global shipping empires with offshore companies and flags of convenience and led the way to the global shipping business group that prevails the shipping industry today. Their choices in the 1940s and 1950s were new and unusual. Today they have become common practice in the global shipping business. European and world shipping was transformed in the post-World War II period. The 'new men' in Europe, who changed the face of world shipping and undertook European leadership, were involved in oil and tankers, belonged to the European periphery, they came from Greece and Norway. But it was businessmen from the South of Europe that led the way and helped the North to keep European primacy in global shipping.

Bibliography

Unpublished Sources

Archives of the Federal Bureau of Investigation (FBI), 'Aristotle Onassis'.
Bundesarchiv Koblenz, Germany: B102/15552, and B102/75949.
Bundesarchiv Koblenz, Germany: B108/5149.
Nikolaos I. Makarezos Archive, Institute for Mediterranean Studies-Foundation for Research and Technology Hellas, Rethymno, Greece.
Onassis Business Archive, Alexander S. Onassis Foundation, Athens, Greece.

Published and Online Accessible Sources

Central Intelligence Agency (CIA), Nazi War Crimes Disclosure Act (FOIA)/ESDN (CREST): 519a2b7b993294098d50ffcd. https://www.cia.gov/library/readingroom/. Accessed 30 June 2016.
Foreign Relations of the United States (hereafter FRUS), 1958–1960, VI.

Press and Official Reports

Handelsblatt.
Jahresbericht des Bundesverbandes der Deutschen Industrie 1 Mai 1954–30. April 1955.
Naftika Chronika.
O Oikonomikos Tachydromos.
Schiff und Hafen.
The New York Times.
UNCTAD. 2017. *Review of Maritime Transport.*

Secondary Literature

Achee-Thornton, R., & Thomson, P. (2001). Learning from Experience and Learning from Others: An Exploration of Learning and Spillovers in Wartime Shipbuilding. *The American Economic Review, 91*(5), 1350–1368.

Boie, C. (1993). *Schiffbau in Deutschland 1945–52. Die verbotene Industrie.* Bad Segerberg: Detlefsen.
Boyce, G. (2003). Network Knowledge and Network Routines: Negotiating Activities Between Shipowners and Shipbuilders. *Business History, 45*(2), 52–76.
Cafruny, A. (1987). *Ruling the Waves: The Political Economy of International Shipping.* Berkeley: University of California Press.
Carlisle, R. P. (1981). *Sovereignty for Sale: The Origins and Evolution of the Panamanian and Liberian Flags of Convenience.* Annapolis, MD: Naval Institute Press.
de la Pedraja, R. (1992). *Rise and Decline of US Merchant Shipping in the Twentieth Century.* New York: Maxwell Macmillan International.
Eden, R. J., et al. (1981). *Energy Economics: Growth, Resource and Policies.* New York: Cambridge University Press.
Foreign Relations of the United States (hereafter *FRUS*), *1958–1960*, VI, 980–991 (545) and *FRUS, 1964–1968,* XVI, 174–179 (82).
Harlaftis, G. (1989). Greek Shipowners and State Intervention in the 1940s: A Formal Justification for the Resort to Flags-of-Convenience? *International Journal of Maritime History, 1*(2), 37–63.
Harlaftis, G. (1993). *Greek Shipowners and Greece, 1945–1975: From Separate Development to Mutual Interdependence.* London: Athlone Press.
Harlaftis, G. (1996). *A history of Greek-Owned Shipping: The Making of an International Tramp Fleet, 1830 to the Present Day.* London: Routledge.
Harlaftis, G. (2008). Greek Shipowners and Constantine Karamanlis. In C. Svolopoulos, C. Botsiou, & E. Hadzivassiliou (Eds.), *Constantine Karamanlis in the Twentieth Century, International Conference, June 2007* (Vol. III, pp. 92–112). Athens: Constantine Karamanlis Foundation [in Greek].
Harlaftis, G. (2013). The "J'accuse" of Aristotle Onassis to the Shipowners and the Greek Government in 1947. *Ionios Logos, 4,* 325–400. [in Greek].
Harlaftis, G. (2014). The Onassis Global Shipping Business: 1920s–1950s. *Business History Review, 88*(2), 241–271.
Harlaftis, G. (2019). *Creating Global Shipping: Aristotle Onassis, the Vagliano Brothers and the Business of Shipping, c. 1820–1970.* Cambridge: Cambridge University Press.
Hutchins, J. G. B. (1951). United Merchant Marine Policy and Surplus Ships. *Journal of Political Economy, 59*(2), 117–125.
Ikonomou, H., & Tsakas, C. (2019). Crisis, Capitalism and Common Policies: Greek and Norwegian Responses to Common Shipping Policy Efforts in

the 1960s and 1970s. *European Review of History*. https://doi.org/10.1080/13507486.2019.1592121.

Johnman, L., & Murphy, H. (2002). *British Shipbuilding and the State Since 1918: A Political Economy of Decline*. Exeter: University of Exeter Press.

Marx, D., Jr. (1948). The Merchant Ship Sales Act. *The Journal of Business of the University of Chicago, 21*(1), 12–28.

Metaxas, B. N. (1985). *Flags of Convenience*. London: Gower.

Miller, M. B. (2012). *Europe and the Maritime World: A Twentieth-Century History*. Cambridge: Cambridge University Press.

Moss, M., & Hume, J. R. (1986). *Shipbuilders to the World. 125 of Harland and Wolff, Belfast 1861–1986*. Belfast and Wolfeboro, New Hampshire: The Blackstaff Press.

Perry, H. S. (1946). The Wartime Merchant Fleet and Post-war Shipping Requirements. *The American Economic Review, 36*(2), 520–546.

Ramirez Perez, S. (2010). The European Committee for Economic and Social Progress: Business Networks Between Atlantic and European Communities. In W. Kaiser, B. Leucht, & M. Gehler (Eds.), *Transnational Networks in Regional Integration* (pp. 61–84). Basingstoke: Palgrave.

Ratcliffe, M. (1985). *Liquid Gold Ships: A History of the Tanker, 1859–1984*. London: Lloyd's of London Press.

Rollings, N., & Kipping, M. (2008). Private Transnational Governance in the Heyday of the Nation-State: The Council of European Industrial Federations (CEIF). *Economic History Review, 61*(2), 409–431.

Sawyer, L. S., & Mitchell, W. H. (1973). *The Liberty Ships*. Devon: Newton Abbot.

Shields, J. (1986). *The Invisible Billionaire: Daniel Ludwig*. Boston: Houghton Mifflin.

Stopford, M. (1997). *Maritime Economics*. London: Routledge.

Tenold, S. (2019). *Norwegian Shipping in the 20th Century: Norway's Successful Navigation of the World's Most Global Industry*. Cham: Palgrave.

Tenold, S., Iversen, M. J., & Lange, E. (Eds.). (2012). *Global Shipping in Small Nations: Nordic Experiences After 1960*. Basingstoke: Palgrave.

Theotokas, I., & Harlaftis, G. (2009). *Leadership in World Shipping: Greek Family Firms in International Business*. Basingstoke: Palgrave.

Tsakas, C. (2018). Europeanisation Under Authoritarian Rule: Greek Business and the Hoped-for Transition to Electoral Politics, 1967–1974. *Business History*. https://doi.org/10.1080/00076791.2018.1494156.

Tzamtzis, A. (1984). *The Liberties and the Greeks: The Chronicle of a Peaceful Fleet*. Athens: Estia. [in Greek].

UNCTAD. (2017). *Review of Maritime Transport*.
Wend, H. B. (2001). *Recovery and Restoration: U.S. Foreign Policy and the Politics of Reconstruction of West Germany's Shipbuilding Industry, 1945–1955*. Westport, CT: Greenwood Publishing.

Open Access This chapter is licensed under the terms of the Creative Commons Attribution-NonCommercial-NoDerivatives 4.0 International License (http://creativecommons.org/licenses/by-nc-nd/4.0/), which permits any noncommercial use, sharing, distribution and reproduction in any medium or format, as long as you give appropriate credit to the original author(s) and the source, provide a link to the Creative Commons license and indicate if you modified the licensed material. You do not have permission under this license to share adapted material derived from this chapter or parts of it.

The images or other third party material in this chapter are included in the chapter's Creative Commons license, unless indicated otherwise in a credit line to the material. If material is not included in the chapter's Creative Commons license and your intended use is not permitted by statutory regulation or exceeds the permitted use, you will need to obtain permission directly from the copyright holder.

9

Regional, yet Global: The Life Cycle of Overnight Ferry Shipping

René Taudal Poulsen

Introduction

In the last couple of decades, major geographical shifts have occurred in industries with global competition, and shipping was among the first to experience this. Production has relocated several times to exploit the geographical differentials in labour and capital costs.[1] In 1960 Europe dominated the registration, ownership, management and manning of the world fleet.[2] In subsequent decades, European flags experienced an exodus of tonnage to the open ship registers, while expanding shipowners

---

[1] See Dicken (2015).

[2] Until the middle of the twentieth century, Europe also dominated the global shipbuilding industry, but Asia overtook this position in the second half of the century. On the European decline, see Tenold's chapter in this volume, and Stråth (1987), Lorenz (1991), Johnman and Murphy (2002), and Poulsen et al. (2017).

R. T. Poulsen (✉)
Copenhagen Business School, Frederiksberg, Denmark
e-mail: rtp.si@cbs.dk

and managers from Emerging Maritime Nations such as Singapore, Hong Kong, South Korea and China posed new challenges to European shipping companies, reflecting the acceleration of Asian economic growth. Based on low wages, the Philippines, other South East Asian and Eastern European countries took over the role from Europe as centres for the global supply of seafarers.[3] In short, an eastwards shift transformed the economic geography of shipping.

The causes of Europe's relative decline in the world of shipping have attracted considerable attention.[4] Sturmey's seminal book on British shipping largely attributed the British decline to decisions made by the British shipowners. More recently, Ojala and Tenold attributed Europe's loss of maritime hegemony to the continent's waning position in world politics, the rise of Asia in the global economy and the regulatory innovations associated with the open ship registers.[5] However, they have also reminded us that adaptations by some Greeks, Norwegians and Danes have allowed these nations to continue to play important roles in the global cross trades.

In order to explain geographical shifts in shipping, several analyses of have relied upon the industry life cycle theory, which economist Raymond Vernon publicized in 1966.[6] Originally developed for studies of manufacturing, the theory predicted that companies would compete in different ways and locate in different countries at different stages of a product's life cycle—from early development, over growth and maturity to obsolescence. In the early development or innovation phase, pioneers would locate in high labour cost countries (for Vernon this meant the US) and supply a unique product for demanding customers at home. As demand for the product increased both in the home market and abroad, the technology would gradually diffuse. Late movers would be able to emulate the pioneers' product. As the product matured and finally became standardized, price competition intensified. For this reason, manufacturing would relocate to countries with low labour costs, from where exports to the rest

---

[3] Tenold and Ojala (2017).
[4] Sturmey (1962/2010), Jamieson (2003), and Miller (2012).
[5] Tenold and Ojala (2017) and Ojala and Tenold (2017).
[6] Vernon (1960). See also Dicken (2015, 95–97, 114–15).

9 Regional, yet Global: The Life Cycle of Overnight Ferry Shipping

of the world would occur. Ultimately, demand would fall, as the product entered obsolescence.

The shipping economist Helen Thanopoulou attributed the shifts in the world fleet from Traditional Maritime Nations to open registries and Emerging Maritime Nations in Asia to the product life cycle.[7] The product life cycle has also been used in analyses of the evolution of chemical tanker shipping. During the innovative phase of the life cycle, in the 1950s and 1960s, a combination of cooperation, innovation and vertical integration allowed Norwegian shipowners to build up a global stronghold in the new segment. When chemical tanker shipping matured and services became more standardized, low labour cost newcomers were able to enter the business. The Norwegian pioneers lost some of their competitive advantages, as the segment moved into the standardized phase of the life cycle.[8]

In an industry as global as shipping, the market for ferry services represents a remarkable exception. In fact, there is no global market for ferry services: both in their operations and market structures, ferry services are regional in nature. Year after year, the same ferries transport passengers, cars, lorries and trailers between the same pair of ports. The companies that operate them face only a handful of competitors, if any, and their earnings are much more stable than in the highly volatile global shipping segments.[9] The cargo, of course, differs, as passenger shipping is the only segment where consumers directly face the shipping companies that own the ships—usually, shipping serves business-to-business markets.

In the twentieth century, passenger shipping included three different segments. The first was ferry services for passengers, cars, lorries, trailers and in some cases railway wagons, on short and medium hauls, with voyages lasting between a few minutes and app. 24 hours. The second main segment was the transoceanic liner services for long-haul passenger transportation, such as Southampton–New York, and Genoa–Sydney. The third and final passenger shipping segment was served by cruise lines, where the purpose of travel was holiday onboard, and itineraries of variable

---

[7] Thanopoulou (1995). See also Sletmo (1989).
[8] Murphy and Tenold (2008) and Tenold (2009).
[9] Wergeland (2012).

duration included several port calls and typically followed a circuit.[10] This chapter primarily deals with the first of these three segments.

Although ferries recently represented a mere 0.3% of the world merchant fleet in terms of deadweight, they have fulfilled important infrastructure functions in Northern Europe, the Mediterranean region, the Middle East, Japan, South East Asia, Canada and the Caribbean throughout the twentieth century, and continue to do so in the twenty-first century.[11] However, these markets are regional and appear geographically separate.[12] The question is whether these regional market structures shielded ferry shipping companies against the forces of global competition, which have been so pronounced in the rest of the shipping industry and in many other industries.

In the 1960s, Nordic shipping companies held a prominent position in passenger shipping, as pioneers of overnight car ferry services. Not only did they introduce the most advanced ferries, they also offered innovative onboard services to their passengers. Four decades later, they had arguably lost the edge in service innovation in passenger shipping.

This chapter explores the causes for the Nordic stronghold in ferry shipping and its subsequent decline. Can the decline be attributed to the same processes of global competition as those faced by the rest of European shipping? By studying the evolution of Nordic overnight ferry shipping since 1960, the chapter sheds new light on a previously neglected shipping

---

[10] In the 1950s intercontinental flights started to attract large passenger volumes from the transoceanic liner services, most of which were discontinued in the 1960s or 1970s. Some of the traditional ocean liners regularly found employment in cruise trade, and when the transoceanic lines started to decline, some permanently shifted to the cruise trades. Gradually purpose-built cruise ships became the mainstays of the cruise business. On the evolution of ocean liner and cruise ship designs, see Quartermaine and Peter (2006).

[11] UNCTAD (2016). *UNCTAD Review of Maritime Transport 2016*, p. 31. Capacities for overnight ferries are more commonly measured in terms of gross tons (GT), number of cabins and berths and car deck lane-metres. In 2015, the world fleet of car ferries counted 1222 vessels, ranging from small commuter and shuttle ferries, over large roll-on/roll-off ships with limited passenger capacity to large cruise ferries with relatively small car decks and up to 1200 passenger cabins. On the main regions where ferries are employed, see Louagie (2017).

[12] To the extent that there is competition in addition to other ferry companies, for instance, from other modes of transport, it is also regionally based. Someone wanting to cross the Adriatic from Ancona in Italy to Split in Croatia by ferry are unlikely to consider the North Sea link from IJmuiden in the Netherlands to Newcastle in the United Kingdom or the Alaskan ferry from Juneau to Sitka as alternatives.

niche as well as the manner in which the forces of global competition affect regional markets.

Historiography

Despite their special characteristics and consumer-facing nature, ferry services have received little attention from maritime scholars. One notable exception is a recent textbook chapter by the maritime economist, Tor Wergeland. He observed large variation between routes in terms of customer preferences and vessels deployment, and noted that the fragmented business showed no signs of consolidation. He concluded that '…critical, strategic decisions must be made on a route level, so in a sense each route is a market in itself'.[13] Applying the analytical framework of Porter's Five Forces, Wergeland found a combination of high entry barriers, low competition, high demand growth and low exit barriers, which created a favourable business environment for incumbent firms. Entry barriers existed because companies required access to ferry terminals in central city locations, and often political contacts and local knowledge were required to obtain such access. On most routes, Wergeland saw 'a tendency towards monopoly, or at best oligopoly', although some parallel ferry routes were in more direct competition.[14] Exit barriers were low due to the existence of liquid second-hand and charter markets, where ships were traded and leased, respectively. An important part of this mechanism was that 'less sophisticated markets are happy to take over older tonnage that more sophisticated markets find outdated'.[15] Nordic ferry companies were leaders in terms of advanced tonnage, and Wergeland observed the following 'cascading' pattern:

> Historically, a typical life for a Baltic newbuilding would have been: 1st second-hand sale to Skagerrak or the English Channel; 2nd second-hand

---

[13] Wergeland (2012, 170).
[14] Wergeland (2012, 167).
[15] Wergeland (2012, 176).

sale to the Mediterranean; 3rd second-hand sale to Africa; 4th second-hand sale to Asia, then for demolition.[16]

While Wergeland portrayed many important characteristics of ferry shipping, he did not explain its development, and this topic has attracted only little attention within the maritime economics and transport geography literatures.[17] A few studies have focused on the design of government tenders for subsidized ferry routes (such as island services) or the competitiveness of roll-on/roll-off short sea shipping vis-à-vis road transportation.[18] Within design history, several studies have explored the evolution of ferry designs (i.e., naval architecture and interior designs), and a number of ethnographic studies have been carried out onboard Nordic ferries.[19] However, maritime and business historians have generally not shown great interest in ferry shipping, focusing instead on the naval aspects—war at sea—and cargo shipping.[20]

The most comprehensive study of ferry shipping was published in 2006 by Anders Bergenek and Klas Brogren from ShipPax Information, a maritime publishing and consulting house.[21] Over 441 pages, Bergenek and Brogren presented a systematic and comprehensive overview of the historical development of the extensive network of ferry routes from Sweden. Brogren, a former ferry shipping consultant and journalist, knew the industry very well, but the book lacks references.

Over the last couple of decades, several commissioned histories of ferry shipping companies have been published, and Nordic companies have been particularly prolific in this field.[22] The books were mainly authored

---

[16] Wergeland (2012, 176).
[17] See Luis (2002), Rutz and Coull (1996), Baird (2000), Pantouvakis (2007), Heijveld and Gray (1996), and Baird (1999).
[18] Baird et al. (2011), Baird (2012), Brooks and Frost (2004), and Casaca and Marlow (2005).
[19] On design, see Peter (2004), Peter and Dawson (2010), Peter (2017), and Peter and Id (2017). For ethnographic studies, Hahn-Pedersen et al. (2003, 2004) and Westerlund (2012).
[20] For the mixed fortunes of Nordic cargo shipping companies after 1960, see Tenold, Iversen and Lange (2012). Only the Finnish chapter of the book mentions ferry shipping. On Norwegian shipping, see also Tenold (2019).
[21] Bergenek and Brogren (2006).
[22] Graae (1966), Malmberg and Sjöström (1997), Rinman (1989), Malmberg and Stempehl (2007), Brogren et al. (2012), Tor Line (1985), and Sjöström and Brzoza (2009).

by shipping company employees and maritime journalists, and often published to commemorate corporate anniversaries. Their audiences were the general public, and ferry passengers in particular. A part of the companies' marketing and branding efforts, they were often distributed via onboard shops. A few commissioned histories have focused specifically on individual shipowners and have mainly been directed towards the shipping companies' employees.[23] Unfortunately, the commissioned histories rarely contain references to their sources, which detract from their academic merit. Finally, shipping enthusiast literature has tended to focus on the fates of individual ships.[24]

Methods and Sources

To study the mixed fortunes of Nordic ferry shipping a multiple case study method is employed. The case studies are four overnight car ferry routes: Copenhagen–Oslo, Gothenburg–Kiel/Travemünde, Gothenburg–Great Britain and Stockholm–Helsinki, which served the five largest cities in the Nordic countries, and continuously employed the most advanced and largest ferries, not only in a northern European context, but globally.[25] With the ship as unit of analysis, the chapter reconstructs the life cycles of all the 45 ferries, which were employed on these routes after 1960.[26] Almost all of the 20 largest ferries in terms of gross tonnage and cabin capacity vessels were Nordic ferries throughout the period.

---

[23] Svensson (1986, 1990).
[24] For instance, Widdows (2010, 2011). See also the private webpage www.faktaomfartyg.se for very comprehensive information about the employment of virtually all European ferries since the 1960s (Accessed on 22 July 2018).
[25] Great Britain refers to several ports; Tilbury, Harwich, Immigham, Hull and Newcastle (North Shields).
[26] The analysis focuses on the employment of the ferries during the high season (i.e. the Northern Hemisphere summer). On most routes ferry traffic was highly seasonal. Some ferries were employed on the same routes year round, while others were laid-up or chartered for use as floating accommodation for hotel guests, refugees or oil construction workers during the off-season. On some routes, February was also a busy month due to the winter holidays. Stand-in vessels, which were briefly employed on any of the four case routes, for example, during the dry-dockings of the route mainstays, are excluded from the data set.

The data set is derived from multiple published sources, of which the ShipPax Information represents the key one. Founded by Brogren, ShipPax's first publication appeared in 1974. Gradually expanding, it now provides ferry and cruise market intelligence services and organizes an annual shipping industry practitioner conference, *The Ferry Shipping Conference*. It publishes three annual publications (*Guide*, *Designs* and *Market*) and a monthly newspaper (*Info*) on ferry shipping, for which the audience is ferry and cruise shipping industry professionals.[27] Information on the employment of the individual ferries is also available in several very extensive fleet histories, which have been published by all of the major ferry shipping companies.[28]

To explain the mixed fortunes of Nordic ferry shipping and the changing employments of the 45 ferries, traffic figures provide revealing insights. *Market* and *Statistics* contain detailed traffic statistics on a route basis for 1990 and annually since 1995. It is possible to quality check this with data sets in shipping company fleet histories, ferry shipping company annual reports and national statistical bureaus, which extend back to the early 1960s.[29] Such comparisons show a high degree of accordance between the sources.

Further information is available in annual reports from the publicly listed Nordic ferry shipping companies.[30] They contain detailed corporate information for shareholders, regarding the company's performance (e.g., key financial figures and traffic figures), market situation and strategic considerations. In some annual reports, data for onboard spending per

---

[27] *Guide* contains a full list of ferries world-wide, including technical data (e.g., passenger and car capacity, service speed, gross tonnage) and information on employment, whereas *Designs* provides even more detailed technical data on all new ferries and major conversions as well as interior design reports. In 2000, 64 out of the global fleet of 449 ferries (with more than 99 berths) were employed on ferry routes to the Nordic countries. This represented 14.3% of the global fleet. This estimate is based on the global fleet list published in the supplementary publication to *Guide 00*, which has the title *Pocket Guide* (2000) (Halmstad: ShipPax Information). *Market* contains comprehensive lists of almost all routes and their ferries as well as market reports for the year 1990 and annually since 1995.

[28] Sahlsten et al. (1992), Thorsøe et al. (1991, 2006), and Simonsen and Krogh-Andersen (2016).

[29] For Denmark, see Statistics Denmark (1977–1988). *Danmarks Skibe og Skibsfart 1976–87* (Copenhagen: Danmarks Statistik). For Sweden see Statistiska Central Byrån (various years) *Sveriges Officiella Statistik: Sjöfart* (Stockholm: Statistiska Centralbyrån).

[30] DFDS, Silja Line/Tallink, Viking Line and Stena Line.

passenger and price per ticket, which provides insights on the earning power of the vessels, are also available. These figures are important pieces of evidence for the study of the mixed fortunes of Nordic ferry shipping.

Innovation and Growth, 1960–1990

The Nordic geography is well suited for ferry services, in much the same way as the Mediterranean, South East Asian, Japanese, Caribbean and Canadian coastlines are. In a sense, Sweden, Norway and Finland are island economies, depending on ferry services for international communication, and indeed, passenger ships have plied the Baltic and North Seas for much longer than car ferries. In the nineteenth century, business travellers, politicians and large numbers of migrants sailed on passenger routes over the Baltic and North Seas, and train ferries provided frequent services on many short routes.[31] In the 1930s—in response to the growth of the car economy—the first small drive-through car ferries entered service, offering short day time crossings over the Great Belt, the Øresund, the Kattegat and the Skagerrak.

Car ferries with overnight cabin accommodation were introduced in significant numbers to the Nordic market in the 1960s, coinciding with a period of sustained growth for the Nordic welfare states. The labour market expanded quickly and household incomes in the Nordic countries—and in neighbouring Western Germany—soared. The ownership of private cars also took off.[32] At the same time, new laws provided longer paid holidays for the workforce.[33] Favourable policies, which allowed for duty free sales of alcohol, tobacco, cosmetics and candy onboard ferries on international routes, attenuated the socio-economic growth factors.

Growing welfare and duty free sales provided an ideal cocktail for entrepreneurial shipowners to build up businesses in overnight car ferry

---

[31] For a study on the evolution of the DFDS North and Baltic Seas passenger liner network in the nineteenth and twentieth centuries, see Hahn-Pedersen and Poulsen (2006).
[32] Fellman et al. (2008).
[33] In Sweden, for instance, Parliament enacted a law, which guaranteed all workers three weeks of holidays per year from 1953. In 1963 and 1978, the guaranteed holiday period was extended to four and five weeks, respectively.

shipping. Both existing shipping companies and newcomers were able to grab and form new business opportunities. Companies such as Stockholms Rederi AB Svea, Svenska Lloyd AB, Ångfartygs AB Bore, Finska Ångfartyg, DFDS and Det Bergenske Dampskibsselskab, with origins in nineteenth-century steam-shipping, operated comprehensive networks of passenger routes. To the extent that conventional passenger ships carried cars, these were hoisted onboard in small numbers and stowed in cargo holds. During the 1960s, overnight car ferries, where cars and lorries could roll-on and roll-off easily and quickly, replaced the relatively inefficient, conventional passenger vessels.

The impetus for service innovation, however, came mainly from new players in passenger shipping. The Swedish entrepreneur, Sten A. Olsson entered the Nordic ferry scene in 1962. In a short period of time, his company, Stena Line, attracted substantial numbers of shopping travellers on short day routes between Sweden, Denmark and Germany. Stena Line offered cheap or sometimes free tickets, since earnings were generated mainly from onboard duty free sales.[34] In 1967 Stena Line introduced an overnight car ferry service on the much longer route between Gothenburg and Kiel, and from 1973 two new and larger car ferries offered daily departures in both directions. In the same year a competitor, Sessan Line, introduced an overnight car ferry on a parallel route, Gothenburg–Travemünde. The two companies were also in competition with ferry routes from Scania in Southern Sweden to Germany and the shorter routes from Sweden to Denmark. When Stena Line acquired Sessan Line in 1981, it created a local monopoly on the ferry routes from Gothenburg to Germany and Denmark. It terminated the ferry service to Travemünde to concentrate on Gothenburg–Kiel.

On the Åland Sea, Stena Line also had a brief spell in the 1960s, but other entrepreneurs with similar business models played the key roles here. Carl Bertil Mysten from Swedish Rederi AB Slite, Gunnar Eklund from Vikinglinjen and Ålandsfärjan started short-day car ferry routes with second-hand tonnage on the Åland Sea in the late 1950s, and soon joined forces under the marketing name Viking Line.[35] They had no

---

[34] Bergenek and Brogren (2006).
[35] Svensson (1986, 1990), Harberg (1995), and Karlsson (2007).

prior experience in ferry shipping, but the Åland shipowner community backed them, and introduced novel services to their passengers. Like in the case of Stena Line, tickets were often free to stimulate shopping-based travel, and quickly several new-buildings were introduced. Initially focused on the short Åland Sea routes, Viking Line entered the longer Stockholm–Helsinki route in 1975. Svea, Bore and Finska Ångfartyg, which had operated passenger routes between Finland and Sweden since the nineteenth century, formed Silja Line in 1957. It introduced several car ferries in the course of a few years, and was the first company to provide year-round car ferry services between Stockholm and Helsinki even during the winter season with severe ice conditions.[36]

On the North Sea a newcomer, Tor Line challenged the three incumbents, Ellerman's Wilson Line, Svenska Lloyd and Svea. Backed by a group of Swedish shipping companies, Tor Line introduced two new and fast overnight car ferries between Gothenburg, Immigham and Amsterdam in 1966. The three established shipping companies replaced their conventional passenger ships with three new overnight car ferries on a joint Gothenburg–Hull service in 1966, but the new vessels were costly and suffered from car deck design flaws.[37] According to the commissioned Tor Line history, a 'battle of the North Sea' ensued.[38] Following Tor Line's introduction of two very large and fast overnight car ferries, the *Tor Britannia* and *Tor Scandinavia*, on a service to Felixstowe, in close proximity to London in 1975 and 1976, the competitors withdrew. The two new ferries remained the mainstays on the Swedish North Sea routes for the following three decades.

On the trade between the Danish and Norwegian capitals, DFDS, another shipping line with origins in the mid-nineteenth century, operated a daily passenger service.[39] Here no real contender emerged.[40] In 1957,

---

[36] Malmberg and Stempehl (2007). Silja Line started operating on the Stockholm-Helsinki route in 1972. In 1973 and 1974, Birka Line, an Åland based shipping company, also operated a Stockholm-Helsinki service.

[37] Rinman (1968).

[38] Tor Line (1985).

[39] Graae (1966), Møller (1933), Thorsøe et al. (1991, 2006), and Simonsen and Krogh-Andersen (2016).

[40] Two competing lines briefly operated between Copenhagen and different ports in the Oslofjord area (1966–1968) and between Sandefjord and Hundested (1982).

DFDS introduced the first car ferries, with small car decks with access through side ramps. In the late 1960s, two larger vessels entered service, but the first overnight car ferries with more convenient loading through bow and stern doors entered service on the route as late as 1984.

In the 1960s, traffic volumes climbed quickly on all the routes, often at the rate of 30% annually. Unsurprisingly such growth rates were impossible to sustain (Confer Table 9.1). In the 1970s, annual growth rates were in the range 5–15% despite the slowdown in the Nordic economies after 1973. Ferry shipping was also relatively unaffected by the shipping crisis, which started for crude oil tankers in 1973, and quickly spread to all the other global shipping segments.[41] When tanker, dry bulk and liner shipping companies were struggling for survival, and many Nordic players went out of business, the Nordic ferry companies continued to prosper. Their regional trade shielded them from the volatility of the global freight rates. In the 1980s, growth rates in the passenger volumes were generally below 5%, but the Sweden–Finland routes saw passenger volumes jump by 22–24% annually between 1988 and 1990 in response to the introduction of new ferries.[42]

Even though the Swedish and Finnish capitals were roughly equal in the size to the Danish and Norwegian capitals, the Stockholm–Helsinki routes attracted the highest number of passengers. Annual passenger traffic peaked in 2006 at more than 2.5 million, and bus services extended their catchment area into the interior of Sweden and Finland. On Gothenburg–Great Britain, Gothenburg–Kiel and Copenhagen–Oslo annual passenger traffic peaked at 335,000, 934,000 and 817,000 in 1981, 1997 and 2002, respectively.[43]

Nordic shipowners responded to growth with frequent investments in new and larger vessels. Many of the first-generation car ferries soon proved unsuitable for the traffic for which they were designed. Either car decks had insufficient height, or cabin capacity turned out to be too small. Moreover, they often lacked sufficient numbers of cabins with en suite bathrooms.

---

[41] Tenold (2006).
[42] Tenold et al. (2012).
[43] Statistics Denmark (various years) *Danmarks Skibe og Skibsfart* (Copenhagen: Danmarks Statistik); SCB (various years) *Sveriges officiella statistik: Sjöfart* (Stockholm: Statistiska Centralbyrån/SCB); ShipPax Information (various years) *Markets* and *Statistics* (Halmstad: ShipPax Information).

9 Regional, yet Global: The Life Cycle of Overnight Ferry Shipping

Table 9.1 Decadal changes in the annual number of passengers carried, in percent, by route

	1960s	1970s	1980s	1990s	2000s	2010s[d]
Copenhagen–Oslo[a]	207%	33%	29%	49%	−5%	5%
Gothenburg–Great Britain[b]	207%	113%	5%	−48%	−30%	No service
Gothenburg–Germany	81%	187%	41%	−35%	0%	3%
Stockholm–Helsinki	N/A	N/A	N/A	11%	−10%	−4%
Stockholm–Finland[c]	−19%	250%	59%	20%	3%	−11%
Sweden–Finland[e]	272%	106%	46%	16%	5%	−5%

[a]The 1960s cover 1961–1969 only. The 1970s cover 1972–1979 only. The 1980s includes 1990
[b]The 1960s cover 1961–1969 only. The 1980s cover 1980–1988 only. The service was discontinued in 2006
[c]The 1960s cover 1965–1969 only. The 1980s cover 1980–1988 only
[d]The 2010s cover 2010–2017 only. For Gothenburg–Germany, 2010–2016 only
[e]Figures for Finnlink's Kapellskär–Naantali service are missing for 1999 and 2000
Source Statistics Denmark (various years) *Danmarks Skibe og Skibsfart* (Copenhagen: Danmarks Statistik) for Copenhagen–Oslo for the 1960s, 1970s and 1980s. SCB (various years) *Sveriges officiella statistik: Sjöfart* (Stockholm: Statistiska Centralbyrån/SCB) for all routes calling at Swedish ports for the 1960s, 1970s and 1980s. ShipPax Information (various years) *Markets and Statistics* (Halmstad: ShipPax Information) for all routes for the 1990s, 2000s and 2010s

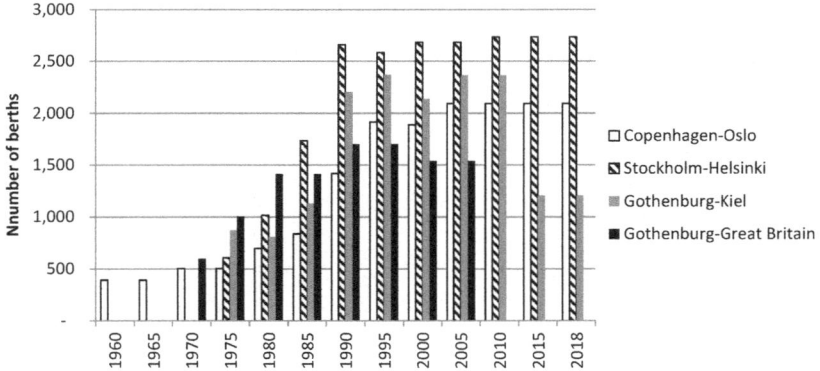

Fig. 9.1 Average number of cabin berths per vessel, by route, 1960–2018 (*Source* Compiled on the basis of ShipPax Information [various years] *Guide*, *Designs* and *Market*, and corporate fleet histories)

Average vessel sizes on the four premier Nordic routes climbed quickly (Fig. 9.1). The ferry shipping companies were able to order new ferries at relatively low prices in shipyards, which were struggling to find new orders due to the crisis.

At the same time, onboard services improved. The ferry generation of the 1980s provided a greater diversity of buffet and à la carte restaurants, bars, casinos and show lounges, swimming pools, and saunas. Tellingly, ShipPax's publications *Guide* and *Designs* on innovative passenger ships focused almost entirely on the Nordic ferries during this period.

Although ferries were designed for specific routes, the owners could still reposition them to secondary routes within their networks. DFDS redeployed vessels from their main routes to secondary routes such as Esbjerg–Torshavn, and Silja Line redeployed old vessels to secondary routes in the Gulf of Bothnia. From the 1960s to the 1990s, several Nordic overnight car ferries were also employed by their owners as cruise ships in the Norwegian Fjords, the Canary Islands, or the Mediterranean during the low season.[44] The Nordic ferries had accommodation of such high quality, that they could offer cruise services to passengers on voyages of several days' duration. This illustrates the high level of service and designs

---

[44]Thorsøe et al. (1991), Malmberg and Stampehl (2007), and Sjöström and Brzoza (2009).

9 Regional, yet Global: The Life Cycle of Overnight Ferry Shipping

of such vessels, which often equalled or exceeded those found on some cruise ships of the period.[45] Former Nordic ferries also found new employment in the North American cruise trades, which emerged in the 1960s and 1970s, a testament to the service innovations in the Nordic business.[46]

When the Nordic lines no longer needed the oldest and smallest ships in their fleets, a liquid second-hand market allowed them to dispose of the vessels for further trading elsewhere. As observed by Wergeland, ferries tended to migrate southwards and then eastwards as they aged (See examples in Table 9.2). Nordic ferries transferred to routes to the British Isles and in the Mediterranean in particular. On the long routes across the Adriatic, from Greece to Italy, and from the European mainland to Corsica and Sardinia, the superfluous Nordic ferries from the 1960s and 1970s proved ideal. Their car and passenger configuration worked well in this context, and in terms of distance and duration the Mediterranean routes resembled the Nordic ones. Most notably, Moby Line of Italy was a frequent buyer of Nordic tonnage. In 2018, six out of Moby Line's nine overnight car ferries originated from Northern Europe.[47] Meanwhile, some of the former Nordic ferries from the 1960s and 1970s had left the Mediterranean, in accordance with the patterns observed by Wergeland. Towards the end of their careers, they found employment in the Red Sea pilgrim trades or in the casino cruise business in the Pearl River Delta, and elsewhere in South East Asia. Even though ferry service markets were regional, the

---

[45] Peter (2004, 2017), Peter and Dawson (2010), and Peter and Id (2017). Several Nordic ferry shipping companies, including Bergenske, DFDS, Lion Ferry, Bore, Rederi AB Sally and Silja Line parent EffJohn International ventured into the dedicated cruise shipping markets at different points in time. None of them, however, was able to leverage the passenger shipping experiences in such a way that they could keep a long-term, profitable presence in cruise shipping. None of the current top four cruise lines, which dominate the global cruise shipping market, ever engaged in ferry shipping.

[46] Due to a location at high northern latitudes, the Nordic countries are widely known for long and dark winters. This has not prevented two cruise lines (Scandinavian World Cruises and Norwegian Cruise Lines) from emphasizing their Nordic origins in marketing and vessel names. In 1982, for instance, Scandinavian World Cruises introduced a former Baltic Sea ferry in the Florida cruise trade for sun-seeking Americans and renamed it the *Scandinavian Sun*.

[47] Louagie (2017).

228 R. T. Poulsen

Table 9.2 Employment of selected ferries, 1957–2018

Original name of vessel	Prinsesse Margrethe	Tor Anglia	Saga	Kong Olav V	Svea Regina	Stena Scandinavica	Prinsessan Birgitta	Tor Britannia	Svea Corona	Mariella	Silja Serenade	Crown of Scandinavia
1957	1.3.											
1958	1.3.											
1959	1.3.											
1960	1.3.											
1961	1.3.											
1962	1.3.											
1963	1.3.											
1964	1.3.											
1965	1.3.											
1966	1.3.	1.2.										
1967	1.3.	1.2.	1.2.									
1968	1.3.	1.2.	1.2.	1.3.								
1969	1.2.	1.2.	1.2.	1.3.								
1970	1.3.	1.2.	1.2.	1.3.								
1971	1.2.	1.2.	1.2.	1.3.								
1972	1.1.	1.2.	1.3.	1.3.	1.1.							
1973	1.1.	1.2.	1.3.	1.3.	1.1.	1.3.	1.3.					
1974	1.1.	1.2.	1.4.	1.3.	1.1.	1.3.	1.3.					
1975	1.1.	1.3.	1.4.	1.3.	1.1.	1.3.	1.3.	1.2.	1.1.			
1976	1.1.	3.1.	2.	1.3.	1.1.	1.3.	1.3.	1.2.	1.1.			

Original name of vessel	Prinsesse Margrethe	Tor Anglia	Saga	Kong Olav V	Svea Regina	Stena Scandinavica	Prinsessan Birgitta	Tor Britannia	Svea Corona	Mariella	Silja Serenade	Crown of Scandinavia
1977	1.1.	3.1.	2.	1.3.	3.1.	1.3.	1.3.	1.2.	1.1.			
1978	1.1.	3.2	2.	1.3.	1.1.	2.	1.3.	1.2.	1.1.			
1979	8.	8.	2.	1.3.	1.1.	2.	1.3.	1.2.	1.1.			
1980	6.	1.4.	2.	1.3.	3.2.	2.	1.3.	1.2.	1.1.			
1981	6.	2.	2.	1.3.	8.	2.	1.3.	1.2.	1.1.			
1982	6.	3.1.	1.1.	1.3.	3.2.	2.	1.3.	1.2.	1.1.			
1983	6.	3.1.	1.1.	1.3.	3.2.	2.	1.3.	1.2.	1.1.			
1984	6.	3.1.	1.1.	5.1.	5.2.	2.	1.3.	1.2.	1.1.			
1985	6.	3.1.	3.2.	5.1.	5.2.	2.	1.3.	1.2.	5.2.	1.1.		
1986	6.	3.1.	3.2.	5.1.	5.2.	2.	1.3.	1.2.	7.	1.1.		
1987		3.1.	3.2.	5.1.	5.2.	2.	1.3.	1.2.	5.1.	1.1.		
1988		3.1.	3.2.	5.1.	5.2.	2.	2.	1.2.	5.1.	1.1.		
1989		3.1.	3.2.	5.1.	5.2.	2.	3.1.	1.2.	5.1.	1.1.		
1990		3.1.	3.2.	5.1.	1.1.	2.	1.2.	1.2.	5.1.	1.1.	1.1.	
1991		3.1.	3.2.	5.1.	1.1.	2.	1.2.	1.2.	5.1.	1.1.	1.1.	
1992		3.1.	3.2.	5.1.	1.1.	2.	1.2.	1.2.	8.	1.1.	1.1.	
1993		3.1.	3.2.	5.1.	1.1.	2.	1.2.	1.2.	8.	1.1.	1.1.	
1994		3.1.	3.2.		1.1.	2.	1.2.	1.2.	8.	1.1.	1.1.	1.3.

(continued)

Table 9.2 (continued)

Original name of vessel	Prinsesse Mar-grethe	Tor Anglia	Saga	Kong Olav V	Svea Regina	Stena Scandi-navica	Prinsessan Birgitta	Tor Britannia	Svea Corona	Mariella	Silja Sere-nade	Crown of Scan-dinavia
1995		3.1.	3.2.		1.1.	2.	1.2.	1.2.		1.1.	1.1.	1.3.
1996		3.1.	3.2.		1.1.	2.	1.2.	3.1.		1.1.	1.1.	1.3.
1997		3.1.	3.2.		8.	2.	1.2.	1.2.		1.1.	1.1.	1.3.
1998		3.1.	3.2.		8.	2.	1.2.	1.2.		1.1.	1.1.	1.3.
1999		3.1.	3.2.		6.	8.	1.2.	1.2.		1.1.	1.1.	1.3.
2000		3.1.	3.1.		6.	8.	1.2.	1.2.		1.1.	1.1.	1.3.
2001		3.1.	3.2.		6.	8.	1.2.	1.2.		1.1.	1.1.	1.3.
2002		3.1.	3.2.		6.	8.	3.2.	1.2.		1.1.	1.1.	1.3.
2003		3.1.			6.	3.2.	3.2.	1.2.		1.1.	1.1.	1.3.
2004		3.1.			6.	3.1.	3.2.	3.2.		1.1.	1.1.	1.3.
2005		3.1.				8.	3.2.	3.2.		1.1.	1.1.	1.3.
2006		3.1.				8.	3.2.	3.2.		1.1.	1.1.	1.3.
2007		3.1.					3.2.	3.2.		1.1.	1.1.	1.3.
2008		3.1.					3.2.	3.2.		1.1.	1.1.	1.3.
2009		3.1.					3.2.	3.2.		1.1.	1.1.	1.3.
2010		3.1.					7.	3.2.		1.1.	1.1.	1.3.
2011		7.					7.	3.2.		1.1.	1.1.	1.3.
2012		7.					7.	3.2.		1.1.	1.1.	1.3.
2013		7.					7.	3.2.		1.1.	1.1.	1.3.
2014		7.					7.	3.2.		1.1.	1.1.	1.3.
2015							7.	3.2.		1.1.	1.1.	1.3.
2016							7.	3.2.		1.1.	1.1.	1.3.
2017							7.	3.2.		1.1.	1.1.	1.3.
2018							3.2.	3.2.		1.1.	1.1.	1.3.

9 Regional, yet Global: The Life Cycle of Overnight Ferry Shipping

Legend

Code	Trade
1.1.	Northern Baltic
1.2.	North Sea
1.3.	Skagerrak
1.4.	Southern Baltic
2.	UK (excl. North Sea)
3.1.	Western Mediterranean
3.2.	Eastern Mediterranean
4.1.	Mediterranean or West Africa (cruises)
4.2.	Americas (cruises)
4.3.	Americas (ferry services)
5.1	China (incl. Hong Kong)
5.2.	South East Asia (cruises)
5.3.	India
6.	Red Sea
7.	Floating accommodation
8.	Laid up/undergoing repair/unknown trade

second-hand market was clearly global. A northwards move of second-hand ferries never occurred. In this way, the migration patterns of ferries reflected general patterns in the global economy.[48]

Maturity, 1990–1999

Around 1990, Nordic ferry shipping was at its peak—both in terms of service innovation and passenger volumes. In particular, the Sweden-Finland trades boomed. Numerous new ships entered service on the Åland Sea, and for every new ship, new service features appeared.[49] Onboard business conferences facilities had first been introduced in the 1960s to attract a new clientele, but with the ferries of the early 1990s they reached a new scale and standard. Moreover, the ferries featured a much wider variety of restaurants, bars and casinos, as well as larger swimming pools and recreational facilities. In 1990, the *Silja Serenade* entered service on the Stockholm–Helsinki route and introduced the most innovative feature of them all—a 140-metre-long internal promenade split almost the entire superstructure in two. This allowed for a large variety of shops and restaurants along the promenade and from cabins on four decks above, passengers had unrestricted views over the promenade. Internal cabins, which had always sold at lower prices than outside cabins, suddenly became very popular among the passengers. In some cases, they sold out before the outside ones.[50] In terms of service offerings, the *Silja Serenade* and its sistership, the *Silja Symphony*, were ahead of even the most advanced cruise ships at

---

[48]Out of the more than 40 overnight ferries currently employed in the Nordics, only the *Stena Germanica* and *Stena Scandinavia* entered service outside the Nordic region (on Stena Line's Harwich–Hoek van Holland route). In 2010–2011, Stena Line redeployed the two on the Gothenburg–Kiel route. In same fleet, the *Pearl Seaways* and *Silja Europa* have returned to Nordic ferry routes after spells as cruise ship and floating accommodation in Asia and Australia, respectively.

[49]The new Stockholm–Helsinki ferry *Silja Europa* was the first to introduce an onboard McDonald's. The onboard report from the vessel, published by Plus 2 Ferry consultation in *Designs 93* made the following observation: 'It has been asked if a McDonald's really suits a ship on which people travel for no other reason than to wine and dine, but when the doors open at 2 pm (four hours before departure) the place becomes something of a magnet drawing not only passengers, but also staff from shore' (p. 21).

[50]Brogren (1991).

9 Regional, yet Global: The Life Cycle of Overnight Ferry Shipping

the time. In an interview, Hans Christner, CEO of Effjohn International, the owner of Silja Line, said:

> We have cruising companies onboard the new Silja-ferries, who spontaneously said that they would be 'money-machines' on 3- and 4-day cruises. And it is with this 'parachute' function we designed the ferries in case everything would go wrong.[51]

The two ferries have remained on the Stockholm–Helsinki route ever since, and Christner was right in his observation on the potential for new features in the cruise business. Subsequently, several cruise ships introduced the promenade feature, closely emulating the *Silja Serenade*.[52]

In the early 1990s, a slowdown occurred in the Swedish and Finnish economies. The breakup of the Soviet Union negatively affected Finnish exports and a Swedish banking crisis contributed to the slowdown.[53] On the Sweden–Finland routes, a large oversupply of passenger capacity was a consequence. In 1990, Viking Line's ferries completed 994 voyages between the two capitals in just one year.[54] Every second evening, two Viking Line and one Silja Line ferry, with overnight capacity for almost 8000 people, departed almost simultaneously from Stockholm to Helsinki.[55] This was too much. And the new ships had been acquired at high prices. Due to the bankruptcy of the Finnish shipbuilder, Wärtsilä Marine, which supplied most of the new vessels, the prices increased significantly after most of the contracts had been signed.[56] Not only did Silja Line and Viking Line compete against each other. Even within Viking Line an element of competition existed, as the ownership of the ferries and investment decisions were entirely in the hands of the two owners,

---

[51] Quote by Brogren (1991, 121).
[52] Royal Caribbean Cruise Line's *Voyager of the Seas* from 1999 was the first cruise ship to adopt the mall, and many subsequent ships have taken up the feature. See Brogren (2000, 205–207; 2010).
[53] Fellman et al. (2008).
[54] Brogren (1998, 105).
[55] In the same evening, another five large ferries and passenger vessels would depart from Stockholm for Mariehamn and Turku in Finland.
[56] Peter and Id (2017, 172–178), Sjöström and Brzoza (2009, 165–170), and Brogren (1991, 120).

Rederi AB Slite and SF Line.[57] In 1993 Slite filed for bankruptcy, and left Åland-based SF Line as the sole owner of Viking Line. The Slite fleet was redeployed to the Southern Balticand UK routes, and in cruising from Hong Kong and Singapore. In the latter case, the new owners converted the car decks into large casinos and subsequently had purpose-built cruise ships derive from the ferry designs.[58]

Further setbacks to the entire ferry business occurred, when two ferries were lost at sea. In April 1990, the *Scandinavian Star* caught fire while *en route* from Oslo to Frederikshavn in Denmark, and 159 people perished onboard. The police suspected arson, and the case has remained controversial ever since. In September 1994, the *Estonia*, the flagship of the Tallinn–Stockholm route, capsized in the matter of a few minutes, causing the death of 852 passengers and crew members. With good reason, the losses brought the question of ferry safety to the front pages of newspapers and high in the general public's attention. The United Nations' International Maritime Organization subsequently tightened safety regulation for ferries.

Throughout the 1990s, traffic volumes stagnated (Table 9.1), and fleet renewal came to a halt. The shipping companies fine-tuned onboard service offerings, and regularly upgraded cabins, restaurants and other public spaces. In the Baltic Sea, the fall of the Iron Curtain, which opened the Baltic States to ferry shipping, partly offset stagnation on the established routes. New routes to Tallinn from Helsinki and Stockholm boomed and provided new revenue streams for Silja and Viking Line, as well as a newcomer, Tallink.[59]

In the 1980s and 1990s, passenger traffic continued to build up on the Copenhagen–Oslo route. In 1983, DFDS had introduced the *Scandinavia* on the route in a defensive move. Built for a new DFDS cruise venture in the US, the vessel threatened the very existence of the company. The US cruise venture went badly wrong, and DFDS repositioned the ship to the

---

[57] Eliasson (2005, 135–147) provides a reprint of the Viking Line strategy dating from 1987. It reveals the competitive dynamic between the two owners.

[58] Brogren (1993, 57–60; 1999).

[59] For a personal account of the introduction of ferry shipping services to the new Baltic States after 1990, see Tolstrup (2012).

Copenhagen–Oslo route to cut losses.⁶⁰ The vessel was too costly to run on this route and DFDS soon sold it to a US cruise company. However, the *Scandinavia* demonstrated the expansion potential of the route. With the right tonnage, DFDS could attract significant numbers of mini-cruise passengers.⁶¹

On Gothenburg–Kiel annual passenger volumes stabilized around 850,000 passengers in the 1990s, but Stena Line achieved further volume growth through acquisitions. In 1989 and 1990, respectively, it acquired the Dutch Crown Line and Sealink British Ferries, thus extending its network to the English Channel and the Irish Sea.⁶² The growing route network gave Stena Line economies of scale in its administration and procurement, and gave it more opportunities for redeployment of its vessels.

Decline After 1999

In the 1990s, the market reports focused strongly on new challenges caused by the imminent opening of new tunnels or bridges across the English Channel (in 1994), the Great Belt (in 1998) and the Øresund (in 2000), as well as and the European Union's planned abolition of duty free sales. The fixed connections, which were in direct competition with the daytime ferries on short routes, were not a major concern for the overnight ferry lines. The EU's planned abolition of duty free sales, however, posed a major strategic challenge to them. For almost a decade, European ferry shipowners lobbied against the EU decision, arguing that many jobs were at stake and road congestion would ensue.⁶³ However, the lobbying efforts were unsuccessful and in 1995 the market report in *Guide 95* indicated that the 'shipping industry has already given up and believe that the battle will be lost in 1999'.⁶⁴ Indeed, this prediction proved correct, and the

---

⁶⁰Lange (1995, 296–316).
⁶¹In 1989, 1990, 1994 and 2002, and it therefore introduced new ferries, three of which originated from the Stockholm–Finland trade.
⁶²Stena Line AB annual reports (1988–1990), Brogren et al. (2012, 217–247).
⁶³Brogren (various years, 1990–1999) Brogren et al. (2012, 249–253, 295–301); Bergenek and Brogren (2006, 294–299).
⁶⁴Brogren (1995, 118).

termination of duty free sales between EU ports occurred on 30 June 1999.

Immediately, the termination strongly affected Stena Line's earnings. Overnight passenger volumes decreased by more than 25% on most routes and onboard spending on the Scandinavian routes dropped from 278 SEK to 156 SEK per passenger between 1998 and 2000.[65] On the Gothenburg–Kiel route, half of the passengers disappeared between 1998 and 2000. Stena Line's annual revenues contracted by 1 billion SEK, and the company made a loss of more than 600 million SEK in 2000.[66] According to Dan Sten Olsson, CEO, 'Stena Line could not survive as a publicly listed shipping company'.[67] In 2001, the Olsson family's Stena Group took over Stena Line.[68] The Stena Group had diversified in offshore drilling, tanker and ro/ro shipping, real estate and recycling. While the ferry operations were loss making, the other businesses generally remained profitable.[69]

Stena Line immediately responded to the abolition of duty free sales with ticket price increases. Customers with lorries or trailers and travellers with cars usually accepted this, but the price-sensitive shopping passengers did not.[70] In the longer term, Stena Line focused increasingly on trailer traffic, which continued to grow. It maintained passenger services, albeit at a reduced level, and through cost reduction programmes, it gradually returned to profitability.[71] On some routes, Stena Line introduced new, so-called ro-pax vessels, with high trailer intake and reduced passenger accommodation. On the Gothenburg–Kiel route, this happened in 2010–2011. The two replacement ferries reduced passenger capacity by approximately 50%, but trailer capacity grew by more than 150% (Fig. 9.2). Of the four case routes in this study, the Gothenburg–Kiel route is the only one where a major fleet renewal has taken place in the

---

[65] Brogren et al. (2012, 328).
[66] Stena AB annual report 2000, 4–5.
[67] Stena AB annual report 2000, 4–5.
[68] Stena AB annual reports 1999, 2000. The Stena Group had also owned Stena Line until the stock-listing in 1988.
[69] Stena AB annual reports 2000–2008.
[70] Stena AB annual report 2000, 4–5.
[71] Stena AB annual reports 2008–2016.

9 Regional, yet Global: The Life Cycle of Overnight Ferry Shipping

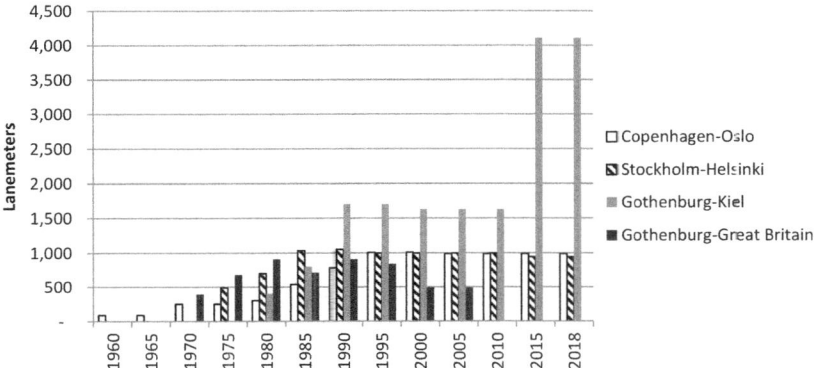

Fig. 9.2 Average number of lane metres per vessel, by route, 1960–2018 (*Source* ShipPax Information [various years] *Guide, Designs* and *Market* and corporate fleet histories)

twenty-first century, and the only one, which succeeded in attracting large trailer volumes to the ferries.

The second—and more fundamental—challenge that all ferry routes faced, came from above. It resembled the situation that transoceanic passenger lines had experienced five decades earlier: competition from airlines. From the late 1990s, several low-cost airlines conquered market shares for passengers' travel.[72] Ryanair and EasyJet, the latter with a Greek shipowner as investor, were the most famous, and benefitted from liberalization in European airline markets.[73] Air travellers saved time and money, and avoided the sometimes rough waves on the North and Baltic Seas. The effects were the strongest on the North Sea, where almost all overnight ferry services disappeared within about a decade.[74] In response to the abolition of the duty free sales and airline competition, DFDS discontinued the Gothenburg–Harwich route, and added a call in the non-EU port of Kristiansand in Norway on the Gothenburg–Newcastle route. Despite continuation of duty free sales, DFDS was disappointed

---

[72] Francis et al. (2006) and Dobruszkes (2013).
[73] The effects of discount airlines on demand for ferry services are discussed in market reports by Brogren (1998–2006). On the liberalization of airlines in Scandinavia, see Sjögren (2015).
[74] Only the routes IJmuiden–Newcastle, Hull–Rotterdam, Hull–Zeebrugge and Harwich–Hoek van Holland remained.

with the results.[75] In 2006, DFDS closed the last passenger service from Gothenburg and sold the last vessel to further trading in the Mediterranean. Instead, it focused on expanding the much more profitable pure roll-on/roll-off freight routes in the North and Baltic Seas.[76]

Duty free sales continued on the Copenhagen–Oslo route, but even here, stagnation set in. Since the late 1990s, the annual passenger traffic on Copenhagen–Oslo has hovered around 770,000, with only small fluctuations and a flat trend line (Table 9.1). The service remains highly profitable, however.[77] In the Stockholm–Helsinki route, passenger trends were in decline after the turn of the millennium. Sweden and Finland had joined the EU in 1996, but the economy of the Åland islands was highly dependent on the ferry business and gained an EU-exemption to continue the duty free sales. Stockholm–Helsinki vessels deviated, to include a call at Åland in the middle of the night. While hardly any passengers disembarked or even noted the night-time call, the manoeuvre enabled Viking and Silja Line to continue duty free sales. Without the Åland exemption, it is clear that the Stockholm-Finland trade would not have continued to sustain the current passenger volumes.

On the Stockholm–Helsinki and Copenhagen–Oslo routes, the current fleets were designed in the early and mid-1980s. Public spaces and cabins on these ferries have been upgraded regularly, but effectively no service innovations have been introduced.[78] In 2018, the average age of the remaining Nordic ferries was historically high (Fig. 9.3). On the Copenhagen–Oslo and Stockholm–Helsinki routes, it approached 27 and 29 years, respectively. In comparison the global average age for bulk carriers, container ships and tankers was 8.8, 11.6 and 18.8 years, respectively.[79] Currently the age of the Nordic ferry fleet is on the same level as the fleet of cargo ships flagged in developing countries (29 years). This appears as a remarkable turn of events. In general, merchant ships flagged in developing economies are on average 10 years older than those flagged

---

[75] DFDS annual reports (2002–2006).
[76] DFDS annual reports (2005–2017).
[77] DFDS annual report (2017, 29).
[78] ShipPax Information (2014, 120–121) contains information on the upgrading of the *Silja Serenade* and *Silja Symphony* after almost two and half decades of service on the Stockholm–Helsinki route.
[79] UNCTAD (2017, 27). Calculations are based on number of ships, not deadweight.

9 Regional, yet Global: The Life Cycle of Overnight Ferry Shipping

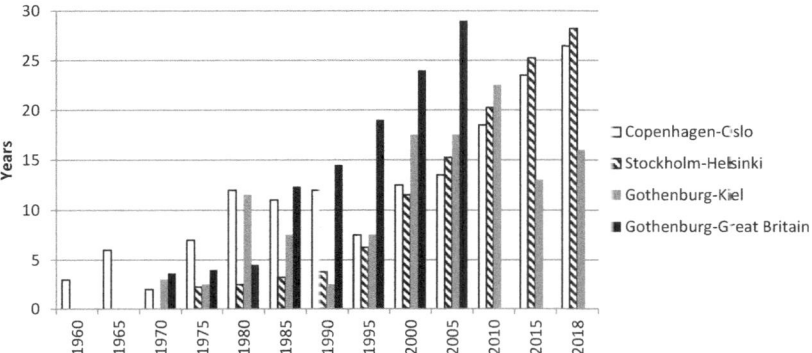

Fig. 9.3 Average age of vessels (in years), by route, 1960–2018 (*Source* ShipPax Information [various years] *Guide*, *Designs* and *Market* and corporate fleet histories)

in developed economies.[80] On average the 45 ferries in the studied sample were withdrawn and recycled after approximately 35 years of service. For the shipping companies vessel age means lower capital costs, but also higher maintenance costs. It seems not unlikely the current, Nordic ferry fleet is approaching the later stage of its life cycle.[81]

The decline in Nordic ferry shipping coincided with a historical boom in the global shipping markets. In the early 2000s, freight rates for tankers, dry bulk carriers and container vessels skyrocketed in particular due to the rapid growth of the Chinese economy. Shipowners responded with large-scale contracting of new-buildings, many of which only entered service after the Financial Crisis of 2008 caused the global freight markets to collapse. Many shipyards started to search for new orders in niche markets, such as passenger shipping, but the Nordic ferry companies did not respond to the drop in new-building prices by new contracting of vessels. The problems that Nordic ferry shipping had encountered were more

---

[80] UNCTAD (2017, 27). Calculations are based on number of ships, not deadweight.
[81] Calculations are based on the data provided in Table 9.1. On the Stockholm–Mariehamn–Turku route, Viking Line introduced a new-building in 2013 and, at the time of writing, it has another ferry on order at a Chinese shipyard for the same route. These two vessels represent the only significant renewal in the fleet for almost two decades.

fundamental than those caused by the traditional shipping cycle. Ferry shipping had entered the declining phase of its life cycle.

After 2000, low cost airlines rapidly gained ground, not only in Europe, but all over the world. As a result, the alternative employment opportunities for second-hand ferries declined and the 'cascading' pattern from previous decades was broken. The Nordic ferries from the 1980s and 1990s, designed for duty-free sales, had high cabin capacity, large public spaces and relatively small car decks. They were not ideal for the Mediterranean routes, where trailer traffic had also become more important.[82] Around 2000, the Adriatic ferry fleet saw renewal with new-buildings and former Japanese ro/ro ships with significantly higher trailer intake and higher service speeds.[83] With rapidly rising household incomes in South East Asia, the interest in the aging tonnage from Northern Europe evaporated. Indeed Chinese ferry trades, in particular in the Bohai Rim in the North of the country, expanded, but new vessels with significantly larger car decks than the Nordic ferries entered service.

One new employment opportunity for a few old ferries did emerge in the 2010s. For a period, four of the 45 vessels in the sample entered service as floating accommodation for offshore wind farm construction workers. Anchored close to the wind farm construction sites, the old ferries provided hotel functions for workers, who therefore avoided the time-consuming transfer between land and the site. While this represented a novel use of the old vessels, the innovation did not come from the ferry companies, but from entrepreneurs within offshore wind shipping. Recently, tailor-made offshore accommodation vessels, however, have taken over the market from the old ferries.[84]

In the global cruise business, where second-hand ferries' large cabin accommodations had been a valuable asset, employment opportunities also vanished. After 2000, cruise shipping grew quickly, but the Nordic ferries were generally too small and had car decks, for which the cruise lines found no use. Instead the global cruise lines built long series of significantly larger vessels, which also featured numerous new service offerings. These

---

[82] Second hand market reports by Louagie (2013–16).
[83] See for example, Brogren (2000) on the new *Superfast* ferries for the Adriatic Sea services.
[84] C-Bed's web-page, https://c-bed.nl/, accessed 27 July 2017.

included ice skating rinks, stages for Broadway shows, numerous specialty restaurants, water sport arenas, climbing walls and other sport facilities. Moreover cruise cabins were larger and of a higher standard, and most featured private balconies. In the booming Chinese cruise trade, which had previously employed former Nordic ferries, tailor-made new cruise ships also entered service in the 2010s.[85] Service innovation in passenger shipping had become the realm of the global cruise lines.

Conclusion

With its regional operations and market structures, ferry shipping represents a small and somewhat unusual niche in the global shipping industry. It differs from most other shipping segments, in which shipping companies take global competition for granted and face very pronounced freight cycles. Yet in the end, the regional markets could not shield ferry companies against the forces of global competition. Ferry shipping evolved over the innovation phase to the mature phase, before it ultimately started to decline.

From the 1960s to the early 1990s, Nordic ferry shipping companies were global leaders in terms of service innovation, pushing the boundaries for onboard amenities and ship designs. They even set the standards for cruise services. As they broadened their service offerings, the Nordic lines frequently introduced state-of-the-art vessels. This resonated well with other shipping niches, such as chemical tanker, car carrier and open hatch bulk shipping, where Nordic shipowners were also at the forefront of innovation in the 1960s and early 1970s. This reflected the innovation phase of the industry life cycle.

The Nordic geography favoured ferry services, but socio-economic factors fuelled growth. Longer holidays for workers and growing household incomes provided shipping lines with a rising market of demanding travellers. Moreover, supporting government policies paved the way for very profitable onboard duty free sales and enabled ferry shipping companies to attract many passengers, who would not otherwise have travelled. The

---

[85] Cruise market reports by Louagie (2013–16).

growth of Nordic ferry shipping mirrored the strong growth of the Nordic economies in the 1960s. Even though ferry shipping was local in its operations, the second-hand market for ferries was global. Regions with lower average household incomes and lower consumer expectations than the Nordics acquired redundant tonnage. The 'cascading' pattern was very pronounced and the south- and eastwards migration of old ferries clearly reflected the interconnectedness of the global economy.

Structural changes caused Nordic companies in global shipping segments to lose momentum in the 1970s and 1980s. In the case of ferry shipping, similar losses occurred. It happened a decade later, due to a combination of adverse socio-economic and policy factors. Policy changes with the abolition of duty free sales within the EU in 1999 reduced revenue streams. Some routes ceased, while others shifted focus towards the more profitable trailer traffic. However, the policy changes were not the fundamental causes for the lost momentum. Stagnation set in even on the routes where duty free sales could continue. In the Baltic Sea and on the Skagerrak, a fleet of large, but ageing overnight ferries continues to operate. Since the late 1990s, most travellers have preferred the much fast and cheaper services of airlines, and the superior service offerings of cruise lines and other holiday alternatives. In the face of intensified competition, the Nordic ferry companies could not find resources to upgrade and improve their service offerings with innovations. Instead, the global cruise industry took over role of service innovation in passenger shipping more broadly.

Even though a new centre for ferry shipping innovation never emerged, the development of Nordic ferry shipping reflected global developments. In the last two decades, the 'cascading' pattern was broken (see Table 9.2). The shipping companies in the Mediterranean and Asia largely lost interest in the ageing Nordic car ferries, originally designed for duty-free sales and with an impractical capacity configuration. Rapidly rising income levels in the South East Asia enabled Asian shipowners to look for new buildings whenever they needed it. The world over, low-cost airlines had also carved out a major share of the passenger market. The industry life cycle theory neatly explains why a new centre for ferry service innovation failed to materialize. Globally the business for overnight ferry services had entered the declining stage of its life cycle. In the end, the regional market structures could not shield ferry shipping against structural changes in the global economy. The development of ferry shipping in the twentieth and early twenty-first centuries is therefore a reminder that global economic processes can have pervasive effects even on regional businesses.

Acknowledgements I would like to thank the editors for their valuable feedback to this chapter. I would also like to thank Niels P. Petersson and Nicholas J. White for organizing the workshop 'Shipping, Globalisation and Structural Change' held at Liverpool in June 2016, where I had an opportunity to present an early version of my work. Finally, I would like to thank Niels Tolstrup and Bruce Peter for valuable comments. The usual caveats apply.

References

Baird, A. J. (1999). A Comparative Study of the Ferry Industry in Japan and the UK. *Transport Reviews, 19*(1), 33–55.

Baird, A. J. (2000). The Japan Coastal Ferry System. *Maritime Policy & Management, 27*(1), 3–16.

Baird, A. J. (2012). Comparing the Efficiency of Public and Private Ferry Services on the Pentland Firth Between Mainland Scotland and the Orkney Islands. *Research in Transportation Business & Management, 4*, 79–89.

Baird, A. J., Wilmsmeier, G., Brooks, M. R., & Frost, J. D. (2011). Public Tendering of Ferry Services in Europe. *European Transport, 49*, 90–111.

Bergenek, A., & Brogren, K. (2006). *Passagerare till sjöss: den svenska färjesjöfartens historia*. Halmstad: ShipPax Information.

Brogren, K. (Ed.). (1991). *Designs 91*. Halmstad: Plus 2 Ferryconsultation.

Brogren, K. (Ed.). (1993). *Designs 93*. Halmstad: ShipPax Information.

Brogren, K. (Ed). (1995). *Guide 95*. Halmstad: ShipPax Information.

Brogren, K. (1998–2006). *Statistics 98–06*. Halmstad: ShipPax Information.

Brogren, K. (Ed.). (1999). *Designs 99*. Halmstad: ShipPax Information.

Brogren, K. (Ed.). (2000). *Designs 00*. Halmstad: ShipPax Information.

Brogren, K. (Ed.). (2010). *Guide 10*. Halmstad: ShipPax Information.

Brogren, K., Bergenek, A., & Sahlsten, R. (2012). *Stena Line – historien om ett färjerederi*. Gothenburg/Halmstad: Stena Line/ShipPax Information.

Brooks, M. R., & Frost, J. D. (2004). Short Sea Shipping: A Canadian Perspective. *Maritime Policy & Management, 31*(4), 393–407.

Casaca, A. C. P., & Marlow, P. B. (2005). The Competitiveness of Short Sea Shipping in Multimodal Logistics Supply Chains: Service Attributes. *Maritime Policy & Management, 32*(4), 363–382.
Dicken, P. (2015). *Global Shift: Mapping the Changing Contours of the World Economy* (7th ed.). New York: Guilford Press.
Dobruszkes, F. (2013). The Geography of European Low-Cost Airline Networks: A Contemporary Analysis. *Journal of Transport Geography, 28,* 75–88.
Eliasson, T. (2005). *Viking Line i bakspegeln.* Mariehamn: Viking Line.
Fellman, S., Iversen, M. J., Sjögren, H., & Thue, L. (Eds.). (2008). *Creating Nordic Capitalism: The Business History of a Competitive Periphery.* Basingstoke: Palgrave Macmillan.
Francis, G., Humphreys, H., Ison, S., & Aicken, M. (2006). Where Next for Low Cost Airlines? A Spatial and Temporal Comparative Study. *Journal of Transport Geography, 14*(2), 83–94.
Graae, P. (1966). *Hundrede år på havene.* Copenhagen: DFDS.
Hahn-Pedersen, M., Bisbjerg, L., Hansen, L. A., Jacobsen, A. L. L., Poulsen, R. T., & Søndergaard, M. K. (2004). Nye tider i Englandstrafikken – På triptur med M/S Dana Sirena. In M. Hahn-Pedersen (Ed.), *Sjæk'len, Årbog for Fiskeri- og Søfartsmuseet 2003* (pp. 98–117). Esbjerg: Fisheries and Maritime Museum.
Hahn-Pedersen, M., Hansen, L. A., Jacobsen, A. L. L., Poulsen, B., Poulsen, R. T., & Søndergaard, M. K. (2003). På triptur med Dana Anglia. In M. Hahn-Pedersen (Ed.), *Sjæk'len, Årbog for Fiskeri- og Søfartsmuseet 2002* (pp. 57–78). Esbjerg: Fisheries- and Maritime Museum.
Hahn-Pedersen, M., & Poulsen, R. T. (2006). Danske passagerlinjer på Nordsøen, ca. 1850–2005. In M. Hahn-Pedersen (Ed.), *Sjæk'len, Årbog for Fiskeri- og Søfartsmuseet 2005* (pp. 8–25). Esbjerg: Fisheries and Maritime Museum.
Harberg, J. (1995). *Åländsk sjöfart med maskindrivna fartyg.* Mariehamn: Ålands Nautical Club.
Heijveld, H., & Gray, R. (1996). The Competitive Environment of a Service Industry: The Examples of the UK-Continent Passenger Sea Ferry Services. *Journal of the History of Economic Thought, 23*(2), 157–166.
Jamieson, A. G. (2003). *Ebb Tide in the British Maritime Industries: Change and Adaptation, 1918–1990.* Exeter: University of Exeter Press.
Johnman, L., & Murphy, H. (2002). *British Shipbuilding and the State Since 1918: A Political Economy of Decline.* Exeter: University of Exeter Press.
Karlsson, A. (2007). *Det åländska sjöklustret. En studie i den ekonomiska tillväxtens entreprenöriella och instiutionella förutsättningar.* Mariehamn: ÅSUB.

Lange, O. (1995). *Logbog for Lauritzen 1884–1995, historien om konsulen, hans sønner og Lauritzen Gruppen* (pp. 296–316). Copenhagen: Handelshøjskolens Forlag.

Lorenz, E. H. (1991). An Evolutionary Explanation for Competitive Decline: The British Shipbuilding Industry, 1890–1970. *The Journal of Economic History, 51*(4), 911–935.

Louagie, M. (Ed.). (2013–16). *Market 13–16*. Halmstad: ShipPax Information.

Louagie, M. (Ed.). (2017). *Market 17*. Halmstad: ShipPax Information.

Luis, J. Á. H. (2002). Temporal Accessibility in Archipelagos: Inter-Island Shipping in the Canary Islands. *Journal of Transport Geography, 10*(3), 231–239.

Malmberg, T., & Sjöström, P. (1997). *Bore 1897–1997: ett sekel finländsk sjöfart*. Turku: Bore Shipowners.

Malmberg, T., & Stempehl, M. (2007). *Femti år med Silja*. Esbo: Tallink Silja Oy.

Miller, M. B. (2012). *Europe and the Maritime World: A Twentieth Century History*. Cambridge: Cambridge University Press.

Møller, A. M. (1983). København-Kristiania: Fra sejlpaket til konferenceskib. *Maritim Kontakt, 6,* 115–132.

Murphy, H., & Tenold, S. (2008). Strategies, Market Concentration and Hegemony in Chemical Parcel Tanker Shipping, 1960–1985. *Business History, 50*(3), 291–309.

Ojala, J., & Tenold, S. (2017). Maritime Trade and Merchant Shipping: The Shipping/Trade Ratio Since the 1870s. *International Journal of Maritime History, 29*(4), 838–854.

Pantouvakis, A. M. (2007). Who Pays the Ferryman? An Analysis of the Ferry Passenger's Selection Dilemma. *Maritime Policy & Management, 34*(6), 591–612.

Peter, B. (2004). *Danish Ship Design: The Work of Kay Fisker and Kay Kørbing*. Ramsey: Ferry Publications.

Peter, B. (2017). *Knud E Hansen A/S 80 Years*. Ramsey: Ferry Publications.

Peter, B., & Dawson, P. (2010). *The Ferry: A Drive-Through History*. Ramsey: Ferry Publications.

Peter, B., & Id, K. (2017). *Innovation and Specialization: The Story of Shipbuilding in Finland*. Lyngby: Nautilus Forlag.

Poulsen, R. T., Jensen, K., Christensen, R. S., & Jiang, L. (2017). Corporate Strategies and Global Competition: Odense Steel Shipyard, 1918–2012. *Business History Review, 91*(4), 707–734.

Quartermaine, P., & Peter, B. (2006). *Cruise: Identity, Design And Culture*. London: Laurence King Publishing.

Rinman, T. (1968). *Svenska Lloyd gennem etthundra år*. Gothenburg: Zinderman.

Rinman, T. (1989). *Rederiet: Johnson Line under 100 år*. Gothenburg: Rinman & Lindén AB/Johnson Line AB.
Rutz, W. O. A., & Coull, J. R. (1996). Inter-Island Passenger Shipping in Indonesia: Development of the System—Present Characteristics and Future Requirements. *Journal of Transport Geography*, 4(4), 275–286.
Sahlsten, R., Söderberg, B., & Bång, K. (1992). *Stena Lines fartyg 1962–1992*. Gothenburg: Stena Line AB.
ShipPax Information. various years. *Markets and Statistics*. Halmstad: ShipPax Information.
Simonsen, P., & Krogh-Andersen, S. (2016). *The DFDS Fleet 1991–2016*. Copenhagen: DFDS A/S.
Sjögren, H. (2015). *Högtryck: SAS och omvandlingen*. Stockholm: Dialogos Förlag.
Sjöström, P., & Brzoza, K. (2009). *Vägen över havet – från pionjärer till marknadsledare*. Gothenburg: Breakwater Publishing AB/Viking Line.
Sletmo, G. K. (1989). Shipping's Fourth Wave: Ship Management and Vernon's Trade Cycles. *Maritime Policy & Management*, 16(4), 293–303.
Stråth, B. (1987). *The Politics of De-industrialisation: The Contraction of the West European Shipbuilding Industry*. London: Croom Helm.
Sturmey, S. G. (1962/2010). *British Shipping and World Competition*. St. John's, NL: International Maritime Economic History Association.
Svensson, H. (1986). *En man och hans linje: Gunnar Eklund och färjtrafiken Sverige-Åland-Finland*. Mariehamn: Viking Line.
Svensson, H. (1990). *Med Carl Bertil Myrsten från ö till ö: En envis gottlänning och färjtrafiken Sverige-Åland-Finland*. Mariehamn: Viking Line.
Tenold, S. (2006). *Tankers in Trouble: Norwegian Shipping and the Crisis of the 1970s and 1980*. St. John's, NL: International Maritime Economic History Association.
Tenold, S. (2009). Vernon's Product Life Cycle and Maritime Innovation: Specialised Shipping in Bergen, Norway, 1970–1987. *Business History*, 51(5), 770–786.
Tenold, S. (2019). *Norwegian Shipping in the 20th Century: Norway's Successful Navigation of the World's Most Global Industry*. Cham: Palgrave Macmillan.
Tenold, S., Iversen, M. J., & Lange, E. (Eds.). (2012). *Global Shipping in Small Nations: Nordic Experiences After 1960*. Basingstoke: Palgrave Macmillan.
Tenold, S., & Ojala, J. (2017). How to Sail a Sinking Ship: Regulatory Innovation and the Competitiveness of the European Shipping Industry. In B. Bouwens, P. Donzé, & T. Kurosawa (Eds.), *Industries and Global Competition: A History of Business Beyond Borders* (pp. 215–234). New York: Routledge.

Thanopoulou, H. A. (1995). The Growth of Fleets Registered in the Newly-Emerging Maritime Countries and Maritime Crises. *Maritime Policy & Management, 22*(1), 51–62.

Thorsøe, S., Simonsen, P., Krogh-Andersen, S., Frederichsen, F., & Vaupel, H. (1991). *DFDS 1866–1991: Skibsudvikling gennem 125 år fra Hjulpdamper til Rulleskib/ DFDS: Ship Development through 125 years – from Paddle Steamer to Ro/Ro Ship.* Copenhagen: DFDS A/S/World Ship Society.

Thorsøe, S., Simonsen, P., Krogh-Andersen, S., & Vaupel, H. (2006). *DFDS 1991–2006 Skibsudviklingen forsætter/ DFDS 1991–2006 Ship Development Continues.* Copenhagen: DFDS A/S/World Ship Society.

Tolstrup, N. (2012). *Pionerer mod øst: Personlige fortællinger om DSB Rederis/Scandlines' indtog i den østlige del af Østersøen.* Lyngby: Nautilus Forlag.

Tor Line. (1985). *Tor Line: 20 years.* Gothenburg: Tor Line.

UNCTAD. (2016). *UNCTAD Review of Maritime Transport 2016.* Geneva: UNCTAD.

Vernon, R. (1960). International Investment and International Trade in the Product Cycle. *Quarterly Journal of Economics, 80*(2), 190–207.

Wergeland, T. (2012). Ferry Passenger Markets. In W. K. Talley (Ed.), *The Blackwell Companion to Maritime Economics* (pp. 161–83). Malden, MA: Wiley-Blackwell.

Westerlund, K. (Ed.). (2012). *Färjefart: Historiska og etnologiska perspektiv på färjetrafiken mellan Finland och Sverige* (Meddelande från Sjöhistoriska Institutet vid Åbo Akademi 33). Turku: Sjöhistoriska Institutet vid Åbo Akademi.

Widdows, N. (2010). *Stena Line: The Fleet.* Ramsey: Ferry Publications.

Widdows, N. (2011). *DFDS: The Fleet* (2nd ed.). Ramsey: Ferry Publications.

Open Access This chapter is licensed under the terms of the Creative Commons Attribution-NonCommercial-NoDerivatives 4.0 International License (http://creativecommons.org/licenses/by-nc-nd/4.0/), which permits any noncommercial use, sharing, distribution and reproduction in any medium or format, as long as you give appropriate credit to the original author(s) and the source, provide a link to the Creative Commons license and indicate if you modified the licensed material. You do not have permission under this license to share adapted material derived from this chapter or parts of it.

The images or other third party material in this chapter are included in the chapter's Creative Commons license, unless indicated otherwise in a credit line to the material. If material is not included in the chapter's Creative Commons license and your intended use is not permitted by statutory regulation or exceeds the permitted use, you will need to obtain permission directly from the copyright holder.

10

Conclusion

Niels P. Petersson, Stig Tenold and Nicholas J. White

Global history, transnational history and the history of globalization are among the key trends in historiography over the past two decades.[1] To an extent, these are fashionable buzzwords, made attractive and plausible by

---

[1] For a recent discussion of approaches to global history, see Osterhammel (2019).

N. P. Petersson (✉)
Sheffield Hallam University, Sheffield, UK
e-mail: n.p.petersson@shu.ac.uk

S. Tenold
Department of Economics, NHH – Norwegian School of Economics, Bergen, Norway
e-mail: stig.tenold@nhh.no

N. J. White
School of Humanities and Social Science, Liverpool John Moores University, Liverpool, Merseyside, UK
e-mail: n.j.white@ljmu.ac.uk

our present-day experience of ever-increasing connections across countries and continents. But these trends have also helped enrich historiography by opening up new areas of study and encouraging historians to ask new questions and transcend boundaries not just of a geographical but also of a disciplinary nature. The challenges of getting to grips with a range of new phenomena and topics have made historians more open towards combining social, cultural, political and economic approaches and encouraged dialogue with neighbouring disciplines. In particular, interest in economic history has increased due to the obvious importance that businesses, markets, infrastructures, and economic policies have had for global flows of all kinds.

Deep-sea shipping is inextricably linked to notions of transnationalism and globalization. Over centuries, transnational and transcontinental spaces were opened up by ships and defined by shipping routes.[2] The integration of the world economy and world markets in the nineteenth century has been explained by the impact of low-cost transportation made possible by the introduction of steamships.[3] In his excellent history of Europe and the maritime world, Michael Miller presents maritime infrastructures as an essential ingredient in all key processes of twentieth-century history.[4] At the same time, historians have studied the transformation of shipping from an activity recognizably anchored in specific nation-states into 'the world's most global industry'.[5] Thus, the history of shipping can illustrate and illuminate the characteristics of different periods in the history of globalization[6] and help explain the changes that occurred.

This volume focuses on the transformations of the second half of the twentieth century. There has been considerable discussion on periodization as well as on how to characterize changes that have been summed up as the 'shock of the global'.[7] For both purposes, the question of continuity and change in the run-up to present-day globalization has been important. For Miller, the transnationalism of the maritime world and its cross-border

---

[2] Fusaro and Polónia (2010).
[3] Kaukiainen (2006), Kaukiainen (2012), Harley (2008), and O'Rourke and Williamson (1999).
[4] Miller (2012, 3).
[5] Kaukiainen (2008) and Tenold (2019).
[6] Hopkins (2002) and Osterhammel and Petersson (2005).
[7] Ferguson et al. (2010).

networks underpins the continuity of globalization throughout the twentieth century, including the interwar years that are often regarded as a period of deglobalization.[8] Nonetheless, Miller also sees a switch, in the final third of the twentieth century, from networks that were Eurocentric, imperial, and fragmented to ones that were multipolar and almost seamlessly global. His account of the relationship between shipping and globalization in the twentieth century is a story of progressions and mutations rather than interruptions and new beginnings.[9] Miller focuses on the expertise that was available to overcome obstacles to global flows—but it is equally possible to highlight instead the variety and importance of such obstacles, and how they fell away once the old world of protected national markets, cargo liners and conferences gave way to that of liberalized world trade, container ships and cut-throat competition.[10] We have to take a closer look at particular contexts, companies and connections and find out about mutations, interruptions and new beginnings and how they relate to the wider histories of globalizations.

Contexts

Highly important in these mutations, interruptions and new beginnings were the process of decolonization and the accompanying economic nationalism (not just in the developing world but in the US and the Soviet bloc too, and supported by the UN's drive towards trying to create a more egalitarian world-trading regime from the 1960s). This was hardly surprising since, as Tenold argues in his overarching chapter, European, and especially British, dominance at the beginning of the twentieth century in global shipping was due to a 'leading position within production and trade' and 'superior access to technology, capital [including human know-how] and sufficiently skilled labour' but also 'imperial ambitions and structures that ensured political support for maritime activities'. Before World War

---

[8] Miller (2012, 6, 11). For a different discussion of changes and continuities in interwar global networks, see Dejung and Petersson (2013, 12–16).
[9] Miller (2012, 12).
[10] Levinson (2006).

II it was only Japan outside Europe which proved capable of breaking into this maritime system through a combination of defensive industrialization and defensive imperialism.[11]

With a few exceptions, such as Singapore's Neptune Orient Line, new national shipping lines were often ineffective in the longer-term. Yet, the efforts of European shipping companies to manoeuvre around obstacles (both real and perceived) in the decolonized world led onto the adoption of containerization (as White demonstrates in the British case). This was a new beginning which suggests that, as Tenold also stresses in his chapter, European shipping companies were innovative and adaptive, for example, employing multinational crews and exploiting liberalized trading regimes, and that entrepreneurial/commercial stasis was not the crucial factor in European decline as Sturmey once argued in the British case.[12] As distinct from European shipbuilders, European shipping firms in Tenold's schema continued to play 'a crucial, albeit reduced, role'. This is a theme explored further in the 'companies' part of this volume. Moreover, while part of the OCL strategy after 1965 was to defend imperial market shares, notably in the politically stable and culturally familiar old Dominions, diversification and redeployment by Britain's leading shipowners also represented a chance to tap further into the dynamic Asia-Pacific trading and investment realm. That reflected not only a quantitative upsurge in world trade but also a qualitative shift in which the real value-added in global trade was now to be found in increased exchanges between industrialized countries rather than between European industrial and financial 'metropoles' and primary-producing 'peripheries' in the developing world.[13]

This trend towards global intra-industrial trade reinforces Tenold's 'swing to the East' and his emphasis in this collection on the changing gravity of the world economy as western Europe lost its hegemony in both ocean-going shipping and shipbuilding (but particularly the latter and for Britain most starkly). Japan had already surpassed the UK in 1956 as the world's leading shipbuilder, and that was followed from the mid-1970s by

---

[11] On Japan's defensive modernization and imperialism, see Young (2018, 216).
[12] Sturmey (1962/2010).
[13] Hopkins (2002) and Cain and Hopkins (2016, 714–717).

South Korea and subsequently China. Asian dominance by the twenty-first century, as Tenold tells us, was even greater than Europe's had proved a century earlier. In the maritime industries, at least, Asia finally caught up from Pomeranz's 'Great Divergence' in which, around 1800, well-placed coal supplies and resource-rich colonies across the Atlantic allowed the western rather than the eastern end of Eurasia to suddenly and unexpectedly leap forward. In this bit of geographical luck, the particularly 'fortunate freak' was Britain. Highly significant for later maritime dominance was that Britain's plentiful coal supplies were close to lots of water and conveniently-located ports which made steam power cost-effective. Plantations in the Americas, meanwhile, provided a superabundance of raw materials for further industrialization as well as the development of ocean-going maritime trade.[14] In what might be termed a 'Great Convergence', Tenold shows that East Asians had acquired capital and skills to succeed in shipping by the later twentieth century. Transnational business networks in the burgeoning intra-Asian economy, government support, low wages, limited unionization, reliable domestic supplies of steel, and easily transferrable technology allowed for the emergence of large-scale and globally competitive Asian shipbuilding. To maintain competitiveness, European shipping companies turned to Japanese yards for the building of their vessels—as early as 1965 for Blue Funnel, Britain's leading cargo line in East and Southeast Asia, and even earlier in the late-1950s for the Greek bulk carriers (as Harlaftis's and Tsakas's chapter in this volume illustrates).[15]

As Tenold argues, the draw towards Asia entailed considerable 'dislocation' effects in the combination of production creation and production diversion that characterized post-war globalization. That mirrors Levinson's notion that containerization broke the link between ports and production centres—the ultimate 'shock city' of this post-colonial deglobalization in the 1970s and 1980s probably being Liverpool whose position as the second city of the British Empire had been based upon the port's

---

[14] Pomeranz (2000, 207) and Perdue (2000, 1–3).
[15] White and Evans (2016, 233).

proximity to northern England's manufacturing powerhouse and a shipbuilding complex at Birkenhead.[16] At a geo-political level, the 'Global Cold War' can be brought into this transnational maritime narrative too because, as also addressed by Tenold, the Japanese and South Korean take-off in shipbuilding was greatly assisted by US aid, investment and technology transfer in the broader context of containing Communist China.[17]

What emerges equally from the 'contexts' section of this volume, is the reduced (or, at least, changing) role of the nation-state in the postwar globalization of the maritime industries. The shift towards a more 'conglomeratic approach' in the regulation of maritime shipping, Reiling points out, was reflective itself of the decline of state supervision at a national level and the multinational nature of shipping through flags of convenience and open registries. Also stressed by Tenold, these are developments in business forms which make it difficult to precisely identify ownership patterns and, hence, the European share in shipping, the decline of which was offset by European-owned vessels flying foreign flags. On top of this, was the internationalization of cargoes and crews. As Harlaftis's and Tsakas's chapter shows, Greek shipowners-cum-shipbuilders pioneered these business practices in 'mammoth' bulk carriage (especially oil, the new preferred fuel of post-colonial globalization) in the 1940s and 1950s. That additionally involved a considerable internationalization of capital in shipping as the Greeks contracted with American oil companies, utilized US bank finance and invested in American and later northern European shipyards. White's discussion of Nigeria shows that multinational crewing was hardly unknown under the old globalization and the politicization of non-European seafarers, as well as dockworkers, should not be neglected in explaining increasing costs. But, in the British case, the use of Nigerian, Kru, Lascar, Malay and Chinese crews (many of the latter from Singapore and Hong Kong) was clearly linked to empire. The more recent widespread use of Filipino labour, for example, in international shipping emphasizes this multinationalization and the decoupling of colonialism and maritime dominance.[18]

---

[16]Levinson (2006), D'Eramo (2015), and Lane (1997).
[17]Westad (2005), Forsberg (2000), and Duara (2011).
[18]Alderton et al. (2004), Ruggunan (2011) and Swift (2011).

The transboundary, de-territorialized nature of shipping and multiple actors involved, in which open registries had 'neither the capacity nor inclination' to provide regulation frameworks, led, as Reiling shows, to a parallel multiplication and broadening out of standard-setting and quality-monitoring bodies. These took a particular role in labour, safety and ecological issues and encompassed international organizations (often under UN auspice), regional bodies like the EU, port-based public authorities, transnational classification societies and P&I clubs. This medley of regulatory inputs and oversight bodies was a far cry from the self-governance of the European-dominated liner conference system of the old 'colonial' globalization.

This is not to say that the nation state disappeared. White's analysis of British containerization points to the central role in the 1960s and 1970s of governmental actors in the assertive ex-Dominions and in Southeast Asia (and later in Sri Lanka as well). Tenold also notes the 'controlled economic development model' in the East Asian NICs. Furthermore, as Reiling emphasizes, there are still 'many weak points' in international regulation which have tended to set minimum standards only and in which implementation still relies on individual states and 'opting out' remains more than possible. The latter phenomenon is indicated in White's discussion of the limitations of the UNCTAD liner code, and the US's non-compliance during the 1980s. EEC reservations, meanwhile, 'disappl[ied] crucial parts of the Code to trades between EEC members and, on a reciprocal basis, between EEC members and the OECD countries'. An EEC regulation, moreover, required that 'shippers and ship-owners of Member States shall not insist on applying the procedures for settling disputes provided for in…the Code'. As Sturmey argued, these revisions effectively jettisoned 'the fundamental principle of the equality of the two groups of lines of the trading partners in trades with developing countries'.[19] This suggests that the convergence (or equalization) of shipping relationships between Europe and the developing world in post-war globalization have been limited. Indeed, in 1983, an angry Mahathir Mohamad, Malaysia's Prime Minister, accused western governments of obstructing UNCTAD and denying developing countries the opportunity to carry more freight

---

[19] Sturmey (1986, 197).

on their own ships.[20] As O'Brien argued in reviewing the historiographical debate (ten years on) from the publication of Pomeranz's influential book, the 'Great Divergence' between western Europe and East Asia remained 'important for social scientists to address simply because it is still with us as a North-South divide'.[21]

Nor was the global shock, as far as western Europe was concerned, that immediate. Tenold shows that Europe's leading maritime position at the start of the twentieth century was maintained well into the post-war period with Britain, 'the retired empire-builder', continuing to control the world's largest fleet at the end of the 1960s. This lag time suggests that a combination of the old and the new globalization characterized the post-war era for at least a quarter of a century. It was not until the mid-1970s that Asia's new found shipping and shipbuilding advantages became manifest. The big spur here were the OPEC-induced oil price hikes (indicative themselves of a greater balancing and multi-centring of global economics and politics as extra-European producers used their collective muscle in the wake of decolonization). Reiling, likewise, finds that it was not until the 1970s that the conglomeratic approach in maritime regulation tended to replace the flag-state principle and when key IMO interventions were accepted and adopted.

To recap then on contexts, what does shipping/shipbuilding tell us about post-war globalization? Shipping has clearly been an important factor in the changing gravity of the world economy and the changed significance of the nation state. The declining role of Europe in the international economy is starkly illustrated by Tenold's data on the world's largest ports (in 1910 more than half of the world's 15 busiest ports by cargo volume were European; one hundred years later, there was only one European port in the top 15). In Reiling's analysis, meanwhile, new conceptions of maritime international law are a key example of global governance in a 'typically globalized industry'. Yet, disengagement from pre-war colonial structures and patterns was not as complete as might be suggested

---

[20] Central Intelligence Agency (United States), EA 83-10111, Directorate of Intelligence, Office of East Asian Analysis, 'Malaysia: Economic Policy at the Crossroads', 8 June 1983.
[21] O'Brien (2010).

in the term 'post-colonial globalization'. Indeed, Darwin defined decolonization in the 25 years after 1945 as 'a partial retraction, redeployment and redistribution of British and European influences in the regions of the extra-European world whose economic, political and cultural life had previously seemed to flow into Western moulds'.[22] Periodization and chronology remain important, therefore, and the broad brush stroke concept of a distinctive 'post-war globalization' requires modification. In shipping, the 1970s seem to be the breakpoint rather than 1945 or 1990 (as Baldwin's study of information technology suggests for the 'Great Convergence' between 'Global North' and 'Global South').[23]

Yet, the changing nature of business models in which international shipping companies seized upon the opportunities provided by tax havens and off-shore companies, and their investors became more short-termist and profit-oriented and less community-centred, appears to have a longer trajectory. That stretched back to the 1940s and 1950s with innovations introduced by the Greek shipping barons. Moreover, the nationality of those European companies which succeeded in the post-colonial maritime world—the cross-traders of Greece and Scandinavia notably—did not come with the old 'imperial' baggage.[24] This points to the agency of shipping companies in these transformations, as well as the forging of new connections, which are the next two themes of our conclusion.

Companies

Business historians have long stressed the crucial role private firms and entrepreneurs played in economic globalization through their decisions to invest, adopt new technologies, or seek out new markets. Shipping firms have been singled out as key drivers of economic globalization.[25] The companies examined in this volume contributed and reacted to globalization in a variety of ways, and some did so more successfully than others.

---

[22] Darwin (1988, 7).
[23] Baldwin (2016).
[24] In cruising, meanwhile, it has been American 'parvenus' who have come to dominate. Miller (2012, 326–330).
[25] Boon (2017), Ekberg and Lange (2014), Jones (2002), and Miller (2012).

In the 1950s, shipping entrepreneurs began ordering supertankers and large bulk carriers, and created new blueprints for global business organization that appeared exotic to some, illicit to others, but eventually were widely adopted within and beyond the shipping world.[26] In the 1960s, liner shipping firms had to respond to decolonization and developmentalist economic nationalism, while also engaging with the technological and strategic challenges of the container revolution.[27] The 1970s brought a much more difficult environment with macroeconomic instability, stagflation and currency fluctuations. Rising costs, overcapacity and increased competition were the key challenges shipping firms had to face, and their responses led to a fundamental transformation of the international shipping industry. Container transport gained in importance over the 1980s and by the 1990s became a key ingredient in the global integration of production chains spurred on by economic liberalization, while tanker and bulk shipping grew in response to the rising industrial economies' hunger for raw materials.

Business history focuses on corporate success and failure and the reasons behind it. The three chapters in the 'companies' section invite approaching this issue via a comparison of the very different strategies and trajectories of three container shipping firms. Ocean / OCL,[28] EAC and Maersk differed in their basic approaches to containerization; in the timing of market entry and (in the case of Ocean and EAC) market exit; in the resources they could draw on and chose to develop; in the resulting organizational ability to control and coordinate operations effectively on a global scale; in overall corporate strategy; and in the extent to which their strategies and strengths were compatible with a changing external environment. Perhaps the most obvious difference between the three companies lies in where they ended up: Maersk nowadays is well known as the world's largest liner shipping firm with well over 600 ships, including 'megaships' of over 18,000 TEU carrying capacity. Ocean and OCL no longer exist as corporate entities; Ocean sold its stake in OCL in 1986, abandoned its shipping activities

---

[26] See the chapter by Gelina Harlaftis and Christos Tsakas in this volume.

[27] See the chapters by Martin Jes Iversen, Niels P. Petersson, Henrik Sornn-Friese and Nicholas J. White in this volume.

[28] Overseas Container Lines (OCL) was a joint venture established by Ocean, P&O, Furness Withy and British & Commonwealth in 1965.

and developed into a successful logistics business that was acquired by DHL in 2000, while OCL ended up as part of P&O and, ultimately, Maersk. EAC, meanwhile, also left shipping, selling its fleet to Maersk in 1997 and never really recovering from the losses incurred in shipping.

Did Maersk succeed where others failed, and get things right that others got wrong? And, if so, can any of the differences between the three companies be singled out as decisive? Did Maersk, for example, benefit from being a 'late mover' into containerization? OCL certainly incurred its fair share of learning costs as a result of being an early mover. Technologies and processes had to be developed from scratch, and new terminals and facilities built in Europe, Australia and East Asia.[29] Maersk moved into the market once such teething problems had been overcome, and once major port operators had begun building the infrastructure required to handle large-scale container flows. On the other hand, OCL remarkably soon became a successful and profitable operation, which suggests that both early and late entry into the market may have represented viable strategies. (In contrast to EAC, Ocean also proved rather adept at exiting the market as both the sale of OCL and later the takeover of Ocean by DHL were very profitable for the shareholders.)

Were Maersk superior in exploiting and nurturing corporate resources? A slightly flippant point about resources is that it always helps to own an oil well—and Maersk were a large player in the oil business until they decided to focus exclusively on container shipping in 2017.[30] More seriously, containerization represented investment on a much larger scale than liner shipping companies were used to, and neither Ocean, who in the late 1960s were sitting on substantial reserves and unused tax allowances, nor Maersk faced significant financial constraints when they decided to containerize. OCL's fortunes changed in the early 1970s when Ocean and its other three parent companies decided that they wanted OCL to pay dividends rather than reinvest and expand. From then on, OCL's frustrated managers described their business model as simply 'a milch cow followed

---

[29] See Niels P. Petersson's chapter in this volume and Bott (2009).
[30] As of the time of writing, Maersk were planning to complete the sale of Maersk Oil to Total and offering their other oil-related businesses for sale: https://www.maersk.com/news/2018/06/29/values-and-opportunities (last viewed 1 February 2019).

by a coffin'.[31] EAC, during the same period, were also held back by the debt taken on to build the Liner Replacement Vessels, a type of ship that turned out to be unsuited to the market.[32] Thus, from the mid-1970s, OCL and EAC faced tighter restrictions on the investment they could undertake in container shipping than Maersk.

For business historians, the notion of corporate resources covers far more than material and financial ones. Explicit and implicit knowledge, corporate culture, and the often elusive 'dynamic capabilities' are all equally important. The shipping industry did not invent the systematic nurturing of corporate resources, but the three firms examined here certainly went with the times, applying professional management methods, adopting modern personnel development systems, introducing the latest information technologies, and making use of other innovations as they became available. Both Maersk and Ocean placed great value on systematically increasing efficiency and quality throughout all business processes, as captured in Maersk's slogan 'service all the way', and both firms seem to have believed that globally integrated, standardized operations, reporting and control were required to achieve this. In contrast, EAC, rather than aiming to build a standardized, frictionless operation on a global scale, seem to have continued to rely on decentralized ad hoc problem-solving, assuming that significant friction as a result of technological, political and administrative obstacles was unavoidable in maritime transport.

Control and coordination, emphasized so much by Maersk and Ocean, seem to have played an important role both in turning shipping firms into powerful engines of global economic integration and in making their operations profitable. Moreover, institutional and organizational factors also played a role in strategic decision-making far removed from day-to-day business. Of the three companies, Maersk seems to have given the shipping business the largest amount of autonomy over the long term, even though it still was part of a conglomerate. Maersk's container services largely remained outside the shipping conferences through which the traditional operators sought to coordinate their activities and regulate supply and prices. Maersk operated as an outsider competing on cost and

---

[31] Bott (2009, 155 and Chapters 12 and 13).
[32] See Martin Jes Iversen's chapter in this volume.

quality in a free market. OCL initially seemed to enjoy substantial autonomy, having been created as a new organization with the sole purpose of becoming the dominant force in container shipping, unencumbered by any responsibilities in the traditional liner business. Soon, however, it became apparent that OCL as a joint venture had to follow a strategic direction set by its four parent companies. By the mid-1980s, managers at Ocean had come round to the view that OCL required control over its own affairs, and that they would have to either acquire sole ownership of the container shipping consortium or (as they eventually did) sell their stake in it.[33] Another respect in which OCL's autonomy was constrained by the parent companies was that OCL always operated as a conference line. Early on, it had been considered to run container services free from the conferences and the 'inhibitions and barriers' they imposed, but Ocean's view that container services should be used for 'strengthening the conference hold over shippers' prevailed.[34] In this case, corporate culture acted as an internal constraint, restricting the options OCL would consider.

Like OCL, EAC was a conference line. EAC also was held back by unhappy relationships, power struggles and miscommunication within the alliances with other container lines that most operators believed were necessary in order to be able to offer frequent sailings while also using large ships. In another respect, however, EAC's senior managers seem to have had too much autonomy for their own good: at key points in the company's history, including the decisions to order the Liner Replacement Vessels and to pour resources into gaining a foothold in the Chinese market, stronger oversight and critical questioning of top-level strategic initiatives could have prevented costly mistakes.

Entrepreneurial autonomy thus needs to be used wisely, in pursuit of a strategy that is in tune with a company's internal capabilities and with the opportunities offered by the external environment. The strategy literature insists that strategy does not necessarily have to imply the systematic pursuit of an elaborate long-term master plan; equally, it can emerge gradually as a pattern of successful activity or manifest itself in the culture and skills

---

[33] Again following Bott (2009, 144, Chapters 12 and 13).
[34] Bott (2009, 86).

that exist within an organisation.[35] Sornn-Friese argues that Maersk pursued just such an emergent strategy over much of their history, reacting flexibly to business opportunities that presented themselves, while also systematically building up commercial and organizational capability. By the mid-1980s, however, a more explicit strategy was chosen as Maersk set out to become the world's most profitable container operator through offering customers the best possible integrated service. Ocean/OCL embraced formal strategic planning with far more enthusiasm. However, the resulting strict focus on business metrics such as profits and share price eventually led to the decision to reduce the company's involvement in shipping activities which seemed to offer inadequate returns, and to concentrate on logistics services instead.[36] EAC, as Iversen demonstrates, seems to have pursued a succession of opportunistic moves. In terms of their time scales, investment requirements and fundamental importance for the company, both the LRV project and the work done in connection with containerizing China's trade were of strategic importance. They were undertaken based on an assessment of long-term term trends in shipping markets and in the global economy, required substantial investments and engaged the future of the company. However, as so many company strategists found out in the 1970s, perceived long-term trends could end abruptly or proceed through cycles of stops and starts, markets moved in unpredictable swings and once resources had been committed to a failed initiative, they were no longer available for anything else.

The ability to make and implement strategy is clearly one of the factors explaining success and failure in the three cases presented here. However, it is likely that EAC was handicapped not only by internal shortcomings and flawed strategy but also by changes in the external environment that, broadly speaking, devalued its strengths and highlighted its weaknesses. For Maersk, the opposite was the case, while Ocean/OCL occupied a middle ground. The external environment may be analyzed from a macro perspective, with a focus on regimes of political economy and global trade. From such a perspective, the liberalization of trade and investment, the

---

[35] Mintzberg et al. (1998).
[36] Barber (2003) offers a succinct analysis of Ocean's and OCL's strategic options.

opening up of once closed economies—foremost among them China—and the growth of non-Western industries and global supply chains are key trends since the late 1970s. Freer trade and level playing fields both allowed and rewarded the investments firms such as Maersk and Ocean made to set up efficient, standardized, customer-focused, globally integrated logistics networks. Firms with a focus on doing business in the cartel-like structures of the conferences, such as Ocean and EAC, found the increased competition from non-conference lines difficult to deal with, whereas Maersk's experience of operating as an outsider firm was increasingly relevant as the conferences eroded and the shipping world became more and more competitive. Meanwhile, the local knowledge and political connections that allowed a company such as EAC to navigate politicized markets in closed economies were no longer of such crucial importance in an era of liberalization. Borders, political economy and institutional regimes matter. Changes in the external environment require firms to adapt and change; however, such change was much easier where it could draw on existing strengths and resources. Different company cultures and the weight of past decisions—path dependency—go some way towards explaining the varied experiences of the three companies in this respect.

A complementary perspective on the external environment would be a local one. Maersk and EAC, along with the entire Danish maritime industry, probably benefited from being important players in a small, open European economy. They enjoyed political clout and social prestige and were part of an industrial cluster which made it easy to recruit talented people and exchange information. Ocean/OCL were located in the UK, exposed to the erosion of colonial and Commonwealth economic ties, to the decline of British industry and British long-distance trade and to industrial unrest. The economic revival of the 1980s bypassed the shipping sector, while capital market liberalization increased the pressure to achieve short-term gains for shareholders and attracted promising young managers to careers in the City. All of this pointed to building Ocean's future in logistics rather than shipping.

Both on a local and on a global level, the factors that made for success were linked to an ability to organize processes in networks of vessels, places, systems and people. In the globalized free-trading world of the 1980s and beyond this was a completely different challenge to what it had been over the middle decades of the twentieth century when the business of moving goods by sea was governed by large numbers of political controls, tariffs, quotas, capital controls and local idiosyncrasies which limited, but did not eliminate, the ability of private firms to pursue truly global strategies and to contribute to global economic integration. Once again, the relationship between shipping and changes in the nation state is crucial.

Connections

Globalization transformed the relationship between countries and between companies—new connections were forged and old ones were transformed. The global nature of shipping demand put the industry in a special position. Shipping companies could challenge the nation state in ways and to a degree that would be difficult for companies in more location-bound industries. We can call this development deterritorialization—the link between the economic activity and the national jurisdiction was severed. Shipping entrepreneurs would transcend traditional borders, and break free from national regulatory regimes, in their attempts at producing shipping services as efficiently and as profitably as possible. This was accomplished by creating a new international division of labour, where countries, companies and workers reconstituted their positions within a global system.

More than anyone else, Greek shipowners contributed to the reconfiguration of the global shipping industry, challenging the role of the nation state and finding alternative ways of organizing their business. Among these Greek pioneers, Aristotle Onassis was the first and foremost. As the chapter by Harlaftis and Tsakas shows, he became one of the world's greatest shipowners by establishing a new institution: 'the global shipping company'.

Two factors enabled Onassis and the other Greeks to do this. First, their 'home bias' was limited, and it was primarily related to cultural, rather than economic or financial, factors. Like the Norwegians before them, the Greeks had built up their position within shipping as cross-traders, fulfilling other countries' transport needs, rather than transporting their own imports and exports. Moreover, there was a long tradition of a Greek diaspora. These merchants and shipowners were originally based in the Mediterranean and the Black Sea, but in the interwar and post-war periods also located in leading metropolises such as London and New York.

The second factor that enabled the Greeks to build global companies was their willingness to undertake organizational innovation—to do business in new ways, which gave them a competitive advantage. The Greeks managed to build up an international system where companies in different countries played specific roles, while the Greek owners at the helm oversaw the activities. By slicing up the value chain, and sourcing inputs where the costs were low, high profits paved the way for further expansion.

As Gelina Harlaftis and Christos Tsakas show, owners such as Aristotle Onassis and Stavros Niarchos pioneered 'business beyond borders'. They combined Greek entrepreneurship with customers and financing from the United States and with German shipbuilding capacity. The corporate model that enabled them to do this was 'global', with a complex legal structure, often impenetrable from the outside. Onassis was an international man. He controlled hundreds of companies in different domiciles, often 'offshore companies' in countries with limited transparency. He registered his ships in a number of countries, both Traditional Maritime Nations and Flags of convenience. Organized in a strictly hierarchical manner, Onassis' companies in different jurisdictions all played special roles, for finance, operation, management, agency or ownership. The basis of this model, the element that made it viable and successful, was Aristotle Onassis and his reputation.

The Greek experience illustrates the manner in which shipping challenged the nation state, utilizing resources from different countries and creating or institutionalizing novel transnational systems. While shipping companies in some countries gained competitive advantage by technological innovation, the Greeks based their competitiveness on organizational innovation.[37] Important ingredients here were offshore companies and Flags of convenience.

Flags of convenience were originally a refuge for owners that wanted to escape strict domestic rules, double taxation and the effects of the Prohibition. The Greeks refined the model, and today such flags have

---

[37] See Tenold and Theotokas (2013).

become the dominant way of organizing vessel ownership. While the vast majority of the world's ships in 1900 was registered in Great Britain, the United States and Germany, the leading flags today are Panama, Liberia and the Marshall Islands.

In 1919 the *Belen Quezada*, a former US navy ship, became the first foreign-owned vessel registered in Panama, often seen as the 'original' Flag of convenience.[38] Slightly less than a century later, the country became the foremost example of tax evasion, greed and an uncontrollable global financial architecture. The leaking of *The Panama Papers*, more than ten million secret files from a lawyer's office, showed how individuals and businesses used offshore companies to avoid the regulations and restrictions of the nation state for personal gain. For many, *The Panama Papers* provided the first glimpse of an economic system that was alien, a rogue system where the nation state had been forced to play second fiddle. In the press, the practice of 'offshore holdings' was linked to the increased international flows of money, to technological improvements that made it possible to distribute incomes and funds among different jurisdictions in a rapid and concealed manner. While many of the businesses involved in the inquiry were legitimate, the leak also revealed a surprisingly large amount of suspicious actions by politicians, athletes and businessmen. For shipping insiders, the practices that were revealed in connection with *The Panama Papers* were neither new nor surprising. Shipping had transcended borders for a long time. The globalized world—and the technological developments that have made this world possible—simply meant that other industries were gradually catching up with shipping.

The new, global shipping regime that emerged on a large scale after World War II was based on new connections, but this also implied that some of the older connections were replaced. The link between (British) shipowners and (British) shipyards, which had given both a dominant position at the start of the twentieth century, was severed. Greek shipowners helped the expansion of German yards in the 1950s and 1960s, and they also embraced low-cost shipyards in Asia, contributing to the shift in

---

[38] See Carlisle (2009, 2017). In the slipstream of *Belen Quezada* came two American cruise ships, encouraged by the owners' desire to avoid being 'dry' during Prohibition. There were long traditions for using foreign flags in times of war, and there had also been instances of 'tactical registration' in foreign countries before this, see Tenold (2019, 38).

the shipbuilding industry. Similarly, the links between shipping companies and their home country—in terms of flag, labour and regulatory and political regime—were cut with the advent of the global and transnational shipping companies.

The majority of the chapters in this book treat shipping demand as a global concept. One of our underlying theses is that the production of shipping services after World War II was transformed from a national frame to a global or transnational frame, parallel with the increasing integration of the international economy. However, René Taudal Poulsen's analysis of the ferry segment shows that this picture is not applicable to all parts of the shipping industry.

The demand for ferry services has a clear national or regional component and is a 'remarkable exception' to the global nature of maritime transport. Consequently, competition and other market processes differ from shipping in general. Focussing on the ferry market in the Nordic countries, Taudal Poulsen shows how important political decisions might be for shipping. For instance, the emergence of a common European market and the termination of 'duty free' sales of alcohol and cigarettes clearly reduced the attractiveness of short sea shipping. Similarly, the 'opening up of the skies' and the growth of low-cost air carriers have provided ferry companies with new types of competition. As such, the basis for the decline of the European ferry market was different from the basis for the decline of European shipping in general.

During the first decades of the post-war period, there was a 'life cycle' that ferries tended to go through.[39] Starting their careers in the Nordic countries, as the ferries aged they were sold on to lower-income markets in the Mediterranean, then moved on to local markets in Africa and Asia before the ship was scrapped. As a result of, among other things, high-income growth in Asia and limited investment in new capacity in the Nordic countries, this life cycle pattern has disappeared today. Due to the fact that regional markets have become more similar, and the segment has become mature, the previous connections in the market for second-hand ships have been severed. As such, it is evident that globalization

---

[39] The existence of life cycles in shipping has been discussed in for instance Thanopoulou (1995).

has influenced not only the global shipping segments, but also the locally based ones.

Concluding Comments

This book has discussed the intimate relationship between shipping and globalization in the post-war period. To some extent, the growth of the shipping industry and the increased economic integration have been two processes that have reinforced each other, two feedback loops.

The shipping industry has contributed to changing the centre of gravity of the world economy. For instance, low and decreasing transport costs have been a necessary condition for the integration of Asian countries in the world economy to the extent that we see today. This pertains to containerization and the low cost of moving manufactured goods from Asia to markets in North America and Europe, but it is also a result of the manner in which technological and organizational innovations have lowered the cost of transporting inputs to Asia. Moreover, the growth of Asian shipbuilding—with subsidies and political priority in Japan, South Korea and China—has reduced the cost of the ships needed to produce shipping services, and thus the cost of providing these services. This is the first of our feedback loops—shifts in production and growing seaborne trade pave the way for reductions in maritime transport costs, and these cost reductions encouraged trade and division of labour.

The shipping industry has also been a frontrunner in the development of 'global companies', organizations that have challenged the role of the nation state in the search for lower costs. Such companies were originally the preserve of shipowners from a handful of countries—Greece and the United States in particular. However, as it is difficult to regulate an industry that primarily operates outside national borders, the liberal regime spread from country to country. The detrimental market conditions during the shipping crises of the 1970s and 1980s implied that countries were forced to liberalize, or see their shipping activities disappear.

Today, the majority of the shipping companies operating in the international market have a high degree of autonomy in questions of localization, and there has been a levelling of tax policies and of registration requirements. This is the second of our feedback loops—when shipowners from one country challenge the regulatory regime, other countries are forced to follow, as the alternative is that their 'own' shipowners lose competitiveness. This exodus triggers further pressure on countries trying to avoid liberalization.

The two feedback loops reflect how shipping has become more global, but the industry still has an important national dimension. Port states still maintain an element of autonomy and authority, and many Traditional Maritime Nations still benefit from having a business culture that promotes maritime activities. Moreover, it is easier to uphold a regulatory regime with regard to coastal transports and short sea shipping, a topic that we have not discussed in detail in this book.

At the beginning of the twentieth century, the shipping industry reflected the primacy of Western Europe and North America, and the political and economic linkages on which this hegemony was built. Today, the shipping industry reflects the global nature of international economic relations. It reflects the constant search for cost reductions in the sourcing of raw materials, and in the production of goods and services.

Shipping is crucial for the smooth functioning of the world economy. It is mainly in the rare instances where this part of the global production system does not perform optimally—for instance when the South Korean container operator Hanjin was facing bankruptcy and their ships were left at sea—that ships and shipping gets any mainstream attention. The maritime transport system that has emerged since World War II is both an important engine—and an important example—of globalization.

References

Alderton, T., Bloor, M., Kahveci, E., Lane, T., Sampson, H., Thomas, M., et al. (2004). *The Global Seafarer: Living and Working Conditions in a Globalized Industry.* Geneva: International Labour Office.

Baldwin, R. (2016). *The Great Convergence: Information Technology and the New Globalization.* Cambridge, MA: Belknap Press of Harvard University.

Barber, N. (2003). Ocean as a Liner Shipping Company. *Nestorian, 20,* 11.

Boon, M. (2017). Business Enterprise and Globalization: Towards a Transnational Business History. *Business History Review, 91,* 511–535.

Bott, A. (Ed.). (2009). *British Box Business: A History of OCL.* SCARA.

Cain, P. J., & Hopkins, A. G. (2016). *British Imperialism, 1688–2015* (3rd ed.). Abingdon: Routledge.

Carlisle, R. (2009). Second Registers: Maritime Nations Respond to Flags of Convenience, 1984–1998. *The Northern Mariner/le marin du nord, 19*(3), 319–340.

Carlisle, R. (2017). *Rough Waters: Sovereignty and the American Merchant Flag.* Annapolis: Naval Institute Press.

Darwin, J. (1988). *Britain and Decolonisation: The Retreat from Empire in the Post-war World.* Basingstoke: Macmillan.

Dejung, C., & Petersson, N. P. (2013). Introduction: Power, Institutions, and Global Markets: Actors, Mechanisms, and Foundations of Worldwide Economic Integration, 1850–1930. In C. Dejung & N. P. Petersson (Eds.), *The Foundations of Worldwide Economic Integration: Power, Institutions, and Global Markets, 1850–1930* (pp. 1–17). Cambridge: Cambridge University Press.

D'Eramo, M. (2015). Dock Life. *New Left Review, 96,* 85–99.

Duara, P. (2011). The Cold War as a Historical Period: An Interpretive Essay. *Journal of Global History, 6*(3), 457–480.

Ekberg, E., & Lange, E. (2014). Business History and Economic Globalisation. *Business History, 56*(1), 101–115.

Ferguson, N., Maier, C. S., Manela, E., & Sargent, D. J. (Eds.). (2010). *The Shock of the Global: The 1970s in Perspective.* Cambridge, MA and London: Belknap Press.

Forsberg, A. (2000). *America and the Japanese Miracle: The Cold War Context of Japan's Economic Revival, 1950–60.* Chapel Hill: University of North Carolina Press.

Fusaro, M., & A. Polónia (Eds.). (2010). *Maritime History as Global History.* St. John's: International Maritime Economic History Association.

Harley, C. K. (2008). Steers Afloat: The North Atlantic Meat Trade, Liner Predominance, and Freight Rates, 1870–1913. *Journal of Economic History, 68,* 1028–1058.

Hopkins, A. G. (2002). The History of Globalization—And the Globalization of History? In A. G. Hopkins (Ed.), *Globalization in World History* (pp. 11–46). London: Pimlico.

Jones, G. (2002). Business Enterprises and Global Worlds. *Enterprise & Society, 3,* 581–605.

Kaukiainen, Y. (2006). Journey Costs, Terminal Costs and Ocean Tramp Freights: How the Price of Distance Declined from the 1870s to 2000. *International Journal of Maritime History, 18*(2), 17–64.

Kaukiainen, Y. (2008). Growth, Diversification and Globalization: Main Trends in International Shipping Since 1850. In L. R. Fischer & E. Lange (Eds.), *International Merchant Shipping in the Nineteenth and Twentieth Centuries: The Comparative Dimension* (pp. 1–56). St. John's: International Maritime Economic History Association.

Kaukiainen, Y. (2012). The Advantages of Water Carriage: Scale Economies and Shipping Technology, c. 1870–2000. In G. Harlaftis, S. Tenold, & J. M. Valdaliso (Eds.), *The World's Key Industry: History and Economics of International Shipping* (pp. 64–87). Houndmills: Palgrave Macmillan.

Lane, T. (1997). *Liverpool: City of the Sea*. Liverpool: Liverpool University Press.

Levinson, M. (2006). *The Box: How the Shipping Container Made the World Smaller and the World Economy Bigger*. Princeton: Princeton University Press.

Miller, M. B. (2012). *Europe and the Maritime World: A Twentieth Century History*. Cambridge: Cambridge University Press.

Mintzberg, H., Ahlstrand, B., & Lampel, J. (1998). *Strategy Safari: A Guided Tour Through the Wilds of Strategic Management*. New York: Free Press.

O'Brien, P. (2010, November 30). Ten Years of Debate on the Origins of the Great Divergence. *Reviews in History*. Available at https://www.history.ac.uk/reviews/review/1008.

O'Rourke, K. H., & Williamson, J. G. (1999). *Globalization and History: The Evolution of a Nineteenth-Century Atlantic Economy*. Cambridge: MIT Press.

Osterhammel, J. (2019). Global History. In M. Tamm & P. Burke (Eds.), *Debating New Approaches to History* (pp. 21–48). London: Bloomsbury.

Osterhammel, J., & Petersson, N. P. (2005). *Globalization: A Short History*. Princeton: Princeton University Press.

Perdue, P. C. (2000, August). *Review of Pomeranz, Kenneth: The Great Divergence: China, Europe, and the Making of the Modern World Economy*. H-World, H-Net Reviews. Available at https://www.h-net.org/reviews/showrev.php?id=4476.

Pomeranz, K. (2000). *The Great Divergence: China, Europe, and the Making of the Modern World Economy*. Princeton: Princeton University Press.

Ruggunan, S. (2011). The Global Labour Market for Filipino and South African Seafarers in the Merchant Navy. *South African Review of Sociology, 42*(1), 78–96.

Sturmey, S. G. (1962/2010). *British Shipping and World Competition* (2nd ed. 2010). St. John's: International Maritime Economic History Association.

Sturmey, S. G. (1986). The Code of Conduct for Liner Conferences: A 1985 View. *Maritime Policy & Management, 13,* 185–221.

Swift, O. (2011). Seafaring Citizenship: What Being Filipino Means at Sea and What Seafaring Means for the Philippines. *South East Asia Research, 19*(2), 273–291.

Tenold, S. (2019). *Norwegian Shipping in the 20th Century: Norway's Successful Navigation of the World's Most Global Industry.* Cham: Palgrave Macmillan.

Tenold, S., & Theotokas, I. (2013). Shipping Innovations: The Different Paths of Greece and Norway. *International Journal of Decision Sciences, Risk and Management, 5*(2), 142–160.

Thanopoulou, H. A. (1995). The Growth of Fleets Registered in the Newly-Emerging Maritime Countries and Maritime Crises. *Maritime Policy and Management, 22*(1), 51–62.

Westad, O. A. (2005). *The Global Cold War: Third World Interventions and the Making of Our Times.* Cambridge: Cambridge University Press.

White, N. J., & Evans, C. (2016). Holding Back the Tide: Liverpool Shipping, Gentlemanly Capitalism and Intra-Asian Trade in the Twentieth Century. In U. Bosma & A. Webster (Eds.), *Commodities, Ports and Asian Maritime Trade Since 1750* (pp. 218–240). Basingstoke: Palgrave Macmillan.

Young, L. (2018). Rethinking Empire: Lessons from Imperial and Post-imperial Japan. In M. Thomas & A. S. Thompson (Eds.), *The Oxford Handbook of the Ends of Empire* (pp. 212–230). Oxford: Oxford University Press.

Open Access This chapter is licensed under the terms of the Creative Commons Attribution-NonCommercial-NoDerivatives 4.0 International License (http://creativecommons.org/licenses/by-nc-nd/4.0/), which permits any noncommercial use, sharing, distribution and reproduction in any medium or format, as long as you give appropriate credit to the original author(s) and the source, provide a link to the Creative Commons license and indicate if you modified the licensed material. You do not have permission under this license to share adapted material derived from this chapter or parts of it.

The images or other third party material in this chapter are included in the chapter's Creative Commons license, unless indicated otherwise in a credit line to the material. If material is not included in the chapter's Creative Commons license and your intended use is not permitted by statutory regulation or exceeds the permitted use, you will need to obtain permission directly from the copyright holder.

Index

A

Abs, Hermann 205
ACE Group 118
Adenauer, Konrad 204, 205, 207
Adriatic Sea 240
A-Fleet 136
Africa 4, 69, 75, 116, 119, 218, 267
A.G. Weser 194, 197, 199, 202
Airlines 206, 208, 237, 240, 242
Åland 223, 234, 238
Åland Sea 222, 223, 228
Alexander, Sir Lindsay 71, 168
Alfred Holt & Co. 14, 70
Algeciras 120
Alleppey 111
Allied Powers 110
Al-Malik Saud Al Awal 200
America 4, 76, 116, 137, 191, 196, 253
American oil companies 187, 190, 205, 254
American President Lines 92, 125
American Racer 134, 135
American shipowners 189, 191
American shipyards 193, 196–198, 200
American Sparrow Point Shipyards 196
Amoco Cadiz 48, 58
Amsterdam 84, 117, 194, 223
Andersen, H.N. 145
Anderson, Sir Donald 73, 164
Andreades 194
Andros 194
Anglo-American Corporation 111, 125
Antwerp 22, 117
Apapa 81

AP Moller-Maersk Group 104, 105, 108, 111–114, 118–121, 125, 126
APM terminals 104
Aramco 205
Argentina 79
Artificial tween-decks 121
A-series, container vessels 126
Asia 2–4, 20, 22, 25, 27, 28, 33, 49, 68, 69, 73, 80, 86, 89, 91, 108, 109, 112, 113, 117, 119, 120, 127, 138, 142, 146, 166, 193, 213–215, 218, 232, 242, 252, 253, 256, 266–268
Assab 111
Associated Container Transportation 94
Ateliers & Chantiers de la Seine Maritime (Worms & Cie) 194
Atlantic Container Line (ACL) 137
Austin & Pickersgill (shipyards) 207
Australia 4, 17, 69, 70, 72, 78, 86–91, 93, 94, 117, 137, 143, 164, 232, 259
Australia Japan Container Line (AJCL) 90
Australian National Line (ANL) 90, 91

B

Baldwin, Richard 257
Balikpapan 84
Baltic Mercantile and Shipping Exchange 16
Baltic Sea 51, 221, 227, 234, 237, 238, 242
Baltic states 234
Baltimore 111, 115
Bangkok 110, 111, 136
Barber, Nicholas 77, 167–172, 174–176, 179, 262
Bartram & Sons Ltd. 194
Bay of Bengal 127
Beckvard, L. 147
Beijing 147, 149–151
Belgian shipyards 197, 201
Belgium 118, 186, 192–194
Ben Line Containers 142
Bethlehem 196, 197
B.H. Sobelman & Co 111
Bibby Line 82
Black Star Line (BSL) 74, 76–78
Blue Funnel Line (BFL) 70, 74, 76, 86, 92
Blue Star Line 139
Blythswood Shipbuilding Co. Ltd. 194
Bohai Rim 240
Bore, Ångfartygs AB 222, 223, 227
Boston 111
Boston Consulting Group 170
BP 189
Bremen 117, 188, 194, 197–199, 202
Brisbane 117
British America 68
British Australia 68
British & Commonwealth (B&C) 79, 80, 88, 164, 258
British India Steam Navigation Company (BI) 79
British Isles 227
British shipowners 10, 13, 14, 23, 72, 89, 214
British Shipping and World Competition (book) 10, 22

British shipping companies 13, 23, 24, 32, 79, 93, 94, 142
British shipyards (shipbuilding industry) 193, 207
Broeze, Frank 68, 72–74, 77, 89, 91, 103
Brogren, Klas 218, 220, 222, 232–237, 240
Broströms 140
bulk carriers 38, 143, 160, 165, 192, 238, 239, 253, 258
Burma (Myanmar) 76
Busan 22
business model 122, 124, 222, 257, 259
Butterfield & Swire (B&S) 85
B&W 139

C

Cable & Wireless 118
Calicut 111
Canada 17, 49, 69, 92, 109, 116, 193, 216
Canary Islands 226
Cantieri Riuniti dell'Adriatico 194
capital 10–12, 16, 17, 26, 30, 31, 56, 67, 72, 73, 80, 89, 145, 151, 167, 168, 173, 174, 178, 198, 207, 213, 223, 224, 233, 239, 251, 253, 254, 263, 264
Cardiff 22
cargo handling 82, 87, 162–166
cargo liners 82, 140, 160, 166, 171, 178, 251
Caribbean 49, 69, 82, 83, 116, 171, 216, 221, 233
Carras 194–196
Carson Cumberbath & Co 111

cascading 217, 240, 242
Castenskiold, Holger 136
Castle, Barbara 89
Caterpillar 121
Central America 116
Cephalonia 196
Ceylon. *See* Sri Lanka
Ceylon Shipping Corporation (CSC) 92, 93
Chandris 194–196
Chantiers & Ateliers de St. Nazaire-Penhoët, S.A. 194
Chantiers Navals de La Ciotat 194
Charleston 111, 115
chemical tanker shipping 215, 241
Chevron 189
Chicago 111, 135
China 4, 18, 19, 27, 29, 30, 33, 39, 68, 69, 83, 85, 90, 104, 116, 127, 134, 147–153, 185, 214, 231, 253, 254, 262, 263, 268
China Navigation Company (CNC) 85, 89, 90
China Ocean Shipping Agency (COSA) 85
Chios 196
Christiansen, Hakon 145
Christner, Hans 233
City of London 16
civil war 83, 108, 207
Clan line 79
classification societies 53, 54, 255
Clyde (river) 11, 12, 194
Cochin 111
Cold War 28, 68, 109, 186, 197
Colombo 22, 82, 92, 93, 111
Common Shipping Policy (EU) 186

Compañía General de Tabacos de Filipinas ('Tabacalera') 108, 111
Compagnie Générale Maritime (CGM) 140
Compagnie Générale Transatlantique 137
competitive advantages 83, 125, 158–160, 166, 176, 178, 207, 215, 265
conferences 42, 50, 57, 71, 74–78, 86–88, 90, 93, 104, 113, 134, 141, 146, 147, 163, 167, 220, 232, 251, 255, 260, 261, 263
Connecting Point Spain (CPS) 120
Constantinople 22
container shipping/containerization 1, 3, 38, 67–72, 78, 79, 86, 88–95, 103–107, 109, 112, 113, 117–124, 127, 134, 135, 137, 138, 148–153, 162–168, 172, 178, 179, 252, 253, 255, 258–261, 268
content management 107
context management 106
cooperation 37, 48, 49, 51, 52, 57, 78, 106, 109, 112, 137, 138, 140–142, 151, 205, 207, 215
Copenhagen 105, 109–116, 118, 125, 128, 135, 137, 138, 140, 141, 148, 150, 219, 220, 223–225, 234, 235, 238
Corsica 227
Cory (full company name) 172, 173, 175, 177
COSCO 134, 150–153
crew size 161
Crown Line 235
cruise business 216, 227, 233, 240

cruise lines 215, 227, 233, 240–242
cruise shipping 220, 227, 240
Cuba 186
Cunard 94, 137

D

Dalian 22
Danish International Ship Register (DIS) 141
Davies, Peter 17, 27, 77, 78, 95
declining phase 240
Delmas Vieljeux 78
Deng Xiaoping 29, 147–149
Denmark 15, 16, 25, 26, 104, 109, 118, 134, 144, 153, 220, 222, 224, 225, 234
Det Bergenske Dampskibsselskap 222
Detroit 111
Deutsche Werft 198
Deutsche Werke (Kiel) 205
DFDS 133, 220–224, 226, 227, 234, 235, 237, 238
Dharmasena, K. 73, 82, 92, 93
Dichmann, Wright & Pugh 111
diesel engines 14, 165
diversification 72, 167, 168, 170–174, 176, 179, 252
Djakarta 75, 84, 111
Djakarta Lloyd (DL) 69
Djibouti 111
dockworkers 67, 68, 84, 160, 165, 254
Drucker, Peter 175
dry bulk ships 32, 224
Dubai 22
Dublin 117
Dunkirk 194

Dutch shipyards 13, 197, 201, 206
duty free sales 221, 222, 235–238, 241, 242
Dynamic capabilities 105, 158, 159, 260

E

EAC-BenLine 142
East Asia 71, 86, 87, 136–140, 146, 256
East Asiatic Company (EAC) 117, 133–153, 258–263
Eastern Europe 116, 117
EasyJet 237
economic integration 11, 260, 264, 268
economic nationalism 75, 251, 258
economies of scale 12, 24, 25, 72, 106, 107, 143, 199, 235
Economist, The 2, 23
EffJohn International 227, 233
Eklund, Gunnar 222
Elder Dempster 70, 74, 76–78, 81, 89
Ellerman (shipping group) 94
Ellerman's Wilson Line 223
El Suleiman (minister) 205
Embiricos 194–196
Emerging Maritime Nations 214, 215
empire 16, 26, 70, 81, 85, 208, 253, 254
English Channel 217, 235
entry barriers 217
Erika 49, 58
Eriksberg Shipyard 140
Esbjerg 226
Esso 189

Estonia (ferry) 234
Europe 2, 4, 9, 11, 14, 17–20, 24–33, 49, 50, 53, 71, 73, 75, 79, 86–88, 90, 94, 109, 112, 113, 117–119, 134, 136–138, 140, 142, 186–188, 192, 193, 197, 201, 206–208, 213, 214, 240, 250, 252, 253, 255, 256, 259, 268
European integration 187, 207, 208
European shipyards (shipbuilding industry) 28, 186–188, 192, 193, 196, 197, 200, 201, 208, 254
European Union (EU) 87, 89, 94, 235, 255
Eurosclerosis 29
Evergreen 107
exit barriers 217

F

Fairfield Shipbuilding & Engineering Co. 194
Falstria 139
Far East 91, 108–110, 121
Far Eastern Freight Conference (FEFC) 118
Far East Line 117
F.C. MacFarlane Steamship Agency 111
Federal Maritime Commission (USA) 76
Federal Republic of Germany (FRG) 186, 197–199, 203, 206
Ferry Shipping Conference 220
Fieldhouse, D.K. 80
Finland 221, 223–225, 232, 233, 235, 238

Finska Ångfartyg 222, 223
Flags of convenience 25, 26, 30, 37, 187, 188, 190–192, 201, 208, 254, 265
floating accommodation 219, 231, 232, 240
France 12, 13, 15–17, 26, 40, 48, 78, 186, 192–194
Frankfurt 117
Fred. Olsen Line Agency 111
Freetown 83
Fremantle 117
French shipyards (competition) 197, 198, 200, 201
Furness Shipbuilding Co., Ltd. 193
Furness Withy 14, 79, 88, 93, 164, 258

G

Gellatly, Hankey & Co 111
geographical shifts 213, 214
George, Prince 149
German economic miracle/*Wirtschaftswunder* 188, 197, 208
Germany 12, 13, 15, 17, 26, 39, 118, 185, 192–194, 201, 204, 222, 225, 266
Germany (West) 92, 221
Ghana 74, 76, 86
Glenlyon 161, 162, 167
global competition 213, 216, 217, 241
globalization 2–4, 9, 31, 37, 38, 57, 68, 69, 81, 86, 87, 95, 153, 179, 192, 249–251, 253–257, 264, 267–269
globalization, first era of 11

global shipping company (multinational company) 187, 191, 192, 264
global shipping markets 239, 262
Gothenburg 117, 219, 222–225, 232, 235–238
government support 27, 28, 253
Great Britain 26, 32, 188, 191, 193, 198, 200, 219, 224, 225, 266
'Great Convergence' 253, 257
'Great Divergence' 253, 256
Greece 14–16, 25, 39, 185, 186, 206–208, 227, 257, 268
Greek shipowners (Greeks) 185–188, 190–197, 199–201, 207, 208, 214, 254, 264, 266
Grimsby and Immingham 21
Guangzhou 127
Gulf 39, 189
Gulf of Bothnia 226
Gulf of Mexico 110
Guofeng, Hua 147

H

Hamburg 22, 92, 117, 136, 187, 194, 197–200, 202, 204, 205
Hampton Roads 111
Hapag-Lloyd 146
Harland & Wolff (shipyards) 207
Harrisons & Crosfield Ltd 108, 110, 111
Hartlepool 193
hegemony 9, 10, 16, 19, 20, 31, 33, 188, 252, 269
Hellenic Shipyards 206, 207
Helsingborg 117
Helsinki 50, 51, 117, 219, 223–225, 232–234, 238

Hoegh Line 77
Hoek van Holland 232, 237
Holland 12, 13, 137
Holtegaard, Erik 113
Honduras 190, 203
Hong Kong 22, 30, 87, 89, 91, 108, 109, 111, 113, 117, 120–122, 124–127, 136, 214, 231, 234, 254
    Port of Hong Kong, 124
Hopkins, A.G. 68, 69, 81, 85–87, 89, 94, 250, 252
Høst, Thorkil 109, 115
Houston 22
Howaldtswerke A.G. 194, 198, 199, 202–206
Hull 13, 50, 54, 199, 219, 223
Hummels, David 95
Hurtigruten 136
Hyundai Heavy Industries 30

I

IJmuiden 216, 237
Immingham 21
imperial ambitions 17, 251
India 73, 79, 82, 87, 104, 108, 137, 231
individual companies 266
individual countries 128
Indonesia 69, 70, 75, 84, 108–110, 112, 137, 161
Industrial Revolution 12
industry life cycle 214, 241, 242
innovation 26, 30, 140, 160, 162, 163, 178, 199, 215, 240–242, 257, 260, 265, 268
innovation phase 214, 215, 241
interior designs 218, 220

International Labour Organization (ILO) 43–47, 56
International Maritime Organization (IMO) 42–54, 57, 234, 256
International Transport Workers' Federation (ITF) 41, 53, 55, 56
Interseas Shipping Company 109
investment 26, 27, 31, 33, 71, 80, 89, 104, 105, 119, 121, 122, 134, 135, 137, 139, 141, 142, 145, 152, 170, 172, 174, 177, 192, 204, 206–208, 224, 233, 252, 254, 259, 260, 262, 263, 267
Irish Sea 235
Iron Curtain 234
Isbrandtsen, Hans 108
Isbrandtsen-Møller Company (ISMOLCO) 108, 109
IT 113, 118, 126
Italian shipyards (competition) 198
Italy 13, 15, 119, 193, 194, 216, 227
Iversen, Niels Jørgen 113
Ivory Coast 119

J

Jacksonville 111
Jacobs, Flemming 113, 120, 121
Jahre, Anders 202
Japan 13, 15, 17–19, 24, 27, 29, 30, 33, 39, 69, 72, 77, 87, 89–91, 108–112, 117, 121, 123, 124, 134, 136–139, 144, 185, 193, 197, 216, 252, 268
Japanese 195
Japanese shipyards (competition) 193, 198
J. Boel & Fils 194

Jebsen & Company/Jebsen & Co. 108, 111, 125
Jephson, Chris 104, 108, 109, 112, 124, 125, 127
J.H. Vavasseur & Co (M) Ltd 111
John Scott & Co. 14
Johnson Line 139
Johnson ScanStar 139, 143
Jones Act 11
Jones, Geoffrey 153, 172, 257
Jørgensen, Niels Lillelund 125
Jutlandia 139–141, 143

K

Kaohsiung 22, 124, 125
Karamanlis, Constantinos 206, 208
Kasos 196
Kaukiainen, Y. 95, 250
Keelung 111, 124, 125
Keville, Sir Errington 93
Kiel 188, 194, 197–199, 202, 204, 206, 219, 222, 224, 232, 235, 236
King Saud 205
Kleiman, Ephraim 76
'K' Line 112
knowledge 14, 18, 26, 33, 48, 50, 107, 113, 134, 157–160, 162, 163, 165–168, 171, 172, 174–179, 217, 260, 263
Kobe 22, 110
Kockums Mekaniska Verkstads Aktiebolag 194
Kontena Nasional 92
Korean War 186, 193, 207
Kristiansand 237
Kruse, Ib 104, 113, 119, 125
Kuala Lumpur 91, 92, 126

Kulukundis (brothers) 186, 188, 194–196, 207

L

La Ciotat 194
Lamark Shipping Agency 111
Lane, F.L. 78
Lemos, C.M. 194, 195
Levinson, Marc 3, 67, 68, 72, 76, 83, 91, 103, 122, 135, 251, 253, 254
Liberia 30, 39, 190, 266
Liberian company/flag 39, 187, 191, 201, 208
Liberty ships (liberties) 190
Lindblad, J. Thomas 69
Liner Replacement Vessels (LRV) 134, 142, 144, 146, 147, 152, 260–262
Livanos, Stavros 186, 188, 194–197, 200
Liverpool 22, 80–82, 84, 85, 169, 243, 253
Liverpool Bay 167
Liverpool Steam Ship Owners' Association (LSSOA) 82, 83
Lloyd's 12, 16, 21
London 14, 16, 18, 21, 22, 39, 52, 54, 79, 92, 109, 118, 163, 193, 207, 223, 265
London and Overseas Freighters (tanker company) 207
Los Angeles 109, 111
Ludwig, Daniel 191, 200
Lund, Christian 125
Lycaon 84
Lykiardopulo 194–196
Lyras (brothers) 200

M

Macao 125
MacArthur, Douglas 110
Maersk Air 126
Maersk-blue brotherhood 114
Maersk Container Line 113
Maersk Data 118, 126
Maersk Drilling 126
Maersk Inc. (New York) 109, 116
Maersk International Shipping Education (M.I.S.E) 115
Maersk Line 104–122, 124–128, 142, 152, 153
Maersk Line's Master Plan 123
Maersk Supply Services 126
Maersk Top 112, 128
Malaysia 70, 72, 73, 75, 77, 84, 91, 92, 117, 122, 125, 126, 151, 255
Malaysian International Shipping Corporation (MISC) 73, 74, 77, 92
Malmö 194
management 3, 27, 53, 70, 81, 83, 106, 108, 109, 113, 114, 118, 128, 136, 138, 139, 144, 145, 150–152, 158, 159, 168–176, 178, 213, 260, 265
Manila 42, 85, 108, 109, 111, 138
Mao Zedong 147
The Maritime Company of the Philippines 86
maritime hegemony 29, 31, 214
Maritime Labour Convention (MLC) 42–44, 46, 47, 56
marketing 25, 74, 113–116, 118, 150, 171, 219, 222, 227
MARPOL 42, 45, 47, 58
Marseille 22

Marshall, Sir John 88, 94
Massawa 111
mature phase 241
Mavroleon, Basil Emmanuel 207
MCC Transport 117
McKinney-Møller, Mærsk 104, 109, 110, 112, 114–116, 153
McLean, Malcom P. 134
Medan 111
Mediterranean 49, 90, 194, 206, 216, 218, 221, 226, 227, 231, 238, 240, 242, 265, 267
Melbourne 117
Melchers & Co. 108
Memphis 111
Meonia 139
Merchant Marine Act of 1920 11
Meyer Werft 20
Middle East 93, 116, 119, 205, 216
migration patterns 232
Milford Haven 21
Miller, Michael B. 85, 164, 166, 187, 214, 250, 251, 257
Mitsubishi 108
Mitsui-OSK 77
Mitsui Shipyard 144
Mobil 189
Moby Lines 227
Mohamad, Mahathir 255
Møller, A.P. 108, 109, 112, 113, 115, 125, 133, 134
Moller Steamship Company 109, 111, 116
monopoly 46, 85, 205, 217, 222
Montreal 111
Munich 117
Myrsten, Carl Bertil 222

N

Nakskov Shipyard 139, 144, 145
National Bulk Carriers (company) 200
National shipping lines 71, 73, 77, 94. See also individual companies
naval architecture 218
Nederlandsche Dok & Sheepsbouw Maatschappij V.O.F. 194
Nederlandsche Stoomvaart Maatschappij 'Oceaan' (NSMO) 84
Nedlloyd Lijnen 140
Neptune Orient Lines (NOL) 73, 91, 92, 146, 252
Nestor 171
Netherlands, The 26, 69, 118, 186, 192, 194, 206, 216
Newcastle-upon-Tyne 200
New Jersey 116, 205
Newly Industrialized Countries 27
New York 22, 39, 80, 108, 109, 134, 135, 186, 191, 196–198, 200, 206, 215, 265
New Zealand 17, 69, 87, 88, 94
Niarchos, Stavros 185, 188, 194–197, 200–207, 265
niche markets 14, 119, 239
Nicholson, Sir John 72, 74, 86–90, 163
Nigeria/Nigerian 77, 78, 81, 83, 86, 254
Nigerian National Shipping Line (NNSL) 77, 78
Nihon 141
Ningbo 22
Ningbo-Zhouzhan 22
N.J. Goulandris (sons) 194, 195

Nomicos 194–196
Norden 133
North America 2, 11, 17, 86, 90, 113, 127, 147, 149, 268, 269
Northern Europe 75, 134, 136, 139–141, 152, 153, 193, 216, 227, 240
North Europe 90, 120
North Sea 194, 216, 221, 223, 231, 237
North Shields 194, 219
Norway 15–17, 25, 26, 29, 77, 118, 133, 186, 208, 221, 237
Norwegian fjords 226
Norwegian shipowners (Norwegians) 140, 202, 215
Nürnberg 117
N.V. Macba 111
N.V. Wilton Fijenoord Dok-en Werf Maats 194

O

O'Brien, Patrick 256
Ocean/Ocean Transport and Trading (OTT) 4, 40, 49, 55, 70, 77, 79, 157, 158, 160–163, 166–179, 258–263
Ocean Steam Ship Company (OSSCo) 14, 70–72, 75, 77–80, 83–86, 89, 92
OECD 21, 30, 57, 255
oligopoly 217
Ollendorff, Finn 136
Olsson, Dan Sten 236
Olsson, Sten Allan 222
O.L. (Ollie) Stevens 111
Olympic (fleet) 196, 201
Olympic Airways 206

Olympic Arrow 203
Olympic Challenger 200
Olympic Champion 203
Olympic Chaser 203
Olympic Conqueror 203
Olympic Cruiser 203
Olympic Explorer 203
Olympic Fame 200
Olympic Fighter 203
Olympic Flame 200
Olympic Games 196
Olympic Hunter 203
Olympic Lightning 203
Olympic Maritime (agency, Hamburg) 202
Olympic Promoter 203
Olympic Rider 203
Olympic Runner 203
Olympic Tracer 203
Olympic Victor 203
Olympic Winner 203
Onassis, Aristotle 185, 187, 188, 191, 192, 194–207, 264, 265
Onassis, Tina 200
OPEC 29, 256
open ship registers 213, 214
order book 20
Øresund 221, 235
organizational processes 106
Osaka 110
Oslo 51, 219, 224, 225, 234, 235, 238
Overseas Containers Ltd (OCL) 68, 70–72, 79, 86–94, 138, 163, 164, 166, 167, 172, 252, 258–263
OY Jacobsen Shipping Ltd 117

P
Pagh, Mogens 135, 136, 139, 142–145, 148, 149, 151–153
Pakistan 79, 82, 137
Palmer, Sarah 30, 31
Panama 30, 39, 41, 116, 190, 266
Panama Canal 108
Panamanian company/flag 187, 191, 201, 203, 208
Panama line 108, 109, 112, 115, 117–119, 121, 123, 127
Papadakis 194–196
Paris 49, 51, 117
Parliament (UK) 23, 24, 32
Pateras, Diamantis 200
Pearl River Delta 227
Penang 91, 111, 126
Peninsular and Oriental Steam Navigation Company (P&O) 70, 72, 73, 79, 90, 91, 142, 163, 164, 258, 259
Penrose, Edith 158
Persian Gulf 110
Petersberg Agreement 198
Petros Goulandris (sons) 194, 197
Pferdmenges, Robert 205
Philadelphia 111
Philippines/Filipino 4, 30, 85, 86, 104, 108, 214, 254
P&I clubs 53–55, 57, 255
Pilferage 67, 71, 83, 94
Ping Xiang Cheng 150
Pittsburg 111
Plantations des Terres Rouges 111
Poland/Polish 75
Pollard, Sidney 12, 13
Pomeranz, Kenneth 253, 256
port congestion 71, 82, 83
Porter's Five Forces 217

Port Hedland 22
Port Klang 22, 91, 92, 122, 126
ports 2, 21, 22, 45, 46, 49, 53, 72, 82, 83, 107, 108, 115, 117, 120, 122, 136, 138–140, 161, 162, 165, 187, 192, 194, 197, 215, 219, 223, 225, 236, 253, 256
port state control 4, 46, 47, 49, 56, 58
Post-WWII 116, 185, 188, 190, 208
Predictive Index (PI) 114
Prestige 49, 58
Priam 161, 162
Principal Agents' Meeting 110, 112
product life cycle 215
profitability 78, 87, 160, 162, 163, 172, 176, 236

Q

Qingdao 22
Qinhuangdao 22
Quality Control 116

R

Raphael, Lutz 177
Rasmussen, Poul 115
Red Sea 92, 117, 227, 231
Rees, John D. 174, 175
Regional Seas Organizations (RSOs) 48, 50–52
regional shipping markets 3, 18, 23, 30, 73, 145, 185, 188
regulatory innovations 214
Reiter, Kurt W. 202
research 22, 30, 153, 158–162, 177, 178, 187

research & development (R&D) 25
Rhodesia (Zimbabwe) 80
Riisager, Birger 113
risk 37, 54, 55, 67, 71, 72, 79, 84, 86, 145, 146, 165, 169
Robert C. Herd & Co 111
The Robert Reford Co 111
Robinson, Ronald 76
Rotterdam 22, 39, 53, 92, 117, 194, 237
Royal Mail Lines 79
Royal Netherlands Lloyd 138
Ruhly, Alfred B. ('Ted') 115
Ryanair 237

S

Safety of Life at Sea (SOLAS) 42, 45–47, 58
Safmarine 90, 105
Saigon 111
Sally, Rederi AB 227
San Francisco 109, 111
Santorini 196
Sardinia 227
Saudi Arabia 205
Saudi Arabian Tankers Co. (company) 200
Savannah 111
ScanAustral Carriers 140
Scandinavia 26, 117, 232, 234, 235, 237, 257
Scandinavian Star 234
Scandinavian Sun 227
ScanDutch 118, 134, 138, 140–143, 152
Scania 222
ScanService 138, 139, 141
Schäffer, Fritz 204

Schmith, Wøldike 146
Scotts' Shipbuilding & Engineering Co., Ltd. 194
seafarers 24, 26, 37, 38, 42, 43, 47, 55, 56, 160, 161, 196, 214, 254
Sea-Land 71, 88, 90, 105, 116, 125, 134, 137, 138
Sea-Land Service, Inc. 67
Sealink British Ferries 235
Selandia 134, 139–141, 143
Senegal 119
service innovation 216, 222, 227, 232, 238, 241, 242
Sessan Line 222
SF Line 234
Shanghai 22, 85, 108, 136, 148, 150, 151
Shaw, Savill & Albion 88
Shell 189
Shenzhen 22
shipbuilding 9–14, 17–20, 22, 23, 25–33, 69, 139, 143, 186–189, 192, 193, 196–202, 206, 208, 213, 252–254, 256, 265, 267, 268
ship design 30, 160, 165, 178, 216, 241
ShipPax Information 218, 220, 224–226, 238
shipping 1–5, 9–12, 14, 16–18, 20, 22–33, 37–42, 44–59, 67, 69–71, 73, 75–78, 84, 85, 88, 93, 94, 103, 108, 113, 116, 120, 124, 125, 127, 133–144, 146–148, 152, 153, 157–160, 162–164, 166–168, 171–173, 178, 179, 186–188, 190, 192–194, 196, 197, 199, 201, 202, 204, 205, 207, 208, 213–216, 218–224, 226, 232, 234–236, 239–243, 250–260, 262–269
shipping agents 92
shipping cycle 240
shipping niches 217, 241
Sierra Leone 83
Silja Line 220, 223, 226, 227, 233, 234, 238
Silja Serenade 232, 233, 238
Silja Symphony 232, 238
Singapore 22, 30, 70, 73, 76, 89, 91, 92, 111, 113, 117, 120–122, 124–126, 136, 137, 161, 169, 185, 214, 234, 252, 254
Sir James Laing and Sons Ltd. 194
Skagerrak 217, 221, 231, 242
Slite, Rederi AB 222, 234
Smith, Bell & Co 85
Smith & Kelly Co 111
Smith's Dock Co. Ltd. 194
Société Anonyme Cockerill-Ourge 194
Société des Ateliers et Chantiers de France 194
Songkhla 146
South Africa 69, 87, 90, 91
South America 79, 116. *See also* individual countries
Southampton 21, 215
Southeast Asia 21, 26, 32, 70, 74, 83, 87, 91, 107, 117, 121–123, 126, 136, 143, 253, 255
Southern Baltic Sea 231, 234
Southern New England 111
Southern Shipping Company 111
Southern Sweden 194, 222

South Korea 18, 19, 27, 30, 33, 214, 253, 268
South Louisiana 22
Soviet bloc 69, 75, 251
Soviet Union 233
Spain 15, 120
Sparsø, Henning H. 136–143, 146–148, 151, 152
Sprague Steamship Company 111
Sri Lanka 92, 93, 255
standardization 14, 166
Standards of Training Certification and Watchkeeping (STCW) 42
steam engines 165
steamships 12, 13, 15, 69, 84
Stena Line 220, 222, 223, 232, 235, 236
St. Johnston, Kerry 70, 71, 74, 76, 87, 93
St. Nazaire 194
Stockholm 117, 219, 220, 223–225, 232–235, 238, 239
Storm-Jørgensen 136
Straits Steamship Company 92
strategy 17, 27, 71, 72, 78, 93, 94, 104, 105, 107, 119, 139, 158, 159, 168–172, 177, 178, 206, 208, 234, 252, 258, 261, 262
strikes 67, 72, 80–83, 163, 204
Sturmey, Stanley 10, 22–24, 27
Stuttgart 117
submarine cables 16
subsidies 10, 22, 24, 28, 39, 268
Sudan 76, 111
Suez Canal 144
Suez crisis 161
Suez line 110, 117, 118
Sumbawa 146
Sunderland 194, 207

support 17, 28, 30, 50, 52, 55, 56, 70, 75, 85, 88, 89, 107, 148, 168, 169, 176, 189, 204, 206, 251
Svea, Stockholms Rederi AB 222
Svenska Lloyd AB 222, 223
Sweden 12, 15, 29, 118, 186, 192–194, 198, 218, 220–225, 232, 238
Swedish American 137
Swedish East Asian Company 137, 138
Swedish shipyards 140, 198, 199
Switzerland 118
Sydney 117, 150, 163, 215

T

Taichung 125
Taipei 120, 124
Tait & Co. 108, 111
Taiwan 107, 108, 110, 117, 121, 124, 125
Tallink 220, 234
Tallinn 234
tankers 3, 32, 38, 48–50, 55, 76, 135, 138, 144, 160, 171, 185–194, 196–202, 204, 205, 207, 208, 215, 224, 236, 238, 239, 258
tax 3, 31, 33, 39, 167, 168, 257, 259, 266, 269
technology 10, 11, 14, 15, 17, 19, 25, 27, 28, 30, 33, 67, 68, 73, 92, 135, 137, 145, 147, 148, 153, 159, 160, 165, 177, 178, 189, 194, 199, 201, 214, 251, 253, 254, 257, 259, 260
telegraph 16, 162
Texaco 189

Index

Thai State Railways 110
Thailand 109, 110, 112
Tianjin 22, 148, 150
Tilbury 219
Timm Steamship Agency West Redding, Connecticut 111
Titanic 42, 58
Toffler, Alvin 175
Togo 119
Tokyo 49, 110, 111
Tokyo Bay 92
tonnage, compensated 15
tonnage, estimated 15
tons, dead weight 19
tons, gross register 19, 204
Tor Britannia 223
Tor Line 218, 223
TORM 133
Toronto 111
Torrey Canyon 58
Tor Scandinavia 223
Torshavn 226
Toyama 141
Traditional Maritime Nations 26, 215, 265, 269
Trait 20, 194
Transatlantic 110, 137, 140
Transnational, transnationalization 3, 41, 58, 104–107, 113, 128, 166, 249, 250, 254, 255, 265, 267
Transocean 140
transoceanic liner services 215, 216
Transport Committee (UK) 23, 32
Trans World Airlines 135
Travemünde 219, 222
Trieste 194
Trio 118
TRIO consortium 142

Truman, Harry S. (President) 190
Tschudi & Eitzen 133
Tuticorin 111
Tyne 22, 193
Tyne and Wear 11, 12

U

Uddevalla 194
Uddevallavarvet Aktiebolag 194
UK West Africa Lines (UKWAL) 78
UN Conference on Trade and Development (UNCTAD) 21, 39, 75, 77, 185, 216, 238, 239, 255
Union-Castle line 79
United Kingdom (UK) 9, 11–14, 16–18, 21, 23–27, 30–32, 46, 69, 70, 72–75, 79, 82–84, 87, 94, 122, 157, 164, 166–168, 231, 234, 252, 263
United Nations (UN) 43, 75, 234, 251, 255
United Nations Convention on the Law of the Sea (UNCLOS) 40, 42, 47, 48, 57
United States (USA) 4, 12, 17, 18, 25, 108, 109, 112, 115–117, 121–123, 125, 146, 186–191, 193, 196–198, 200, 207, 208, 214, 256, 265, 266, 268
United States Lines (USL) 134, 137
United States Maritime Commission (USMC) 189, 190, 196
US Defense Department 110

V

Vergottis 194–196

Vernon, Raymond 214
vertical integration 215
Vickers-Armstrongs Ltd. 193, 200
Vietnam 68, 88, 127
Vietnam War 68
Viking Line 220, 222, 223, 233, 234, 238, 239
Vikinglinjen 222
Voyager of the Seas 233

W

Wärtsilä Marine 233
wage costs 25, 67
Wallenius 137
Wallenius Lines 90
Washington D.C. 52, 76, 111, 197
Wergeland, Tor 215, 217, 218, 227
Werring Jr., Niels 140, 141
West Africa 70, 79, 82, 83, 86–89, 95, 110, 119, 120, 231
Westerman, Sir Alan 88
Western Europe 9, 18, 20, 21, 24, 32, 86, 117, 147, 149, 252, 256, 269
Western offshoots 17
West German shipyards (shipbuilding industry) 198, 199, 201, 202, 205
West Hartlepool 194
Westphal, Adolf 203

W. Gray & Co. Ltd. 194
'White' Dominions 87. *See also* Australia; Canada; New Zealand; South Africa
Wilhelm Wilhelmsen 137, 138, 140
William Denny and Brothers 14
William Doxford & Sons Ltd 194
William J. Spurrier 111
Woermann Line 74
World Enterprise 200
World fleet 11, 13, 15, 20–22, 29, 32, 213, 215, 216
World Glory 197
World War I 11, 17, 27, 38, 108, 145, 199
World War II 2–4, 9, 10, 17, 18, 27, 33, 39, 68, 107, 109, 116, 124, 188, 189, 191, 193, 196, 207, 252, 266, 267, 269

Y

Yokohama 110
Young & Rubicam 118
Yugoslavia 76, 192, 193

Z

Zeebrugge 237
Zim Line 76
Zurich 135

The manufacturer's authorised representative in the EU is Springer Nature Customer Service Centre GmbH, Europaplatz 3, 69115 Heidelberg, Germany. If you have any concerns regarding our products, please contact ProductSafety@springernature.com

Printed and bound by CPI Group (UK) Ltd, Croydon, CR0 4YY

23/03/2026

02076667-0003